MW01283332

THE JAPANESE DISCOVERY OF CHINESE FICTION

The Japanese Discovery of Chinese Fiction

THE WATER MARGIN AND

THE MAKING OF A NATIONAL CANON

William C. Hedberg

Columbia University Press
New York

Columbia University Press wishes to express its appreciation for assistance given by the Wm. Theodore de Bary Fund in the publication of this book.

Columbia University Press
Publishers Since 1893
New York   Chichester, West Sussex
cup.columbia.edu

Library of Congress Cataloging-in-Publication Data
Names: Hedberg, William C., author.
Title: The Japanese discovery of Chinese fiction : The water margin and the making of a national canon / William C. Hedberg.
Description: New York : Columbia University Press, [2019] | Includes bibliographical references and index.
Identifiers: LCCN 2019008386 (print) | LCCN 2019018582 (ebook) | ISBN 9780231550260 (electronic) | ISBN 9780231193344 | ISBN 9780231193344 (cloth : alk. paper) | ISBN 9780231550260 (electronic)
Subjects: LCSH: Shui hu zhuan—Appreciation—Japan. | Japanese literature—Chinese influences. | Chinese literature—Yuan dynasty, 1260–1368—History and criticism.
Classification: LCC PL2694.S53 (ebook) | LCC PL2694.S53 H686 2019 (print) | DDC 895.13/44—dc23
LC record available at https://lccn.loc.gov/2019008386

Columbia University Press books are printed on permanent and durable acid-free paper.

Printed in the United States of America

Cover design: Chang Jae Lee
Cover image: Color woodblock print depicting Du Xing, one of the "One Hundred and Eight Heroes of the Water Margin," by Utagawa Kuniyoshi, courtesy of Bridgeman Images.

CONTENTS

CONTENTS

Chapter Four
Civilization and Its Discontents: Travel, Translation,
and Armchair Ethnography   145

Epilogue
A Final View from the Margins   178

ACKNOWLEDGMENTS

Although it took longer to finish than I anticipated, writing this book has been, on the balance of things, a tremendous amount of fun. It is, after all, a study of obsession, and an examination of the ways in which a particular Chinese text captivated and held spellbound a Japanese audience separated from its composition by nearly insurmountable language barriers, perilous geography, and the passage of centuries. Being suddenly and inexplicably gripped to the point of mania by a foreign literary artifact is a feeling that most of us who teach literature for a living can identify with, and one that we hope to inculcate in our own students. At the risk of relaxing my critical guard too much, I still find myself in sympathy with the irrepressible enthusiasm of Meiji- and Taishō-period readers, who—objective and "scientific" methodologies notwithstanding—found themselves reduced to the status of giddy fans when explicating what Akutagawa Ryūnosuke termed the "*Shuihu*-esque."

The writer of any book amasses a number of academic and personal debts, and it stands to reason that a study of two national literatures should require twice as much room for its author to adequately thank his supporters. The roots of my fascination with *Shuihu zhuan* stretch back a decade and a half to my years as an undergraduate at the University of Kansas, where I read Sidney Shapiro's translation with my first teachers of Chinese, Keith McMahon and Deborah Peterson. I read the original(s) in full viii

during my graduate years, and my deepest gratitude goes to my former advisers—Wilt Idema, Karen Thornber, David Der-wei Wang, Edwin Cranston, and Wai-yee Li—whose constant encouragement in my unusual research trajectory allowed me to reinvent myself as a comparatist halfway through my graduate career. Stephen Owen, Michael Puett, Eileen Chow, Xiaofei Tian, David Gundry, Emanuel Pastreich, Ōki Yasushi, David Rolston, and Hu Siao-chen have all provided invaluable advice and support during my research time in the United States, Tokyo, and Taipei. Many of the ideas explored in this book were formulated and refined through workshop and conference presentations, invited lectures, and informal conversations. Among my friends, collaborators, and supporters, I would especially like to thank Will Fleming, Matthew Fraleigh, Ariel Fox, Brian Skerratt, Andy Rodekohr, Scott Gregory, Fumiko Jōo, Mengjun Li, Andre Haag, Paul Vierthaler, Heng Du, Josh Schlachet, Erin Brightwell, Jeff Moser, Suyoung Son, David Atherton, Lorie Brau, and Seth Jacobowitz.

Arizona State University's School of International Letters and Cultures was an instantly welcoming home for me and my family, and I am eternally grateful to be in the company of friends, mentors, and senior colleagues extraordinaire Steve West, Young Oh, Steve Bokenkamp, Xiaoqiao Ling, Mark Cruse, Rob Tuck, Dan Gilfillan, Joe Cutter, Jiwon Shin, Joanne Tsao, Lisa Berkson, Hilde Hoogenboom, Hoyt Tillman, Peter Suwarno, Françoise Mirguet, Andrew Ross, Claudia Brown, Juliane Schober, Anne Feldhaus, Jim Rush, Angie Chau, Jianling Liao, and Ebru Türker. Nina Berman has been eternally supportive of me both professionally and personally, and my colleagues in the Japanese section—Tomoko Shimomura, Bradley Wilson, Kumiko Hirano, and Eiji Suhara—are an inspiration and delight to work with. It is often said about teaching that you learn as much from your students as you yourself hope to impart, and this is especially true when you have students as brilliant as Sebastian Xin, Kimberly Harui, Jin Zhang, and Sarah Gossett. This project would have taken much longer to complete had my friends and colleagues not so often allowed me to be selfish with my research time. I received additional support from both ASU's Institute for Humanities Research (IHR) and the School of International Letters and Cultures, who provided me with generous subvention grants that assisted me greatly in the final publication of my manuscript. Final thanks go to our dear family friend, Rachel Reinke, whose help during the 2017–2018 year made it possible for me to go on leave.

ACKNOWLEDGMENTS

This book could not have been written without profoundly generous financial and institutional support. The lion's share of the writing was completed during a year of research leave, made possible by grants from the American Council of Learned Societies, the Social Science Research Council (SSRC), and the Institute for Advanced Study (IAS) in Princeton. Two SSRC workshops in Chiang Mai and New Delhi, led by Prasenjit Duara, Engseng Ho, Srirupa Roy, and Seteney Shami, were instrumental in helping me formulate the methodological underpinnings for my work, as well as think about how to put my research in dialogue with other scholars working on inter-Asian topics. Under the auspices of a Mellon Fellowship for Assistant Professors at the IAS, I had the tremendous good fortune to work with Nicola Di Cosmo, whose limitless erudition, hospitality, and sense of humor made for a deeply enjoyable year. Special thanks go to the members of the IAS East Asian Studies seminar—Miriam Kingsberg Kadia, Catherine Clark, Eugenia Lean, Ying Zhang, Tim Brook, Marta Hanson, Connie Cook, Weijing Lu, Kwangmin Kim, and Minoru Inaba—for their feedback and friendship, as well as to Peter Coviello, John Modern, Andrew Zimmerman, Julie Orlemanski, and Jamie Kreiner, for their late-night insights into the usefulness of üseless knowledge. Proximity to Princeton and Columbia allowed me to take part in a wonderfully stimulating intellectual community, and I cherish the conversations and time spent with Paize Keulemans, Tom Hare, Atsuko Ueda, Xin Wen, Brian Steininger, Ksenia Chizhova, Benjamin Elman, Federico Marcon, Anna Shields, Ying Qian, and John Phan. My final thanks go to my editors at Columbia University Press, Christine Dunbar, Christian Winting, and Leslie Kriesel; my copyeditor, Mike Ashby, and indexer, Alexander Trotter; and my anonymous reviewers, whose knowledge, generosity, and thoughtful feedback have made this a much better book.

The ultimate place of honor goes to the members of my family. I am reduced to *haohan*-esque inarticulateness when it comes to thanking my parents, Melida and Steve, and it is with tremendous love and gratitude that I give them a long overdue copy of this book. My siblings Gina and Rob and my in-laws Sergej and Irina have been inexhaustible sources of enthusiasm and optimism, even when—especially when!—I had trouble summoning that enthusiasm and optimism myself. My wife, Ana, has supported me unequivocally in everything I've done, and she and my son, Alan, provide a center that makes all peripheries lose their luster and pale in comparison. This book is dedicated to my grandmother, Jean Hedberg, who gave me a bilingual edition of the *Daodejing* when I was fourteen, and in doing so arguably set me off on my life's trajectory. Although she passed away before the book was finished, my grandmother impressed upon me the importance of following one's passions to even the most distant margins, and demonstrated through her own outlaw example that the people worth knowing and the things worth doing are all to be found beyond the borders of convention.

Much of chapter 1 first appeared in *The Journal of Japanese Studies* 41, no. 2 (2015) as "Separating the Word and the Way: Suyama Nantō's *Chūgi Suikodenkai* and Edo-Period Vernacular Philology." A section of chapter 2 was published in the *International Journal of Asian Studies* 12, no. 2 (2015) as "Reclaiming the Margins: Seita Tansō's *Suikoden hihyōkai* and the Poetics of Cross-Cultural Influence." I am deeply grateful to the editors and publishers of both journals for their permission to reprint material in this volume.

NOTE ON FORMATTING

Since I hope that my study will be of equal interest to scholars of Japanese and Chinese literature, I have struggled with the issue of how to present non-English terms in a way that would be recognizable and accessible to both groups. I have limited my use of characters to proper names, titles, and a handful of essential terms (i.e., *Tōwagaku* in chapter 1), all of which can be found in a list at the end of the study. In the case of shorter translations, I have provided a transliteration of the Chinese or Japanese if I felt that the author's phrasing or use of a particular term was unusual and required explication (i.e., the many uses of *bungaku* in chapter 3). Otherwise, I have simply provided the reference for the translation in question.

One of the central arguments made in this study is that Japanese aficionados of Chinese fiction did not read a single, stable novel called *The Water Margin (Shuihu zhuan)*; rather, they encountered *Shuihu zhuan* (and other Chinese novels) in a wide variety of editions and titles that differed from one another dramatically in terms of printing quality, illustration, volume of paratextual material, and especially the trajectory of the narrative itself. The situation only becomes more complicated once writers and authors in Japan begin creating their own translations, adaptations, and illustrations. To help the reader keep the potentially bewildering variety of *Shuihu zhuan*s examined in this volume straight, I have described the features of many of the editions and translations I discuss at the beginning of my bibliography.

One deliberate idiosyncrasy requires brief justification. The pronunciation of *Shuihu zhuan* in Japanese is, of course, *Suikoden*. However, throughout this study I use the Chinese reading to emphasize the text's foreign genesis and general linguistic and cultural "Otherness," a quality that, as I demonstrate, it never entirely shed, no matter how deeply it worked itself into the fabric of Japanese literary culture. For this reason, I also leave the title of *Shuihu zhuan* untranslated throughout my study, even when I have chosen to translate the titles of other novels like *Romance of the Three Kingdoms* (*Sanguo yanyi*) and *Journey to the West* (*Xiyouji*) into English. The translation of the title as *The Water Margin* dates to a 1937 English-language edition by J. H. Jackson and now serves as a widely accepted and instantly recognizable rendition. When appropriate, I have elected to use this as an English-language translation.

THE JAPANESE DISCOVERY OF CHINESE FICTION

ENTERING THE MARGINS—READING
SHUIHU ZHUAN AS JAPANESE LITERATURE

It is an apparent irony of East Asian literary history that one of the texts at the center of the traditional canon is explicitly concerned with marginality. The Ming-dynasty novel *Shuihu zhuan*, variously translated into English as *All Men Are Brothers*, *Outlaws of the Marsh*, and most literally, *The Water Margin*, details the gradual assemblage and subsequent adventures of 108 outlaws in the backwaters of what is now Shandong province in northeastern China. The riverbank, edge, or "margin" (*hu*) alluded to in the title of the novel is a topos intended to be taken both literally and figuratively. After falling afoul of the law as enforced by the corrupt ministers of the Song emperor Huizong (r. 1100–1126), the outlaws find refuge in the swampy mazes and riparian byways of the Liangshan marshes, a region sufficiently removed from the Song-dynasty court that the refugees are able to establish parallel systems of government, subsistence, and ethics in exile. Not until the eighty-second chapter of the novel, when Huizong offers the group amnesty in exchange for military service against other groups of bandits and invaders, do the Liangshan outlaws relinquish their existences in the periphery and reenter (in many cases, with great trepidation) the gravitational pull of the central court.

As premodern readers quickly noted, however, the margin is also a political status and a state of mind. In an essay that was appended as a preface to many editions of the novel, the iconoclast philosopher Li Zhuowu

(1527–1602) presented the Liangshan outlaws as casualties of a world in which traditional moral hierarchies had been inverted, where "men of great virtue were forced to the bottom, the unworthy rose to the top," and loyalty and justice were forced into abeyance along the peripheries of empire.[1] Li's concern about the misrecognition of the protagonists' value is a theme that runs like a leitmotif throughout both the reception of the novel and the text itself. Like all great works of literature, *Shuihu zhuan* can be interpreted along any number of interpretive axes, but it is without question a narrative about ways of seeing and the proper recognition of worth, a theme that is as true for the characters themselves as it is for the novel's readers. When an outlaw encounters other outlaws along the rivers and lakes where such men dwell, he is likely to hail them with the greeting, "I have eyes but failed to recognize Mount Tai!" and the first half of the novel ends with the outlaws taking their assigned seats in the Hall of Loyalty and Duty (Zhongyitang), a public and highly visible ritual of recognition intended to confirm that everyone and everything is in its proper place. But the appearance of order can be illusory, and other readers of *Shuihu zhuan* observed that outlaw justice was as inconsistent, violent, and cruel as the official persecution they were allegedly fleeing. Although the 108 outlaws are unquestionably the heroes of the narrative, they are heroes whose moral behavior is singularly ambiguous—characterized by political insubordination, rampant misogyny, and impulsive violence that, in its most extreme cases, takes the form of cold-blooded murder, infanticide, and even cannibalism.

The locus classicus of the term "water margin" (*shuihu*) is as ancient as Chinese literature itself, taking us back in time an additional two millennia to the Zhou-dynasty Confucian classic *The Book of Odes* (*Shijing*). Poem 237 of the anthology recounts how Danfu, a forerunner of the Zhou royal line, led his people to safety by bringing them to the foot of Mount Qi in what is now Shaanxi province:

The ancient duke Danfu
Came in the morning, galloping his horses,
Along the edges of the western rivers [*shuihu*],
To the foot of Mount Qi.
And there, he and the lady Jiang
Came, and together looked for a site on which to settle.
The plain of Zhou looked beautiful and rich,

With its violets and sow thistles sweet as dumplings.
There he began with consulting his followers;
There he singed the tortoise shell, and divined.
The responses were—there to stay, and then;
And they proceeded there to build their houses.[2]

As the poem suggests, margins do not necessarily need to be thought of as removed or barren. In addition to being sites where exiles bide their time and hatch plans for an eventual return to the center, margins can be centers of generative vitality and creative ferment in their own right, the places where new epistemological paradigms and political regimes take form and previously unacquainted people and beliefs collide, interact, and synthesize. On a bibliographic level, the literal margins above the printed text of Chinese novels like *Shuihu zhuan* were sites of tremendous intellectual activity as the area where Chinese (and later, Japanese) readers recorded their observations and analyses of all matters normative and narratological. A handful of commentators established literary reputations for themselves through the publication of this commentary, and in the case of *Shuihu zhuan*, in particular, the fame of certain celebrity commentators rivaled or even eclipsed that of the text's putative author(s). David Rolston, a leading expert on this commentarial tradition, points out that it is often difficult to discern where the text of the novel ends and the commentary begins: a dilemma that applies, I think, to other manifestations of marginality as well.[3] As the outlaws' cozy fortress in the marshes demonstrates, one man's margin is another man's center, although not all readers were willing to embrace this relativity. The prolific literary commentator Jin Shengtan (1608–1661), writing in the decades directly after the death of Li Zhuowu, argued that the author of *Shuihu zhuan* could not have intended to praise the outlaws, because he had placed them in the margins of empire, where only loathsome things flourish. By virtue of their decentered location, the outlaws—or at least some of them—were ipso facto bereft of such hallmarks of Confucian civilization as duty (*yi*) and loyalty (*zhong*).[4]

One wonders how early modern Japanese readers of *Shuihu zhuan* interpreted Jin's equation of margin and vice, especially those recipients of a classical education that clearly labeled China the "central florescence" (Chūka) and demoted all peripheries to the status of barbarian. From the novel's initial importation in the beginning of the seventeenth century, the history of the Japanese reception of *Shuihu zhuan* is intertwined with a network of debates concerning Japan's cultural status vis-à-vis its continental neighbor. History's primary key is irony, and by the time most Japanese readers got their hands on a copy of the novel, the Ming empire itself had been toppled by Manchu "barbarians" from the north, demonstrating if nothing else the porosity of the borders separating barbarism and civilization. For peripheral readers, *Shuihu zhuan* is a profoundly optimistic text in its suggestion that margins might become centers in their own right. Kyokutei Bakin (1767–1848) developed this idea in his adaptation of the novel, *Nansō Satomi hakkenden* (Eight dogs of the Satomi clan of southern Fusa, 1814–1842), which relates the scattering of eight "dog-knights" (*kenshi*) into different families, and later their reunion and successful defense of Awa, in modern Chiba prefecture. In light of its emphasis on social reversals and changes of fortune, it is small wonder, perhaps, that both Bakin's adaptation and the novel on which it was based reached a zenith of popularity in Japan during the politically and socially tumultuous Meiji period, when even the elite politician Ōkuma Shigenobu (1838–1922) described his Tokyo residence as "Liangshan in Tsukiji" (*Tsukiji no Ryōzanpaku*), the protective place where he and his coterie could plot and scheme, as well as wait out periods of imperial disfavor before being recalled to court by their own Song Huizong.

In its frequent reversals of moral, political, and social expectations, *Shuihu zhuan* is an outlier in the traditional East Asian literary canon. In contrast to so many other works of late imperial Chinese fiction and drama, *Shuihu zhuan* is not necessarily formally structured by the principle of "retribution" (Ch. *bao*, Jp. *mukui*) that rewards virtue and punishes iniquity with near Newtonian accuracy.[5] While it is true that the outlaws meet their demise at the end of all editions of the novel, their comeuppance is a singularly qualified one, as the deaths of characters like the outlaw chief Song Jiang[6] and his irrepressible sidekick Li Kui are unquestionably imbued with an elegiac, and even tragic air. In light of the morally questionable behavior leading up to their deaths, the perennial appeal of the Liangshan outlaws and the sense of identification they inspired in readers demanded explanation. Bakin spent much of his prolific career marveling that a novel sorely lacking in ethical rectitude could be so appealing on a visceral level, and he presented his own *Hakkenden* as an attempt at preserving *Shuihu zhuan*'s attractive qualities while offering a more wholesome message.[7] Many Meiji-period readers analyzed the outlaws' appeal in terms of the author's mastery of characterization, adapting Jin Shengtan's earlier praise of the author's creation of 108 distinctive "personalities" (Ch. *xingge*) to a literary environment that increasingly emphasized the exploration of interiority and an individual's unique "psychology" (Jp. *shinri*). If, as many critics posited, these were the hallmarks of literary modernity, then *Shuihu zhuan* is a precociously modern text, a point made in 1910 by the critic Yamaji Aizan (1865–1917) when he called *Shuihu zhuan* a model for the naturalist novel. Seen in this light, the very moral ambiguity that had necessitated an intervention by Bakin a century earlier could be recast as evidence of a higher, more sophisticated mimetic sensitivity to the contours of lived experience.

One place where borders and distinctions between centers and peripheries remain stubbornly in place is in the contemporary study of the so-called national literatures, a tradition that, in the case of Japanese *kokubungaku*, dates to the second and third decades of the Meiji period (1868–1912), and in the West goes back approximately a century earlier. As the scholarship of Tomiko Yoda, Haruo Shirane, Tomi Suzuki, and others has convincingly demonstrated, scholars of the twenty-first century are still, in many ways, heirs to Meiji-period literary taxonomies and ideas about literature, both in terms of the texts we admit to the canon and the larger institutional structures in which our analyses take place.[8] The overwhelming majority of research on Japanese literature in the United States takes place under the auspices of East Asian language and literature (or civilization) departments, where—despite some inevitable leakage between fields—research agendas, teaching duties, and tenure lines are usually separated by language (Chinese, Japanese, Korean, etc.), disciplinary methodology (literature, linguistics, history, etc.), and usually time frame (premodern/modern). To be clear at the outset: this study is not a polemical call to do away with this model, and I offer only minor suggestions for how it might be tweaked. However, I do want to argue, as others have before me, that the present institutional configuration does little to encourage research on topics that cross linguistic, geographic, and temporal divides. Although the situation is changing rapidly, scholars whose research traverses linguistic and political borders are still generally expected to gravitate toward a particular "side." Joshua Fogel, one of the universally acknowledged giants of contemporary Sino-Japanese studies, acknowledges this pressure in the introduction to a recent publication, where reluctant to identify primarily with either half of the Sino-Japanese dyad, he describes his research process as picking a topic that moves between languages, cultures, and borders, and "go[ing] where the research necessitates I go."[9] In its focus on the act of "going" itself as a target of analysis, Fogel's attractively pithy description bears some similarity to what David Damrosch has termed a "phenomenology of the work of art," a mode of reading that emphasizes the movement and creative transformation of texts and ideas over questions of origin and essence.[10]

This study centers on the movement and creative transformation of a particular work of Chinese fiction and examines the ways in which the Japanese reception of *Shuihu zhuan* and other late imperial novels contributed to a widespread and radical reappraisal of the relationship between language, literature, and cultural identity over a span of two centuries. By virtue of this focus, it positions itself within a growing body of scholarship devoted to previously overlooked connections between the literary corpuses of China and Japan. The past five years alone have seen a sharp rise of interest in scholarship that, to borrow Fogel's formulation once again, selects a topic and follows it across linguistic, cultural, and temporal divides as the research necessitates—and in doing so, forces us to reconsider the terms on which transregional investigations take place. For purposes of disciplinary classification, research of this type is generally subsumed under the rubric "Sino-Japanese literary studies," which, although useful as shorthand, involves its own perils and assumptions. There is, for example, the potential risk of presentism enshrined in the formulation "Sino-Japanese," which takes the contemporary nation-states China and Japan as its basic conceptual starting point.[11] This is tenuous ground in the case of premodern East Asia, where questions of language and identity are often far from isometric with contemporary political demarcation lines. If anything unites the wide-ranging and disparate group of scholars and topics grouped under the categorical umbrella of Sino-Japanese studies, it is an interest in demonstrating how nationalism and its attendant cultural myopias have warped our perception of the ways in which residents of earlier eras conceived of literature, language, script, and culture. At one end of the historical spectrum, for example, David Lurie has challenged the "bilingual fallacy" that pre-Heian scribes considered themselves to be writing "in Chinese" and that readers evaluated the legibility of inscriptions with exclusive reference to a foreign standard; at the other end of the continuum, Matthew Fraleigh has shown that even for literati who considered a lapse from literary Sinitic grammar to be a compositional faux pas, Sinitic genres such as *kanshibun* (the term itself a Meiji-period neologism) were not marked by any sense of foreignness or alienness for their Japanese practitioners.[12] Perhaps most relevant to the scope of this study, Atsuko Sakaki has demonstrated that there is the perennial danger in conceiving of China and Japan within a polarized framework—particularly in the context of the premodern world—that results in the anachronistic projection of essentialized or putatively "national" qualities back onto earlier texts.[13] Early modern hierarchies of interpretive priorities did not necessarily privilege geography and language, and we should not assume that eighteenth-century Japanese readers of texts like *Shuihu zhuan* read them as "Chinese literature" per se. This is not to say that they were unaware that the novel came from a different region and was written in an unfamiliar language (indeed, they were keenly aware of this) but rather that they did not expect the text to function, as readers a century later did, as the reflection of a geographically or linguistically defined cultural or national essence. Prior to the advent of *kokubungaku* and its Sinocentric cousin *Shina bungaku* in the 1890s, commentators like Kyokutei Bakin were far more interested in the structure of the narrative and its conformity to "universal" standards of duty, loyalty, and justice than in the question of what the novel revealed about China in particular.

As faith in the ontological inevitability of the nation-state wavers, there have been numerous eloquent suggestions for how specific texts and ideas might be "rescued" from the teleologies of nationalism.[14] In very different ways, the research of scholars such as Fogel, Lurie, Fraleigh, and Sakaki among others demonstrates the key role that comparative research can play in this process as an avenue for exploring the cultural, textual, and linguistic networks that are occluded and effaced through a paramount emphasis on the modern nation-state as a unit of analysis. My study of the Japanese reception of *Shuihu zhuan* is informed by recent efforts to rethink the "impact-response" model inherited from earlier *kokubungaku* paradigms, in which we begin with a Chinese text, genre, or motif and explore the processes by which it is adapted and reworked into something quintessentially Japanese. Such a schematic undergirds, for instance, Asō Isoji's seminal discussion of Chinese influence on Edo-period fiction and drama, which invoked a process of "Japanification" (*Nihonka*) as a rubric for assessing a given work's significance to early modern literary culture.[15] Similarly, Nakamura Yukihiko and Takashima Toshio, who have focused on translations, adaptations, and annotations of *Shuihu zhuan* in particular, have centered their studies largely on the ways in which Japanese redactors either departed from or preserved the narrative contours of the original Chinese text.[16] Needless to say, I would have been unable to write my own monograph without these foundational works of scholarship, and my objective in reexamining Japanese engagement with *Shuihu zhuan* is not to supplant these studies but to propose a change of conceptual focus by drawing attention to the ways in which various ideas about "Chineseness" and "Japaneseness" were first generated through transregional literary contact. In contrast to the traditional focus on difference and response, some of the most exciting research in recent years has focused on points of affiliation and continuity: from Saitō Mareshi's discussion of Sinitic "écriture" (*kanbunmyaku*) as a unit of analysis to Atsuko Sakaki's historicization and critical interrogation of the Sino-Japanese polarity itself.[17] In his recent discussion of Meiji-period poetry and poetics, Matthew Fraleigh analyzes the late nineteenth-century epistemological contractions that created *kanshi* and *kanbun* out of what were formerly simply poetry (*shifu*) and prose (*bunshō*), thus highlighting how literary historiography imposes nationalities upon texts in ways that would have been unfamiliar to their authors.[18] In his thoughtful justification of the term "Sinitic poetry" over "Chinese-style poetry" or "Sino-Japanese poetry" as a translation for *kanshi*, Fraleigh asks us to consider the potentially anachronistic entanglements of nomenclature, and gestures, I believe, toward a future in which specialization in "Sinitic literature" might seem as natural in the academy as formulations such as "Japanese literature" and "Chinese literature." The understudied history of Japanese engagement with late imperial Chinese fiction has a great deal to contribute to the aforementioned discussion, in terms of historicizing and reconceptualizing the processes by which certain ideas about literary canon and national literatures that continue into the present first took shape.

This study begins with a question: rather than reading works of Chinese fiction like *Shuihu zhuan* as a source of inspiration *for* Japanese literature, what does it mean to read them *as* Japanese literature? For contemporary scholars, weaned on Gideon Toury's characterization of translations and rewritings as "facts" of the target culture, there is perhaps little in this formulation to cause alarm, but it is important to note that this line of inquiry builds on an indigenous precedent that far predates modern translation theory.[19] A similar proposal was made in 1897, for instance, against the backdrop of burgeoning interest in defining and describing parallel lineages of Japanese "national literature" (*kokubungaku*) and Chinese literature (*Shina bungaku*) as academic objects of knowledge. In the preface to the multivolume *Compendium of Chinese Literature* (*Shina bungaku taikō*), the editors of the series invited the reader—within the space of a few lines—to think of Chinese literature as not only the "literature of a foreign country" (*gaikoku no bungaku*) but also the "second national literature of Japan" (*daini kokubungaku*).[20] Recent years have witnessed a vibrant debate over the history and discursive boundaries of the term "Japanese literature," and, on a superficial level, there is a comparison to be made with the period that witnessed not only the publication of the *Compendium* but also the conceptual birth of "literature" (*bungaku*) itself. What if we revisit and take seriously this presentation of Chinese literature as the second national literature of Japan: not in the overtly nationalistic and imperialistic way intended by the *Compendium*'s editors but as a catalyst for new ways of thinking about how the concept of literature itself was codified and defined by writers of the period?

My motivation in selecting *Shuihu zhuan* as a primary focus for my study stems from its early enlistment in broader interrogations of language, literature, and cultural identity in Japan, a process that began with the novel's importation in the early seventeenth century and continued unabated throughout the first half of the twentieth century. This is not a comprehensive catalogue and analysis of all Japanese translations, adaptations, and redactions of *Shuihu zhuan*, although such an account would undoubtedly be fascinating—indeed, as polyvocal, colorful, and complex as early modern literature itself. However, *Shuihu zhuan* is a novel whose significance to the development of early modern and modern Japanese literature simply cannot be overstated; a work whose translation, adaptation, and gradual ubiquitous presence in Japanese literary culture neatly intersects major trends in philology, literary criticism, and interest in Chinese material culture. As a prism for organizing a history of Japanese fiction and literary criticism, its only analogue, perhaps, is the Heian classic *Genji monogatari*, a title that Edo-period authors themselves invoked in comparative discussions of *Shuihu zhuan*'s themes and structures. However, while the *Genji* was beloved by early modern *kokugaku* scholars for its value in constructing a theory of uncontaminated "pure" Japaneseness, *Shuihu zhuan* provides a template for emplotting an alternative history of Japanese literary and cultural identity, one narrated from outside perspectives and characterized by the sense of alterity, Otherness, and cultural difference that scholars such as Motoori Norinaga (1730–1801) sought to isolate and elide in their scholarship on the Japanese classics.

As a work that emphasizes the centrality of linguistic and cultural translation in the formation of Japanese literature, my research is informed by the recent work of authors like Rebekah Clements, Nakamura Aya, and Okada Kesao, who have conclusively demonstrated the connections between engagement with late imperial Chinese fiction and Japanese interest in language and translation. As my opening chapters demonstrate, I am particularly indebted to the pioneering and wide-ranging research of Emanuel Pastreich, who has been largely responsible for a resurgence of interest in the relationship of this corpus to early modern discourses of language and the representation of the quotidian.[21] Pastreich structures his study as an account of literarization, in which, chiefly as a result of their exposure to Chinese fiction, early modern Japanese readers came to read texts as disparate as courtesan biographies, puppet theater, and the *Analects* of Confucius as "literature." While agreeing with many of the points raised in his seminal study, I believe there is still ample room for inquiry into the ways in which the category of literature itself emerged as a result of the textual circulation he and other scholars describe.[22] Specifically, what does it mean to read something in a "literary" way, and how did this change over the two centuries examined in this study? Did the Tendai abbot Tenkai (d. 1643)— owner of one of the earliest imported editions of *Shuihu zhuan* in Japan— consider the work to be "literature," and did Bakin, two centuries later, read *Shuihu zhuan* as "literature" in the sense of the interconnected and hierarchical system of genres described by Meiji-period historians like Mikami Sanji (1865–1939) and Kojō Teikichi (1866–1949)? My answer to these questions is almost certainly not, which means that additional research is required into the process by which a text like *Shuihu zhuan* entered Japan in the early seventeenth century and emerged two centuries later as a "novel," itself the recently crowned apotheosis of the newly constituted field of literature.

This emphasis on historicization would not only contextualize the century-long emphasis on nation-states and national languages as units of literary taxonomy but also draw attention to the alternative cultural and linguistic networks that were hidden through that emphasis. Although literary Sinitic functioned as a lingua franca throughout East Asia for more than a millennium prior to the period of my research, twentieth-century literary historiography has largely downplayed the influence of Sinitic texts in Japan. As Michael C. Brownstein noted more than thirty years ago, this process has reinforced a teleological narrative of the dominance of literature written in native Japanese scripts (kana) and resulted in an ahistorical and unrepresentative understanding of literary canon.[23] China has until recently been similarly erased on a conceptual level in Japanological studies, where the early modern period has traditionally been presented as a rupture in cultural relations as Japanese "nativist scholars" (*kokugakusha*) rejected China as a model for literary emulation and sought an alternative narrative of origins in the ancient Japanese classics.

One of the greatest contributions made by scholars such as Atsuko Ueda, Wiebke Denecke, Kōno Kimiko, Karen Thornber, Satoru Hashimoto, and Saitō Mareshi has been to call into question the extent and nature of this idea of "rupture" by demonstrating lines of continuity and textual circulation that transcend both the Sino-Japanese and premodern-modern binaries. In contrast to unidirectional vectors of cultural influence, Karen Thornber's discussion of "contact nebulae" has drawn attention to the degree to which literary activity in the Japanese imperium was based on the transformation rather than introduction of contact between regional neighbors.[24] Hashimoto and Saitō have analyzed the role of classical Chinese genres like *shi* poetry and *ci* lyrics as an inter-Asian lingua franca in this process of transculturation, well into the modern era.[25] Finally, several recent studies have reevaluated the relationship between the Western concept of "literature" and East Asian theories of composition. Atsuko Ueda's recontextualization of the term *shōsetsu* in Meiji-period discourse, and Kōno Kimiko and Wiebke Denecke's history of Japanese "letterature" ("*bun*"gakushi) are among the critical attempts at highlighting this lack of isometricity between Western "literature" and neologisms such as *bungaku* and the Chinese *wenxue*.[26]

My research joins these welcome critical interventions by exploring the role played by Chinese fiction in the theorization and construction of Japanese and East Asian literary modernity, a process that began in the second and third decades of the Meiji period but, as my first two chapters show, was deeply rooted in compositional theories advanced in critical commentary of the Edo period. During the Meiji, an epoch characterized by the rapid reclassification of literary texts among newly emergent genres and genre hierarchies, traditional novels like *Shuihu zhuan* were defended by both Chinese and Japanese commentators on the basis of the uncannily protomodern—even radical and revolutionary—qualities they were alleged to possess. Whereas genres such as *shi* poetry, *ci* lyrics, and classical prose could be comfortably analyzed within familiar (and, in Japan, fully naturalized) neo-Confucian and Buddhist theories of literary composition, the initially unfamiliar lexicon and thematic range of fiction resisted efforts at normative and epistemological containment. My research complements the aforementioned pioneering contributions by shifting focus away from the canonical genres of classical-language poetry, prose, and historiography toward the controversial and ethically fraught domain of narrative fiction. This shift allows me to examine how works of fiction were legitimated as literary expression and ultimately contextualize the history of the term "literature" itself. As a text that entered Japan at the precise moment attitudes toward China were undergoing a series of fundamental transformations, *Shuihu zhuan*, in particular, was often employed as a starting point for larger discussions of cultural authenticity, (proto)national identity, and literary modernity, from early eighteenth-century lexicographic projects that centered on the temporal divide separating the language of the past from the language of the present, to late nineteenth- and early twentieth-century ethnographic texts that presented *Shuihu zhuan* as evidence of an unbridgeable gap between a reified Chinese and Japanese "national essence" (*kokusui*).

WHAT IS *SHUIHU ZHUAN*?

This is a study of the early modern and modern Japanese reception of Chinese fiction, and it is imperative to note at the outset that not a single key term in this description existed in its present sense during the period I discuss. The chronological scope of my study spans the end of the seventeenth century, when the first works of Chinese popular narrative were imported and translated in Japan, and the first quarter of the twentieth century, by which time Japanese travel to China itself was no longer a remarkable occurrence. The existence of a clean Edo-Meiji divide in the field of literature has been brought into question many, many times, from Peter Kornicki's seminal study of late Edo fiction in the opening years of the Meiji period to more recent discussions by Atsuko Ueda and Jonathan Zwicker, who highlight the entrenchment of certain taxonomies and modes of reading among even the most revolutionary reformers.[27] Despite the fact that all these studies have been extremely well received, it bears periodic reminding that the temporal boundaries created by political revolution do not necessarily delimit literary fields. Although the chapters in my study are structured roughly by chronology, one of my goals is to highlight the continuity of certain expectations about what writing is and the role it plays in the ordering and definition of society, as well as demonstrate how earlier canons of composition, reception, and circulation were seen not as antithetical but, rather, vital to the conceptualization of literary modernity. If anything, the vicissitudes of Chinese fiction in later epochs of Japanese history are a notable case of the entrenchment—and even amplification—of allegedly "premodern" concerns. To chart the trajectory of Chinese fiction in early modern Japan is, in many ways, to experience a kind of hermeneutic déjà vu in which contexts and terminology change but the arguments themselves remain uncannily familiar. When Akutagawa Ryūnosuke (1892–1927) stood on the banks of West Lake in 1921 and mused about the "Nietzschean" elements of Chinese civilization apparent in its fiction, his argument was not radically dissimilar from the interpretive chestnut that fiction directly reflects the circumstances of its composition, an argument made a century earlier by Kyokutei Bakin and a century before Bakin by the historian Seita Tansō (1719–1785), who urged his readers to comb the official history of the Song dynasty and thereby discover the "real water margin beyond the *Water Margin* of the text."[28] If there is a chronological division line to be drawn between the "premodern" and "modern" halves of this study, then it occurs in the late 1880s and 1890s, when the nascent field of literary historiography (*bungakushi*) established a new superstructure for the lateral comparison of texts and genres—even if the arguments raised with respect to individual works continued to bear the clear traces of earlier criticism by Kyokutei Bakin, Jin Shengtan, and Li Zhuowu.

Similarly, rather than treating China and Japan as stable entities that bounced texts and genres back and forth across clearly demarcated cultural and linguistic borders, my discussion highlights the ways in which ideas about culture and identity (ultimately, but by no means inevitably, in the discourse of national culture and identity) emerged through the circulation and translation of texts. That China's status as a locus of cultural, textual, and epistemological authority was the subject of debate throughout much of the early modern era is evidenced by the wide range of toponyms—Chūka, Kan (as in *wakan*), Tō, Shina—applied during the period of my study. What is immediately clear in investigating the deployment of these toponyms is that each enshrines a particular, but by no means unitary or universally agreed-upon, understanding of cultural, geographic, and political relations.[29] A study of *Shuihu zhuan* in early modern and modern Japan inevitably takes the form of an inquiry into changes in relations between subject and object, observer and observed—from early eighteenth-century vernacular philology, which reassessed the applicability of classical scholarship to the study of contemporary China; to early modern interest in Chinese fiction exegesis, which presumed equal authoritative footing between Chinese and Japanese commentators; to the quasi-ethnographic readings of *Shuihu zhuan* and other texts discussed in the second half of my study, which presented a putative "Chinese people" (*Shina kokumin*) as specimens to be observed, chronicled, and explicated by Japanese experts.

The term "fiction" (*xiaoshuo* and *shōsetsu* in modern Mandarin and Japanese, respectively) is the most problematic term in my study. In the interest of avoiding tiresome qualifications and repetitive prose, I refer to *Shuihu zhuan* and other comparable narratives as "fiction" or "novels" throughout this study, but my research is not only an exploration of Chinese fiction in Japan but also a discussion of the ways in which the novel was defined and positioned within a constellation of other genres and modes of reading. My study partakes of the same intervention as Atsuko Ueda's analysis of Tsubouchi Shōyō's (1859–1935) seminal *Shōsetsu shinzui* (*The Essence of the Novel*, 1885–1886), a text traditionally interpreted as a study of the novel in Japan but that Ueda reads instead as an attempt at forging equivalences between very different literary traditions from Japan, China, and the West.[30] Similarly, while modern readers broadly compare the features of *Shuihu zhuan*, Bakin's *Hakkenden*, and *Genji monogatari* as novels or works of fiction, this establishment of conceptual equivalence can, and needs to be, historicized as part of the same processes of "discovery" that uncovered (which is to say, created) narrative continuity and unitary essences in Shōyō's day.

On the level of summary, it is easy to answer the question raised in the preceding subheading. *Shuihu zhuan* is a lengthy prose narrative (consisting of one hundred or one hundred twenty chapters in its longest recensions) chronicling the gathering of 108 bandit-gallants in the Liangshan marshes of northeastern China. Although the majority of the story takes place during the troubled final years of the Song emperor Huizong, the tale opens several decades earlier, against the backdrop of a plague during the reign of Renzong (r. 1022–1063). Marshal Hong Xin, an official at the Song court, travels to a faraway temple to ask the reclusive patriarch Heavenly Teacher Zhang for assistance in controlling the plague.[31] During his time at the temple, the arrogant marshal insists on opening a sealed coffer, which releases the imprisoned spirits of thirty-six Heavenly Spirits (*tiangang*) and seventy-two Earthly Fiends (*disha*) into the ether. These spirits are reincarnated as the 108 outlaws introduced in widely varying degrees of depth in the subsequent chapters of the novel. Much of *Shuihu zhuan* consists of discrete story cycles, usually a few chapters in length, relating the adventures and backstories of specific outlaws.

Perhaps because a full translation of *Shuihu zhuan* was so long in coming, the characters in the first third of the novel were particularly acclaimed in Edo-period Japan: from "Nine Tattooed Dragons" Shi Jin (Jp. Kyūmonryū Shishin), whose fondness for the fraternal company of outlaws results in his own pursuit by the forces of law and order, to his eventual compatriot "The Tattooed Monk" Lu Zhishen (Kaoshō Rochishin), whose penchant for drink and hard living prevents him from leading a quiet, incognito life on the lam. Other well-known characters from the novel include Wu Song (Bushō), who dispatches a man-eating tiger with his bare hands before applying the same skill set to his adulterous sister-in-law and her murderous lover; "Black Whirlwind" Li Kui (Kokusenpū Riki), whose childlike enthusiasm and mindless embrace of violence straddle an uneasy line between psychopathy and Buddhahood; and the refined bon vivant Yan Qing (Ensei), whose sensual appearance, female contacts, and cultured repertoire make him an exotic addition to the stolidly androcentric and misogynistic company of his peers. As the eventual leader of the Liangshan gang, "Timely Rain" Song Jiang (Kyūjiu Sōkō)—mild-mannered clerk turned brigand chief—was a particular flashpoint for interpretation and criticism. Jin Shengtan famously despised Song Jiang for his alleged hypocrisy and duplicity, and devoted much of his commentarial attention (going so far as to rewrite certain sections of the text) to detailing Song's transgressions—a theme that would be taken up and challenged by Bakin and others once the novel made it to Japan.

As mentioned, *Shuihu zhuan* circulated in a variety of recensions in both China and Japan, and the question of edition becomes particularly important in the second half of the novel. In the longest recensions of the narrative (again, usually one hundred or one hundred twenty chapters long), the assemblage of the 108 outlaws in the seventy-first chapter of the novel is followed by their imperial pardon and summons to the Song court. As a means of redemption, the Liangshan gang is dispatched on campaigns against both Khitan invaders from the north and other groups of outlaws that are, at first blush, not at all that dissimilar from Song Jiang and his followers. After the successful pacification of these revolts, many of the surviving outlaws are enfeoffed and granted prestigious positions in the Song bureaucracy. Song Jiang himself becomes a provincial governor, but the corrupt officials at court continue to impugn his loyalty. Finally, Huizong reluctantly agrees to a scheme by which to murder Song through a gift of poisoned wine. After realizing he has been poisoned, Song Jiang, loyal to the last, worries that his brooding and dangerous doppelgänger, Li Kui, will insist on revenge and tricks his compatriot into drinking the wine as well. In the melancholy final chapter, "Song Jiang's Ghost Haunts Liao'er Flats and Emperor Huizong Dreams of the Liangshan Marshes," Huizong himself undertakes an oneiric journey to the abandoned Hall of Loyalty and Duty, where he meets the ghosts of Song Jiang, Li Kui, and other departed outlaws amid the ruins of their former stronghold. The moral complexity of the novel as a whole is epitomized in these final exchanges in which Li Kui is duped by his own outlaw brother, Song Jiang's loyalty is simultaneously punished and memorialized by the emperor, and the fretful apparition of Huizong hovers on the peripheries of his decentered and doomed empire.[32]

This melancholy and ambiguous ending was too much for some readers to bear. Although he was highly sympathetic to many of the outlaws and praised Li Kui in particular as a "living Buddha" (*huofo*), Jin Shengtan was unsparing in his insistence that rebellion against the Song court should be punished. In a seventy-chapter truncated edition of the novel, Jin excised the entire second half dealing with the outlaws' pardon, redemption, and military campaigns. He replaced it with a single chapter in which, immediately following the gathering of the outlaws, "Jade Unicorn" Lu Junyi has a hideous dream in which he and his fellow outlaws are executed by an official from the Song court. The dream is presumably a harbinger of things to come, and despite its "lady-or-the-tiger"-esque qualities, Jin's rewritten ending emphasized his long-standing contention that Song Jiang and his followers should not be granted pardon. Jin justified his emendation by claiming to have unearthed an "ancient edition" (*guben*) of the novel. The subterfuge fooled very few readers in either China or Japan, but the truncated Jin Shengtan edition of *Shuihu zhuan* was immensely popular in both places, owing in large part to the extensive critical commentary that Jin published along with the body of the novel itself.

In its earliest appearance in Han-period bibliography, the term *xiaoshuo* referred to a minor subset of historiography, and like many other works of late imperial Chinese fiction, *Shuihu zhuan* has a verifiable historical source. The official history of the Song dynasty (*Songshi*) records the existence of a certain Song Jiang, who created a series of disturbances in northern China between the years 1117 and 1121 before being pacified by the magistrate Zhang Shuye (d. 1127).[33] The account credits the retired official Hou Meng (d. 1121) with the idea of enlisting Song's forces in a campaign against a far more formidable foe, the Zhejiang-based rebel Fang La, who attracted several tens of thousands of followers to his cause and arrogated the title of emperor to himself in 1120. The *Songshi* does not discuss whether such a plan was employed, but "unofficial histories" (*waishi*) describe Song Jiang's participation in the battle against Fang La, and the stories surrounding Song gradually became entwined with other myths and legends. As early as the Southern Song (1127–1279), Luo Ye's *Zuiweng tanlu* (Accounts of conversations with a drunken old man) attests to the existence of stories about "the tattooed monk [Lu Zhishen]," "the pilgrim [Wu Song]," and other characters who would later be associated with Song Jiang's coterie.[34] During the Yuan dynasty (1279–1368), when China was under the control of Mongol invaders, stories about Song Jiang and his compatriots—especially the impulsive and charismatic "Black Whirlwind" Li Kui—were used as subject material in numerous works of "variety theater" (*zaju*).[35] Some of the titles mentioned in period sources are still extant, while others appear to have been lost, but taken as a whole these plays attest to thriving and continued interest in narratives about Song Jiang's followers and provide a repository for speculation about what the earliest version(s) of the novel might have looked like.[36]

The novel that we are familiar with today appears to be a product of the sixteenth century, although popular lore places its authorship centuries earlier. Traditionally, *Shuihu zhuan* has had two candidates for authorship, both of whom are usually said to have lived during the Yuan or beginning of the Ming: the playwright Luo Guanzhong (1330–1400?), whose existence is attested to in an early Ming-period text, and the more nebulous Shi Nai'an, whose historicity has never been confirmed.[37] Some sources credit either Luo or Shi with sole authorship of *Shuihu zhuan*, while others present the novel as a collaborative venture between the two. Jin Shengtan, for instance, famously claimed Shi Nai'an was the sole author of *Shuihu zhuan* and justified his excision of the amnesty chapters by saying they were a "dog's tail" (*gouwei*) tacked on later by Luo Guanzhong. Barring a remarkable bibliographic discovery, the question of *Shuihu zhuan*'s authorship will probably never be adequately resolved, but it was seen as central to establishing the meaning of the novel in both early modern China and Japan.[38]

Despite perennial speculation about an ur-edition of *Shuihu zhuan* dating from the early Ming or even Yuan period, it is not until the sixteenth century that we see substantial bibliographic evidence of a novel similar to the editions available today.[39] Remarkably, considering the novel's subaltern focus and subversive content, the earliest mentions of *Shuihu zhuan* are to editions produced under partial or full government patronage, including the "Wuding edition" sponsored by the eponymous marquis of Wuding, Guo Xun (1475–1541), and an edition prepared by the imperial Censorate Bureau (*duchayuan*) sometime before 1570.[40] Far from being the direct product or unmediated reflection of a popular milieu, what stands out most about the novel's early history is the elite circumstances under which it was produced, circulated, and presumably enjoyed—an argument made consistently and convincingly by scholars such as W. L. Idema, Andrew Plaks, and Scott Gregory.[41]

The only datable and intact exemplar of the novel that survives from the sixteenth century is an edition published by the Fujian publisher Yu Xiangdou in 1594. The edition was preserved in the library of the aforementioned abbot Tenkai, whose death in 1643 provides us with a *terminus ante quem* for the novel's importation into Japan. In contrast to the scattered handful of references to *Shuihu zhuan* in library catalogues a mere forty years earlier, the preface to this recension of the novel alludes to a superabundance of editions of *Shuihu zhuan* in circulation, evidence of the rapidity with which the novel infiltrated and established its dominance in the late-Ming commercial market.[42] The proliferation of editions in China is reflected in the history of the novel's importation in Japan. Within the span of a hundred years, the Tenkai edition of *Shuihu zhuan* would be joined by myriad other recensions of the narrative, including, but by no means limited to, the one-hundred-twenty-chapter text printed around 1610 and dubbed the Rongyutang edition after its eponymous Hangzhou publishing house; the slightly later "Wu Yuanwai edition" (named for its Suzhou publisher), which like the Rongyutang text included a preface and commentary attributed to Li Zhuowu; the "Catalogue of Heroes edition" (*Yingxiongpu*) that printed *Shuihu zhuan* alongside the text of its perennial travel companion, *Romance of the Three Kingdoms*; the truncated Jin Shengtan "Guanhuatang edition" named for the studio in which it was allegedly unearthed; and the 1657 "Wang Wangru edition," which added additional commentarial analysis to the seventy-chapter Jin Shengtan text.[43] This brief catalogue is provided not to bog the reader down in bibliographic details but to make the crucial point that, beyond the basic level of narrative summary, the question, what is *Shuihu zhuan*? becomes a much more complex and unstable inquiry, one that, as David Damrosch says about world literature in general, resolves always into a variety of worlds and additional questions.[44]

WHAT IS *SHUIHU ZHUAN*? REDUX

As suggested, Japanese readers of the early modern and modern periods did not read a novel called *Shuihu zhuan*; rather, they read one of many *Shuihu zhuan*s, as instantiated in various commercial, critical, and commentarial editions. Despite his prestigious position in the emergent Tokugawa regime, the abbot Tenkai, for instance, encountered the novel in the form of the cheaply printed simplified edition (*jianben*) published by Yu Xiangdou, while other readers became the proud owners (or at least borrowers) of full editions (*fanben*) characterized by more complex language and higher-quality production.[45] Many early modern Japanese readers read the seventy-chapter truncated edition of Jin Shengtan, while others turned up their noses at the abridgement and sought out the one-hundred-twenty-chapter "original" edition (*shōhon*) instead. Those who accepted Jin's attribution of authorship to Shi Nai'an viewed the imperial pardon chapters as the dog's tail appended by Luo Guanzhong, while readers like Bakin believed that the second half of the novel was integral to the conveyance of the author's moral message. Finally, if they were interested in the critical pronouncements of Chinese commentators—and it appears that nearly all Japanese readers were—aficionados of Chinese fiction read with one of a number of loquacious guides looking over their figurative shoulders. Readers of the Rongyutang's *The Loyal and Righteous Water Margin with Commentary by Mr. Li Zhuowu* were told that the inclusion of the terms "loyal" and "righteous" in the title of the text was a means of inculcating a proper understanding of the novel's central protagonists; readers of Jin Shengtan's *The Fifth Book for Men of Genius: Shi Nai'an's "The Water Margin"* were told that the terms had been excised from the title for precisely the same reason. The experience of reading Jin Shengtan's *Fifth Book for Men of Genius* was emphatically not the same thing as reading the Rongyutang's *Loyal and Righteous Water Margin*, and the fact that this critical commentary was excised in twentieth-century editions of the text does not mean that earlier generations of readers ignored it as well.[46]

The existence of multiple recensions of *Shuihu zhuan* in circulation throughout early modern Japanese history (as well as the presence of lexicographic reference works, commentaries, and adaptations in a variety of media) complicates the question of how to structure my account. As a study of how a particular work of Chinese literature assumed a preeminent position in the emergent field of Japanese literature, the usual name for a monograph such as this is "reception history." And while I have no objections to my work's being characterized as such, I have been persuaded by the argument advanced by Michael Emmerich in his masterful study of the *Genji monogatari*, in which he argues that "studies of canonization, or at least the field of canonization studies, would do well to dispense with the inherently passive word 'reception.'"[47] Objecting to the fact that the term (1) implies the existence of a stable text being transmitted intact from one reader to the next and (2) potentially ignores the "mutable history of books and other material forms," Emmerich advocates thinking instead of "canonization as the continual *replacement* of canonical texts by new, different versions of themselves that answer to the needs not only of authoritative institutions intent on preserving and propagating their own values and ideologies, but also of their consumers; the literary canon as an enormous gallery of look-alikes, a string of placeholders."[48] With a few minor adjustments, Emmerich's argument is keenly suited to the case of *Shuihu zhuan*, where any plan to write a reception history is immediately derailed by the fact that, for much of the period under discussion, it is not clear what, if anything, was being received. Throughout the seventeenth, eighteenth, and even nineteenth centuries, there are myriad references to the difficulty of acquiring an edition of *Shuihu zhuan*; there are descriptions of the singular challenges of reading *Shuihu zhuan*; and there is a cacophony of complaints about the inadequacy of available translations of *Shuihu zhuan* on the market. Far more elusive is evidence of readers sitting down and reading *Shuihu zhuan* from start to finish—at least prior to the mass publication of commercial editions of Chinese fiction in translation in the first decades of the Meiji period. Emmerich's argument is that it is often the production of "replacements" like adaptations, parodies, and material paraphernalia that lead to the canonization of particular works, rather than vice versa. In the case of the *Genji*, these replacements range from the prestigious commentaries collected in Kitamura Kigin's *Kogetsushō* and adaptations such as Ryūtei Tanehiko's *Nise Murasaki inaka Genji*, to novelty items like the eighteenth-century "bean-size" illustrated guide to *Genji* and the *Genji monogatari* Millennial Anniversary Matcha Baumkuchen prepared by the Yamazaki Baking Company in 2008.[49] In the case of *Shuihu zhuan*, such replacements might take the form of the stunning tradition of woodblock illustrations inaugurated by artists like Katsushika Hokusai and Utagawa Kuniyoshi; the *Shuihu zhuan*–themed *sugoroku* game now in the possession of the National Diet Library; and works like Santō Kyōden's *Chūshin Suikoden*, which fused the narrative of *Shuihu zhuan* to the far more familiar story of the forty-seven faithful samurai of Akō. By the standards of the fidelity criticism that has traditionally characterized research on literary relations between China and Japan, these works are secondary and derivative, but it is almost certain that far more readers encountered *Shuihu zhuan* through Kuniyoshi's *musha-e* or Kyōden's *yomihon* than through firsthand engagement with the novel itself.[50] In approaching the issue of the reception of *Shuihu zhuan* in early modern Japan, it is imperative to note that consumers (not necessarily readers) of the novel might have been familiar only with a particular story cycle, the visual representation of an individual character, or simply the novel's overarching engagement with the themes of subversion and moral legitimacy. Despite premodern (and even modern) critics' perennial fixation with authorial intention and the recovery of an original urtext, the fact that *Shuihu zhuan* circulated in a variety of recensions with radically different endings and paratextual frameworks should be an invitation to abandon any quixotic quest for a stable text moving intact from reader to reader, generation to generation.

The example of *Shuihu zhuan* demonstrates above all that Japanese readers, rewriters, and literary historians did not simply consume or "indigenize" Chinese texts; rather, these texts engendered radical reconsiderations of both the function of writing and its relation to larger discourses of cultural affiliation, a process that began in earnest in the first decades of the eighteenth century and continued uninterrupted for the next two centuries. Chapter 1 traces the history of the initial importation of *Shuihu zhuan* in the early seventeenth century and outlines its role as a catalyst for a budding tradition of vernacular philology, a systematic study of contemporary Chinese language and culture that ultimately contributed to a reappraisal of China's position as a source of culture and civilization. Although literary Sinitic had functioned as a written lingua franca in Confucian scholarship for more than a millennium in East Asia, the language of *Shuihu zhuan* was largely unfamiliar to Japanese readers. The desire to read recently imported Chinese texts (in particular, works of fiction) resulted in the serial publication of dictionaries, encyclopedias, and other lexicographic reference works devoted to contemporary language. This engagement had a profound effect on the conceptualization of China as a locus of cultural and epistemological authority—in particular, a shift away from the universalized moral inquiry of traditional Confucian scholarship in favor of a narrower interest in cataloguing the concrete and discrete components of contemporary Chinese material and textual culture. This transitional episteme serves as a link between the moral and political concerns of early eighteenth-century classical studies and the more narrowly ethnographic and positivist studies of China discussed in chapters 3 and 4 of my study.

Chapter 2 shifts emphasis from the lexicographic research presented in chapter 1 to explorations of narratology by eighteenth- and nineteenth-century Japanese readers of Chinese fiction. My analysis centers on Japanese discussions of late imperial Chinese fiction exegesis. Nearly all works of Chinese fiction were printed along with elaborate critical commentaries (known as *pingdian*) that glossed difficult terms, passed moral judgment on the characters' actions, and drew the reader's attention to symbolism and other literary techniques. These commentaries were printed in the margins above the body of the text, and scholars of Chinese fiction have increasingly noted the centrality of this commentarial tradition to the late imperial Chinese reading experience—particularly when approaching ethically complex works such as *Shuihu zhuan*. Edo-period readers like Kyokutei Bakin, Seita Tansō, and Santō Kyōden discussed this commentarial tradition extensively, in a manner consonant with the observations of contemporary literary scholars like Linda Hutcheon and Gérard Genette, who have analyzed adaptations and paratextual commentary as a way of presenting and "making present" foreign works of literature in drastically different cultural and literary contexts.

Chapter 3 discusses the establishment of the academic study of literature (*bungakushi*) in the final decades of the nineteenth century and explores the intertwined relationship between national literature and national identity in Meiji-period Japan. My focus is the centrality of Chinese texts—especially the traditional novel—in the Japanese theorization of literary development. I argue that the emergence of literary historiography in late nineteenth-century Japan was, from its inception, a transregional phenomenon characterized not by the passive acceptance of European intellectual models but through a process of active triangulation between Western, Japanese, and Chinese visions of literary composition and canon formation. Until recently, the role of China in this process has been almost entirely effaced, and my study seeks to restore balance to these considerations. Far from being the stagnant Other to be "left behind" in Fukuzawa Yukichi's canonical formulation, China and its body of fiction provided a repository of thought that Meiji-period literary historians reconfigured in their theories of literary evolution. In an academic environment obsessed with the location and identification of racial, cultural, and psychological essences, Japanese literary history was united by the claim that the "real" or authentic China could be found only in previously marginalized genres such as the novel.

The final chapter of my monograph connects interest in Chinese vernacular fiction to a larger discourse about the political and cultural situation of late Qing and Republican-era China (approximately 1890 to 1920). Whereas the Edo-period critics discussed in chapter 2 had explored the significance of *Shuihu zhuan* with respect to "universal" Confucian norms such as duty and loyalty, one hallmark of Meiji- and Taishō-period interest in the novel was an attempt at grounding the work in the context of contemporary Chinese culture. I examine the writing of key authors of the period, including Mori Ōgai, Akutagawa Ryūnosuke, Tokutomi Sohō, and Masaoka Shiki, and discuss the ways in which their deep familiarity with Chinese fiction shaped their imagination and representation of the Chinese nation-state—a process in which China itself was presented as a text waiting to be read, explicated, and ordered through narrative. *Shuihu zhuan*, in particular, plays a central role in the writing of many Japanese commentators on China, as the lens by which they presented the novel as both a symbol of fin de siècle imperial China and a foil to Japanese modernity.

Chapter One

SINOPHILIA, SINOPHOBIA, AND VERNACULAR PHILOLOGY IN EARLY MODERN JAPAN

The past is a foreign country: they do things differently there.

—L. P. HARTLEY, *THE GO-BETWEEN*

China is China, Japan is Japan; the past is past, and now is now.

—HIRAGA GENNAI, *THE BIOGRAPHY OF DASHING SHIDŌKEN*

It is difficult to exaggerate the importance of Chinese fiction and drama to the literary culture of early modern Japan. The rise to ubiquitous prominence of Chinese texts such as *Shuihu zhuan, Xiyou ji* (*Journey to the West*), and the short fiction of Feng Menglong (1574–1646) was a gradual occurrence, however, and the record suggests that Japanese readers' first encounters with these texts were as fraught with uncertainty, contention, and misunderstanding as the importation of Confucian classics and the Buddhist canon had occasioned in past eras. The Edo-period fascination with Chinese fiction has been well noted (if less frequently discussed), and to a certain extent the place of novels like *Shuihu zhuan* and *Sanguo yanyi* (*Romance of the Three Kingdoms*) in the Japanese literary canon is secure. What is considerably less studied, however, is the circuitous route by which these novels first rose to prominence. *Shuihu zhuan*, for instance, appeared in shogunal bibliographic records as early as the beginning of the seventeenth century, but it was not until well over a century later that the work was first translated into Japanese. This is certainly not to say that *Shuihu zhuan* was unknown in seventeenth- and early eighteenth-century Japan. The title was mentioned in numerous documents from the period, and imported copies of the novel excited considerable interest among connoisseurs of Chinese texts.[1] What is less clear is the degree to which Japanese readers *understood* the novel. The difficult language of the text—which included numerous examples of more contemporary and colloquial usage—precluded any large-scale dissemination, and discussion of the text was limited largely to a small group of initiate readers. As late as 1757, when the scholar and enthusiast Suyama Nantō (1700–1766) compiled a reference guide to "difficult vocabulary" in *Shuihu zhuan*, his list of terms included some of the most elementary locutions found in Chinese fiction. Lest the mere acquisition of Chinese novels be mistaken for detailed comprehension, the preface to the work made mocking reference to Japanese readers who eagerly sought out new titles, only to "bundle them up and store them away, unable to read them."[2]

In the writing of early eighteenth-century scholars of Chinese texts, *Shuihu zhuan* was invoked as an example of the linguistic registers known as *zokugo* and *Tōwa*, terms that have both been translated as "vernacular" but that might be better understood as "colloquial" or "contemporary" language. The term *Tōwa*, in particular, was associated with Japanese interest in Chinese spoken language. With the establishment of trade facilities at Nagasaki in the early years of the Tokugawa period, examples of *Tōwa* might be heard firsthand from Chinese sailors in Nagasaki, and as this chapter shows, a number of fiction aficionados had connections to the port city. Both *Tōwa* and *zokugo* also referred to written registers, including, but by no means limited to, the frequently incomprehensible argot of Chinese fiction and drama. The study of these texts was subsumed by the nascent discipline of *Tōwagaku* (the study of *Tōwa*)—a term that appears to have entered the general lexicon in the first decades of the eighteenth century. Although it originally signified the specific dynasty lasting from 618 to 907, the graph *Tō* was widely used in Edo-period Japan to signify a more general sense of cultural, racial, and linguistic Otherness. Keiko Suzuki discusses the use of the phrase "hairy foreigner" (*ke Tōjin*) as a common epithet for European visitors to Japan, and Ronald Toby has demonstrated that the name *Tōjin* was also applied to the Korean envoys who traveled to Edo.[3] The deployment of Tō took on a special meaning, however, among scholars and translators of Chinese texts, who used it to refer to China as the contemporaneous entity that could be juxtaposed with more geographically and temporally abstract toponyms like Kara or Morokoshi. *Tōjin* referred to the Chinese sailors docked at Nagasaki, *Tōsen* denoted the boats that had brought them there, and *Tōwa* served as a blanket term to signify both the various dialects of Chinese spoken there as well as the written language of much of the literature that they imported. The term *gaku* suggests uniformity in focus and methodology and implies a cohesively constituted discipline, but in fact there was a wide spectrum of subjects grouped under this rubric. The common denominator uniting the professional interpreter in the maritime markets of Nagasaki, the Kyoto scholar studying the lecture records of Chinese neo-Confucians, and the Edo aficionado of Chinese fiction was concern with China as a contemporaneous entity and an interest in registers of Chinese more reflective of an oral context than the literary Sinitic that had functioned as a written lingua franca throughout East Asia for more than a millennium.

Although there was disagreement over the boundaries of the *Tōwagaku* scholar's epistemological domain, there was widespread consensus that contemporary novels like *Shuihu zhuan* required training to read. "Retraining" might be a more apt characterization, however, as Japanese aficionados of Chinese fiction perennially complained that the classical scholars who had previously served as interpreters of Chinese texts were woefully ill-equipped to explicate these new works. The scholar and painter Yanagisawa Kien (1704–1758) sounded a familiar refrain in his set of occasional notes, *Hitorine* (Sleeping alone): "For those who wish to study the practice of [oral] interpretation, one should read *Shuihu zhuan*, *Journey to the West*, *Romance of the Three Kingdoms*, and other novels using Chinese pronunciation. . . . Indeed, the *zoku* texts being imported from China are quite unreadable for today's famous scholars, as a result of their not being familiar with the practice of interpretation."[4]

While the term *Tōwa* could refer to a wide range of written and spoken registers, there was a broad consensus among scholars of *Tōwagaku* that their purview constituted a new area of research and a distinct break with earlier ways of approaching texts from China. For even as broadly read and knowledgeable an intellect as the Confucian scholar and philologist Ogyū Sorai (1666–1728), "China" was always an imagined location—a land whose inhabitants were out of immediate physical reach, save for the occasional brush conversation (*hitsudan*) with an Ōbaku monk. Many of the translators and minor scholars who acted as conduits for the influx of contemporary Chinese culture, however, spent extensive time in Nagasaki, sought out Chinese sailors and émigré scholars for conversation, and devoted themselves to the formal study of little-known texts that would hardly warrant mention in one of Edo's Confucian academies. For such men, mastery of more contemporary registers provided a means of reimagining their place in Edo-period intellectual society by presenting themselves as direct links to a live and vibrant contemporary culture across the sea. In the fractious and cliquish world of early Edo-period classical study, what stands out in the prefaces and manifestos published by the self-proclaimed *Tōwagakusha* is the degree to which they attempted to position themselves as outsiders with respect to preexisting schools of scholarship. If Sorai's standard criticism of his peers focused on their unreasonable fixation with abstruse principle and ahistorical universality, we can see men such as Suyama Nantō and Okajima Kanzan (1674–1728) advancing a parallel argument by emphasizing their personal experience and the immediacy of their connection to contemporary language as criteria for scholastic evaluation. The self-appointed custodians of this mission were quick to stress their own qualifications for the task, but they did so not with reference to traditional benchmarks of scholastic achievement but within the conceptual frameworks provided by the material they were digesting.

This chapter explores the epistemic shifts engendered by Edo-period Japanese engagement with Chinese fiction, through a focus on *Shuihu zhuan*. Deemed the repository par excellence of contemporary Chinese language, *Shuihu zhuan* was quickly enlisted in larger discussions of linguistic change and Japan's cultural relationship to China. Starting in the first decades of the eighteenth century, the work received unique attention as the focus of specialized lectures and reading groups, a process seemingly inaugurated by a "Translation Society" (Yakusha) established by Ogyū Sorai in 1711.[5] During the first half of the eighteenth century, at least, the ability to read and explicate a work like *Shuihu zhuan* constituted cultural capital, and most documented instances of Japanese interest in the novel occurred among the educated elite. The diffusion of interest in both *Shuihu zhuan* and other aspects of contemporary Chinese culture was enabled chiefly by the serial publication of dictionaries and reference works written with the goal of initiating a wider circle of readers into the previously abstruse world of contemporary Chinese. Although devoted to noncanonical and, in the case of *Shuihu zhuan*, overtly subversive texts, the prefaces to these reference works explored the relationship between the language of contemporary China and the registers of literary Sinitic familiar to classical scholars—a line of interrogation that collapsed distinctions between elite and popular branches of knowledge and contributed to a wider exploration of the relationship between the refined and canonical (*ga*) and the common and vulgar (*zoku*) in Edo-period cultural production.[6]

I argue that these guides to the language of *Shuihu zhuan* and other contemporary Chinese texts represent a deliberate attempt at severing the nascent discipline of *Tōwagaku* from its roots in the study of the Chinese Confucian classics (*keigaku*)—an attempt possessing important implications for the study of early modern Japanese literary culture, intellectual history, and eventually sinology. In many ways, the status of *Tōwagaku* as an academic discipline vis-à-vis earlier classical studies mirrored the uncertain institutional standing of its participants. By incorporating noncanonical Chinese texts into a curriculum aimed at ethical cultivation and political statecraft, scholars such as Sorai, Itō Jinsai (1627–1705), and his son Tōgai (1670–1736) unquestionably imbued works of Chinese fiction with an aura of elite respectability. On the other hand, the proponents of *Tōwagaku* were never able to completely distance their field of expertise from its associations with the heterodox, plebeian, and morally dubious. The potentially subversive content of *Shuihu zhuan*, for example, which chronicled the insurrectionary actions of a group of outlaws during the twelfth century, engendered considerable unease among Edo-period readers. On a more institutional level, the fact that the most knowledgeable readers of contemporary texts were often commercial interpreters, merchants, and amateur aficionados with connections to the port city of Nagasaki contributed to an unclear and potentially antagonistic relationship with the traditional custodians of Chinese knowledge.

By culling through the writing of these scholars of contemporary Chinese, a consistent strategy for dealing with this exclusion and marginalization emerges. Instead of subsuming their area of interest to the political and ethical concerns of classical scholarship, students of contemporary Chinese often argued that their specialty was ontologically distinct: an epistemological domain overlapping, but by no means perfectly isometric with earlier branches of study. What ultimately emerged from this line of argumentation was a new theorization of what it meant to study China as a contemporary entity, and a new understanding of the applications of philological research.[7] For Ogyū Sorai, whose scholarship provided a set of foundational concepts and vocabulary for nearly all the writers discussed in this chapter, study of contemporary Chinese was a small part of a broader curriculum undertaken with the primary goal of better elucidating the archaic Chinese political and ritual institutions that constituted "the Way."[8] In contrast, the emergent tradition of "vernacular philology" embedded in works like Kanzan's *Tōwa san'yō* (Collected essentials of contemporary Chinese) and Nantō's *Chūgi Suikodenkai* (An explication of *The Loyal and Righteous Water Margin*) suggests an entirely different orientation toward China and its textual culture, one premised on the belief in a fundamental and unbridgeable rupture separating the language and culture of the present and that of antiquity. These works assume that the political and ethical considerations of classical scholarship bear very little relation to the study of recently imported works, and indeed in studies like Nantō's *Chūgi Suikodenkai*, we see a clear movement away from the concerns of the author's predecessors in favor of a narrower interest in cataloguing the concrete and discrete components of contemporary Chinese material and textual culture. This shift from the universal to the specific is instructive. In their attempts at distancing *Tōwagaku* from its roots in classical scholarship, scholars like Kanzan and Nantō advanced a new conceptual framework for the study of China, one in which Chinese texts like *Shuihu zhuan* are treated more as repositories of linguistic and cultural data than as potential sources of political, historical, or ethical truths. In understanding the diffusion of the risqué *Shuihu zhuan* in Edo-period Japan, such an approach provides an avenue for discussing the novel that neatly sidesteps its subversive and morally disquieting dimensions. Furthermore, in terms of emplotting the history of Chinese studies in early modern Japan, this approach is significant in illustrating a transitional episteme, one serving as a potential link between the moral and political concerns of early eighteenth-century classical studies and the more narrowly lexicographic and positivist focus of late-Edo and Meiji-period sinology.

SPACE AND PLACE IN THE EIGHTEENTH-CENTURY STUDY OF CHINA

Although the early Edo period was certainly not the first time in history Chinese texts had been imported into the country en masse, a survey of importation records reveals a previously unprecedented variety of subject materials, genres, and linguistic registers in the works taken into Japan through the port of Nagasaki. Through the pioneering bibliographic research of scholars like Nakamura Yukihiko, Yoshikawa Kōjirō, and especially Ōba Osamu, we have a clearer understanding not only of which titles were imported through customs at Nagasaki but also in many cases the Japanese afterlives of those works fortunate enough to make it into some form of circulation: an unprecedentedly wide array of texts including familiar works of classical thought and history, contemporary gazetteers, "unofficial histories" (*yeshi, waishi*), and increasingly, works of fiction and drama.[9] As Yoshikawa Kōjirō and Emanuel Pastreich have demonstrated, the sheer diversity of materials and the registers in which they were written led to extensive meditation upon language and concern over what observable historical changes in language signified. Although "crisis" would perhaps be too strong a word to discuss this atmosphere, there does appear to have been at least a faltering confidence in Japanese intellectuals' ability to interpret texts, and a concern that the scholar of classical texts was fundamentally alienated from the domain over which he professed mastery, a doubt that, in many cases, created space for alternative claims to textual authority.

In its earliest phases, Japanese interest in more colloquial registers of Chinese stemmed from a confluence of two separate, arguably noninterrelated groups of imported texts. As Tokuda Takeshi has demonstrated, the first wave of engagement with Chinese "fiction" consisted of a string of Japanese translations of Chinese historical texts known as explications (*yanyi*) or chronicles (*zhizhuan*).[10] These Chinese works were simplified, easily read popularizations of the classical histories produced in large quantity during the late Ming and early Qing dynasties.[11] Although these texts are often referred to as early fiction (*xiaoshuo*) in Chinese-literature historiography, this term is anachronistic and potentially misleading. The Chinese editors generally justified the works as attempts at making the difficult classical histories more accessible to a general audience—claiming to stay true to the didactic principles of classical historiography while making them more palatable through the "slight addition of color" (*shao jia runse*).[12] These explications were generally written in simple literary Sinitic, interspersed with occasional "vernacularisms" more reflective of spoken Chinese. For Japanese readers weaned on literary Sinitic texts, these vernacularisms would understandably have been the most difficult parts of the work. By 1705, Japanese translations of these works, alternately called *tsūzoku* (popularizations), *gundan* (military tales), or *gunkan* (military mirrors), were familiar enough to Japanese readers that the prominent Kyoto publisher Hayashi Gitan (d. 1711) could proclaim, "As for these explications of the successive dynasties, there is no household in which they are not being read and discussed. The events they record begin in highest antiquity and cover the period up to the Yuan. But [until now] there has been no work that discusses the history of the Ming."[13] Gitan undoubtedly exaggerated the popularity of these texts in order to vaunt his own publication (a popular history of the foundation of the Ming), but his statement suggests that, by the end of the Genroku period (1688–1704), there was a sizable community of Japanese readers interested in Chinese popular historiography and familiar with a number of works through translation.

Although Gitan emphasized the educational aspects of his publications, it is a safe bet that many readers were more attracted to exciting narratives than to their morally suasive properties. Other Japanese readers, however, undertook the study of more contemporary registers of Chinese in the pursuit of precisely this kind of edification. For scholars who embraced the "neo-Confucian" interpretations of the Chinese classics, there was a pressing need to read the lecture records (*goroku*) of Zhu Xi (1130–1200) and other Song-period commentators, that made frequent use of more colloquial expressions. To the best of my knowledge, the first reference work to address this problem explicitly was published in 1694. Called *Goroku jigi* (Definitions for lecture records), the short text begins by noting the centrality of language study to a classical education.[14] In the body of the work, characters and compounds often found in Chinese lecture records are glossed and defined in Japanese. As the preface promised, the focus of the dictionary was not the complex principles of Chinese thought but the illusorily simple language in which these principles were encoded. Thus in the opening pages of the dictionary, the reader sees the first appearance of the simple demonstrative pronouns *zheige* (this) and *neige* (that), bisyllabic verbs such as *shuohua* (to speak) and *zhidao* (to know), the aspect marker *le*, and seemingly familiar terms that must be relearned in a new context: the character *ye*, for instance, which is glossed as *mata* (again, also) rather than its classical reading as the copula *nari*. Many of these same terms would reappear in later reference works specifically devoted to the reading and enjoyment of Chinese fiction.

Chinese fiction and drama underwent a dramatic rise in visibility during the first quarter of the eighteenth century, and the figure most responsible for drawing attention to Chinese popular texts in Japan was unquestionably Ogyū Sorai. In contrast to the readers of translations mentioned by Hayashi Gitan, Sorai's interest in more colloquial registers of Chinese was related to a larger pedagogical campaign devoted to an exploration of the historical and cultural mutability of language. As Yoshikawa Kōjirō and Emanuel Pastreich have demonstrated, Sorai demanded that his students grapple with the language of the original Confucian classics instead of relying on later commentaries.[15] For Sorai, these later commentaries included both the pronouncements of Chinese classical scholars (most famously, Zhu Xi) and the Japanese system of annotated reading known as *kundoku*. In his *Yakubun sentei* (Trap and snare for translation) of 1711, Sorai famously equated *kundoku* with the act of translation (*yaku*) and argued that, like all translations, *kundoku* inevitably imparted the interpretation of the annotator who affixed the glosses.[16] The only way to avoid misinterpretation, Sorai maintained, was by studying language in a historical context and approaching the text in the original Chinese—thereby avoiding the contamination of later commentarial accretions.

Although Sorai is deservedly famous for his equation of *kundoku* and translation, it is important to note that he was not the only figure from the period to make such a connection. For all that has been written on the substantial and vehemently articulated differences between the leaders of Edo's various Confucian academies, I am inclined to agree with Kiri Paramore that these educators shared a number of concerns and assumptions when it came to Sino-Japanese cultural and linguistic relations.[17] Among the similarities of practice that Paramore notes is an understanding of "contemporary imperial Chinese society as a completely separate and ruptured society from the ideal historic Confucian age of Yao and Shun," a viewpoint that both contributed to and was enabled by the historical study of language. Certainly, Sorai was not the only Japanese scholar to denigrate the linguistic shortcomings of his peers. As early as 1703, in the preface of his *Yōjikaku* (A standard for the usage of characters), Sorai's contemporary Itō Tōgai complained that reliance on *kundoku* had led to the emergence of an inept hybrid writing style in Japan: "The scholars of our realm have long been using the language of China [Kago] to write their own compositions. However, they are constrained by their own [Japanese] language, and so some are unable to avoid doing things backward and misplacing characters. My text is thus titled *Instructions for the Benighted in the Usage of Characters*, which can be taken as a 'trap and snare' for writing."[18] Similarly, Sorai's pupil Dazai Shundai (1680–1747) emphasized the distinction between students of texts and students of glosses and decried the tendency for Japanese Confucians, in particular, to "put the glosses first and the text last."[19]

In many attacks on Japan's linguistic ineptitude, there was a sense of intellectual competition with China. In his posthumously published occasional notes, for example, the Tsushima diplomat Amenomori Hōshū (1668–1755) captured a general sense of unease when he lamented the inherent disadvantage Japanese scholars faced in matters of scholarship: "There are all too many forms of cultivation in the world, and of these, reading books is the most difficult. In particular, using our language to read Chinese texts is one hundred times more difficult than the obstacles a Chinese reader faces. If a Chinese reader does not delight in study, how much worse for the Japanese!"[20] Or, in a later passage, "The way of the Sages is preserved in texts, and the meaning of these texts is conveyed through language. Linguistic meaning is conveyed through characters, and for that reason, the study of characters [*jigaku*] is something that must be illuminated. . . . [However,] for students of the Master[21] like Muro Kyūsō and the rest, it is so very difficult to reach even the hundredth part of a Chinese person!"[22]

Sorai was a vociferous critic of his peers, but he was also, paradoxically, the most sanguine in defending Japanese classical scholarship. He conceded that Chinese scholars of the classics were geographically and culturally closer to their object of study but canceled this advantage through a clever interpretive maneuver:

The path of scholarship lies in rooting oneself in the archaic. The Six Classics, the *Analects*, the *Zuozhuan*, the *Guoyu*, the *Shiji*, and the *Hanshu* are all ancient texts, and nobody leaves them unread. However, there are some who are pained by their difficulty, which is due to the fact that the language of antiquity was different from that of today. Thus, people find themselves compelled to make use of commentaries and explications to make sense of the original. Or else, they go even further by using Japanese *kundoku* to read a Chinese text, which presents one more barrier in interpretation. *Now, commentaries and explications come from later ages, and so the authors were just like us in terms of differences in language.* They used discussions of Transcendent Principle [*ri*] to search for understanding in their own minds; they did not, however, search for meaning in the content and words of the text itself. Thus, they were led into error.[23]

In other words, the linguistic barriers separating Japan and China are neatly paralleled by the temporal gap between Chinese antiquity and the period in which later Chinese scholars composed their interpretive glosses. For Sorai, the self-proclaimed "Eastern barbarian" (*tōi*), this equation of spatial and temporal distances was a legitimating leveling of the field, and one that he invoked repeatedly in his writing. In a letter to Takeda Shun'an (1661–1745), for instance, Sorai claimed, "Even the Cheng brothers and Zhu Xi were benighted when it came to archaic language. Is there any reason we should rely on their 'translations?' Using them is the same as searching for an understanding of Chinese in Korea."[24] And again, in his posthumously published manifesto *Bendō* (A discourse on the Way),

And yet, because the time [of the Warring States philosophers] was not greatly removed from that of Confucius, the customs and ways were still preserved, and name and object still accorded. When we come to the time of Han Yu during the Tang, however, Chinese writing underwent a fundamental transformation. Later scholars such as Zhu Xi and the Cheng brothers—though great men—did not understand the meaning of the ancient words. Because of this, they were unable to understand the Six Classics and delighted only in the easily read *Zhongyong* and *Mencius*.[25]

When Chinese and Japanese alike find themselves distanced from antiquity, the right of interpretation is up for grabs, and the fact of his "barbarian" birth did not prevent Sorai from eagerly taking up Confucius's mantle in a world irreparably decayed since the middle Tang.

Sorai's interest in more recent registers of Chinese was related to his insistence that a Japanese scholar should be familiar with a wide range of styles and genres in their different historical iterations—a point he developed with immense theoretical sophistication in *Yakuben sentei*. Additionally, Sorai demonstrated that the boundary between the *zoku* and the classical or "refined" (*ga*) was often nebulous: even so-called refined Chinese documents might make use of more colloquial expressions. For instance, when Sorai was called upon to assist Tokugawa Tsunayoshi (r. 1680–1709) in the translation and explication of the Ming legal code (Ch. *Da Ming lü*, Jp. *Dai Min ritsu*), he cited his understanding of less-refined registers as the reason for his appointment: "For the most part, the sections of the *Ming lü* that are perceived to be difficult are only so because scholars in Japan are unfamiliar with common language."[26]

A notable innovation to the curriculum in both Sorai Ken'en academy and Tōgai's Kogidō was the introduction of recently imported works of Chinese fiction and drama in addition to more standard classical texts—a development discussed at length by Emanuel Pastreich in the context of Sorai and Nakamura Yukihiko for the Kogidō.[27] Though the fact was not always acknowledged, the philological research carried out by elite scholars like Sorai and his contemporaries was enabled largely by their contact with another branch of Edo-period Chinese studies, the professional and often commercial interpreters (*tsūji* or *shōsho*) connected with the port city of Nagasaki. In 1711, for instance, Sorai established a "Translation Society" (Yakusha) devoted to the reading and explication of more contemporary registers of written and spoken Chinese.[28] His choice of leader for these sessions was the Nagasaki interpreter Okajima Kanzan, who had already made a name for himself in Kyoto as the translator of *Huang Ming yinglie zhuan* (Tales of valor from the founding of the Ming), the aforementioned historical novel published by Hayashi Gitan in 1705. According to the prefaces to his later published works, Kanzan had studied spoken Chinese under the tutelage of both Japanese instructors and Chinese travelers as a young man in Nagasaki. After working as a professional interpreter in both Nagasaki and in the employ of the daimyo of Chōshū, Mōri Yoshinari (1668–1694), Kanzan set off for Kyoto in 1701. From Kyoto, Kanzan traveled east to Edo in 1706, where, aside from a short period in Osaka, he would remain until 1724. During his tenure in Edo, Kanzan studied with both Sorai and the *bakufu* academician Hayashi Hōkō (1645–1732). Contemporaneous records suggest that Kanzan desired to make a name for himself as a scholar of classical texts, but his peers appeared unsure of how to evaluate his credentials with regard to the traditional benchmarks of classical scholarship. A telling characterization of Kanzan is recounted in Yanagisawa Kien's *Hitorine*, where Kien quotes Sorai's pupil, the painter and *kanshi* poet Hattori Nankaku (1683–1759): "Okajima Enshi [Kanzan] was called Nagazaemon in Nagasaki. He was born with preternatural abilities in spoken Chinese. Nankaku had it right when he remarked that Kanzan was a Chinese guest wandering among us Japanese. It is also said that he does not have a great deal of scholastic aptitude [*gakusai*]."[29]

Although Kanzan would ultimately fail in his quest to become a noteworthy classical scholar, he would make a significant contribution to the burgeoning field of contemporary Chinese language studies. During his tenure at the Ken'en academy, Kanzan published a reference work titled *Tōwa san'yō* (Collected essentials of contemporary Chinese, 1716). A guide to both vocabulary and pronunciation, *Tōwa san'yō* presented lists of terms culled from both classical and more colloquial registers, beginning with simple bisyllabic compounds and building gradually to complex phrases and practice dialogues.[30] All entries in the text were defined in Japanese and affixed with phonetic markers indicating how the entry should be pronounced in Chinese (*Tō'on*).[31] *Tōwa san'yō* was followed by a string of similar reference works that were published serially until Kanzan's death in 1728. Although the titles of the dictionaries generally indicated a contemporary focus through the use of the characters *zoku* or *Tō*, an examination of the contents reveals them to be much broader in scope. Archaisms culled from the Confucian classics stand beside vernacular terms that would be more helpful in reading one of Feng Menglong's stories, chatting up a deckhand in Nagasaki, or ordering a meal in a Nanjing restaurant than in reading the Confucian classics aloud. The text played the role of both lexicographic reference work and encyclopedia by introducing its readers to a vast array of discrete objects and specialized vocabulary related to topics like familial relations, household tools, wild animals, insects, birds, fruits, vegetables, plants, herbs, nautical equipment, and arias culled from works of popular drama. *Tōwa san'yō* could be of aid in studying familiar classical-language texts, but it suggested that the scholar's purview had expanded to make room for the contemporary, exotic, and popular alongside the classical and familiar.

Throughout the text, it is immediately clear that Kanzan based a number of his entries on works of Chinese fiction and drama. Many of the longer phrases are culled from the didactic lines that punctuate late imperial Chinese short fiction ("A good deed never leaves the home, while bad things travel a thousand miles," "They stuck to each other like glue and suited each other like a fish in water," etc.). Evidence of the soon-to-be famous *Shuihu zhuan* is apparent in Kanzan's reference works as well. It is difficult to imagine circumstances under which a student would need to say, "With one stroke, he lopped off his head," "I would rather die than become a bandit," or "I don't fear the official; I fear his rod!" unless he were reading *Shuihu zhuan*.[32]

From the beginning, studies of contemporary Chinese occupied an ambiguous position vis-à-vis earlier schools of Chinese learning. Despite their catholic focus and novel emphasis on contemporary Chinese culture, works like Kanzan's *Tōwa san'yō* situated *Tōwagaku* within familiar epistemological hierarchies. The prefaces and postfaces to these works, for example, invariably took pains to relate the colloquial and contemporary to the classical and canonical. Although there was a call for attention to the *zoku*, there was never any suggestion that it should be separated from the study of traditional refined registers—as evidenced in the remarkably recondite applications of study presented in the practice dialogues collected in the second half of the work. These dialogues often take the form of philosophical and legal debate in which students put their new knowledge of spoken Chinese to work by helping their teachers lecture on the Confucian classics or discourse on legal statutes. Despite the fact that the study of *Tōwa* was represented as a fundamentally new discipline, it was simultaneously presented as one indispensable to the traditional scholar and the ordering of the state—a stepping-stone to higher academic pursuits. As a postface to *Tōwa san'yō* explained, "If the vulgar undergoes a transformation, it becomes the elevated; one more transformation, and it partakes of the Way itself."[33] Or, as the preface to a later reference work titled *Tō'on gazoku gorui* (Classified Chinese terms from elevated and vulgar registers, 1726) presented it,

In actuality, *ga* and *zoku* require each other. If one does not understand the vulgar, one will be unable to attain the refined. Similarly, if one does not understand what the refined is, then the vulgar cannot be banished. Thus, each of them have equal use in scholarship. Attainment is nothing more than success in disposal [of the vulgar], and disposal is the epitome of attainment [of the refined]. The refined follows the vulgar and emerges; the vulgar avails itself of the refined and is transformed.[34]

Kanzan and his students were quick, however, to remind the reader of their own unique credentials as interpreters of China. At the same time they emphasized their usefulness to classical studies, many of the earliest reference works to employ the term *Tōwagaku* hinted at a growing gap between classical studies and the new brand of vernacular philology growing out of the tradition of Nagasaki interpretation. Kanzan and his disciples' elevation of contemporary Chinese studies might be interpreted as a response to their marginalization by the elite classical scholars of the day. Although he would be posthumously honored as the founding father of "the study of fiction" (*haishi no gaku*) in Japan, contemporary accounts of Okajima Kanzan paint a portrait of a frustrated savant denied the academic reputation befitting his ability. For example, Moriyama Sukehiro, Kanzan's student and the author of the preface to Kanzan's 1719 magnum opus, *Taiheiki engi* (A vernacular explication of *The Annals of Pacification*), represented the work as a substitute effort, crediting Kanzan's interest in the translation to the fact that fate had prevented Kanzan from advancing in his official career. The preface to *Tōwa san'yō* similarly borrowed the language of Chinese fiction to represent Kanzan as a romantic outcast who, after leaving employment as a commercial interpreter, wandered the "rivers and lakes" (*kōko*) like an unappreciated gallant from *Shuihu zhuan*.[35]

Whereas Kanzan's critics had denigrated his marginal status and lack of traditional credentials, the prefaces to his reference works hailed him as the forerunner of a new linguistic zeitgeist. Taking a page from Sorai's earlier writing on language, Kanzan's disciples based their defense of Kanzan (and *Tōwagaku* as a whole) on the self-apparent reality of linguistic change— borrowing conceptual vocabulary from Sorai but putting it to a new use. As a preface to *Tōwa san'yō* explained,

The educators of this age are often mired in old ways of doing things and regard the study of *Tōwa* as something extraneous.[36] They leave it aside and do not lecture on it. How undiscerning this is! There have been a few who have studied this subject. However, they become constrained by the four tones and mired in questions of pitch—they seek only to ape the shape of the Chinese speaker's mouth and leave it there. Now Nagasaki is on the coast and only a reed's distance from China. Thus, there is need for interpreters, who are able to make a fortune.[37]

In other words, the establishment of Nagasaki trade with China has inaugurated a new period in Sino-Japanese cultural relations. The difference between the *Tōwagakusha* and the "learned of the age" lies in the new porosity of the border enabled by the trade and diplomatic facilities at Nagasaki.

Although, it is implied, some visionaries are quick to see the applications of this new branch of knowledge, others remain mired in what are described as outdated methods of instruction. If Kanzan's lack of academic capability was slighted in the writing of his contemporaries, we see that dismissal reversed here. The themes presented in this first reference work—the temporally contingent nature of language, the need for new methods of approaching imported texts from China, and the growing gap between *Tōwagaku* and earlier branches of sinological study—would become familiar rhetorical maneuvers in reference works published after *Tōwa san'yō*.

SEPARATING THE WORD AND THE WAY: VERNACULAR PHILOLOGY AND *SHUIHU ZHUAN*

Even before becoming a perennial springboard for translation, adaptation, and commentarial exegesis, *Shuihu zhuan* is a title that appears repeatedly in the writing of early aficionados of Chinese narrative in Japan. As discussed in the introduction, *Shuihu zhuan* appears to have entered Japan sometime fairly soon after the founding of the Tokugawa shogunate, and references throughout the seventeenth century attest to continuous Japanese interest in the work. In the preface to Okajima Kanzan's 1705 translation of *Tales of Valor from the Founding of the Ming*, for instance, Hayashi Gitan claimed to have commissioned Kanzan to do a translation of *Shuihu zhuan* as well. Nothing appears to have resulted from the request.[38] Readers able to procure a rare imported copy could potentially read the novel in the original, but among those interested in the contemporary Chinese language, the title often functioned as shorthand for the difficulties inherent in the study of nonclassical-language texts. In the preface to one of Kanzan's later translations, for instance, Kanzan's student Moriyama Sukehiro drew a helpful distinction between the simple literary Sinitic of the equally popular *Romance of the Three Kingdoms* and the more challenging *Shuihu zhuan*: "Now, in our kingdom of Japan, there are only a handful of learned scholars who try to read Luo Guanzhong's two texts. And even though they attempt to read them, they are able to decipher only *Romance of the Three Kingdoms* and are unable to make out *Shuihu zhuan*."[39]

In contrast to China, where discussions of *Shuihu zhuan* focused mainly on the ethical and moral issues arising from the outlaws' rebellion, initial

Japanese engagement with the text was limited primarily to philological analysis. Had Hayashi Gitan fulfilled his promise to produce an easily read translation of the novel in 1705, it is entirely possible that the flood of digests, illustrations, parodies, and sequels produced in the second half of the Edo period would have surfaced much earlier. As it was, a Japanese reader who was curious about *Shuihu zhuan* had little to work with at the turn of the eighteenth century. General reference works like Kanzan's *Tōwa san'yō* might provide a foot in the door for the amateur enthusiast, as could the first Japanese printing of the work, a 1728 edition comprising the first ten chapters of the novel, posthumously credited to Okajima Kanzan. This Japanese reprinted edition (*wakokubon*) glossed the Chinese text with *kunten* annotation that provided verb inflections and indicated how the text should be read in accordance with Japanese syntax. It did not, however, explain the text's difficult vocabulary, making it of doubtful value to a reader unfamiliar with the colloquial Chinese lexicon. For instance, whereas later commentators would dedicate scores of characters to explicating the meaning and nuance of terms like *huashuo* ("The story goes that . . ."), the explicator of the *wakokubon* simply affixed the verb *su* to the compound. Although Sorai had inveighed against *kundoku* as a mode of translation that produced an overdetermined reading by surreptitiously imparting the explicator's interpretation, the *kundoku* edition of *Shuihu zhuan* is sufficient to demonstrate that Japanese punctuation alone does not create a legible text.

More enterprising students of contemporary Chinese could study the novel directly under an instructor. At nearly the same time that the *wakokubon* edition of *Shuihu zhuan* was published, for instance, the Kamigata scholar and literary polymath Oka Hakku (1692–1767) offered a series of lectures on the meaning of specific vocabulary terms in *Shuihu zhuan*, the notes for which have been preserved in manuscript form.[40] A far more systematic and widely disseminated guide to the novel was compiled by the obscure Tosa scholar Suyama Nantō thirty years later. Published in 1757, on the eve of an explosion of Japanese interest in the novel, Nantō's *Chūgi Suikodenkai* marked one of the first attempts at outlining a cohesive methodology for reading Chinese fiction. The scion of a family of domainal physicians to the Yamauchi family in Shikoku, Nantō studied as a young man in Kyoto at the Kogidō academy of Itō Tōgai, a center of Confucian learning where the study and consumption of Chinese fiction was not only tolerated but also encouraged. *Shuihu zhuan* was a source that Tōgai himself utilized in his lexicographic research, and as the archival research of Nakamura Yukihiko has demonstrated, the Kogidō housed its own imported copy of the novel—a copy that, according to the library's records, Nantō and his peers borrowed a few fascicles at a time.[41]

If the Kogidō provided basic access to the novel, Nantō credited his ability to read it to a second teacher, Tanaka Taikan (1710–1735), a classical scholar and Chinese-literature enthusiast whose memory looms large over Nantō's later study. According to the preface to *Chūgi Suikodenkai*, written by Nantō's friend and fellow reader Akutagawa Tankyū (1710–1785), Taikan required his students to read *Shuihu zhuan*, *Journey to the West*, and other works of fiction using Chinese pronunciation. Taikan died an untimely death in 1735, but Nantō continued his former studies, and it is likely that his reference work was based on notes taken under or received from his teacher. What stands out about Nantō's and Tankyū's recollections of Taikan is the seemingly casual atmosphere of their study sessions. The descriptions might be taken as the earliest mention of Chinese popular *pleasure* reading in Japan, and the text makes a distinction between a scholar's primary duty or occupation (*honmu*) and the "hobby" (*konomi*) of reading a novel like *Shuihu zhuan*. In his preface, for instance, Tankyū credited Nantō with the following remark:

When you and I were young, we studied with Master Tanaka Taikan, with whom we honed our skills in colloquial Chinese and mastered novels like *Shuihu zhuan* and *Journey to the West*. In our everyday dealings, we amused ourselves by refusing to use Japanese [and speaking Chinese instead]. Master Tanaka sickened and died young, and you have been frustrated in your ambitions. I have also been rushing about with my duties, never having even a moment's pause to sit and rest. Still, I have not given up my old hobby. I have devoted myself to works of fiction and compiled a reading guide to *Shuihu zhuan*. Even though it is not the primary duty of a scholar, I would like to entrust it to a fellow aficionado and request a preface.[42]

In contrast to Kanzan's students, who lamented the lack of widespread interest in contemporary Chinese, the preface to Nantō's guide suggests a certain pleasure in the exclusive intimacy of their meetings. The study of contemporary Chinese is presented as an undertaking wholly separate from classical study, and rather than emphasize Tanaka Taikan's accomplishments as a classical scholar, the same passage informs the reader that Taikan's erudition was not the result of formal instruction. Taikan's contact with Nagasaki interpreters is noted approvingly, further distancing the study of *Shuihu zhuan* from the more conventional classical scholarship Nantō must have studied with Itō Tōgai at the Kogidō.

The body of Nantō's *Chūgi Suikodenkai* consists of a list of definitions for "difficult terms" (*nankai no mono*) culled from the first sixteen chapters of the one-hundred-twenty-chapter edition of *Shuihu zhuan*. The final pages of the text promised a forthcoming continuation, but this continuation was never published, although it survives in manuscript form. In format, Nantō's guide is almost identical to the earlier reference works compiled by Okajima Kanzan. Definitions for each term are provided in Japanese, with contemporary Chinese pronunciation marks affixed to the right of each entry. The entries in Nantō's guide are divided evenly between the material objects and institutions described in *Shuihu zhuan* (household implements, clothing, legal and religious terminology, government offices, etc.), genre markers and turns of phrase common in Chinese popular narrative, and classical terms that have acquired a new meaning or nuance in the context of the novel. By way of example, the first term presented, the introductory phrase *huashuo*, is glossed and defined succinctly with reference to familiar Japanese literary conventions:

話説 (pronounced *waa se*[43])—this phrase means "And so our story starts from here." It is the same as the opening of Japanese stories, which begin with the words *somo somo*. It is a phrase for starting a tale.[44]

The text continues by glossing terms in the order that they appear in the novel. It is unlikely that a prospective reader would be able to make it through the text equipped only with Nantō's guide, but there is a clear attempt at identifying and defining the most crucial terms. Nantō's larger goal for his readers might best be described as reeducation, since he was interested primarily in correcting bad habits already ingrained in Japanese readers of Chinese texts. Of these bad habits, Nantō stressed throughout the guide, none was more in need of eradication than the tendency of Japanese readers to muscle their way through recently imported texts on the basis of their knowledge of literary Sinitic. In contrast to the reference works of Okajima Kanzan, which presented the vulgar and refined as closely linked, Nantō's glosses posit a rupture between the refined Chinese language familiar to Japanese readers through classical texts and the new, uncertain world of a text like *Shuihu zhuan*. Although any literate reader would recognize the characters used in *Shuihu zhuan*, Nantō argued, true fluency is potentially impeded by the reader's reliance on earlier associations. To illustrate his point, Nantō showed how the familiar term *xiang* (to face) changed in the context of *Shuihu zhuan*.

向 (pronounced *hyan*)—even though this term is glossed *mukatte* [to face], it is usually used in a different sense in the context of the colloquial. It is more akin to the use of [the general preposition] *oite* in more refined registers, and thus it should be glossed.[45]

In his insistence upon acknowledging historical changes in language, Nantō's labors can be clearly situated in a larger discourse inaugurated by works like Sorai's *Yakubun sentei*. What is notably absent throughout Nantō's discussion of *Shuihu zhuan*, however, is any larger normative or ethical application for this observation. Earlier Japanese interest in contemporary Chinese had been justified—even if only nominally—through reference to larger political and moral objectives. Contemporary Chinese language studies at the Ken'en and Kogidō academies were but a minor part of larger pedagogical regimes focused on political economy, statecraft, and moral development, and as shown previously, even the dictionaries of Kanzan and his followers presented mastery of the vernacular as an alternative stepping-stone to the Way. Against this backdrop, what stands out about Nantō's work is his attempt at breaking away from this familiar paradigm in favor of an understanding of China as nothing more than a collection of discrete material objects, institutions, and linguistic signs. He made no suggestion that *Shuihu zhuan* could be of use, however indirectly, in the larger pursuit of moral edification; rather, the novel is presented as an artifact or material object inextricably bound to a particular geographic and temporal context. The self-deprecating tenor of Nantō's earlier characterization of contemporary Chinese studies as a hobby rather than an occupation belies an epistemological shift at work in the text. China has been decentered as a locus of cultural and textual authority and reimagined as a normatively neutral space with no ontological superiority—or even particular relevance—to Japan. By isolating contemporary language as a discrete area of inquiry, Nantō posited a clear separation between language (*ji*) and any form of transcendent "Way" (*michi*)—an orientation that moved against the philological projects of the previous fifty years.

This was not to say that the study of the colloquial should be undertaken lightly. One of the central arguments made in *Chūgi Suikodenkai* was that study of this register requires systematic diligence. A correct understanding of the novel and its cultural context began with the correct selection of editions, and in his choice of *Shuihu zhuan* editions, Nantō was unequivocal: "In recent years, the seventy-five-chapter edition of *Shuihu zhuan* prepared by Jin Shengtan has flourished in Japan. But what I am using as my base text is the one-hundred-twenty-chapter *original* text as a correction."[46] As discussed in detail in the next chapter, many editions of fiction and drama printed in late imperial China included critical commentary outlining a method for reading the novel through the inclusion of prefatorial essays, interlineal comments, and critical evaluations of specific characters. In China, the inclusion of such commentary by a well-known critic was a selling point in a competitive publishing market. Edo-period Japanese importation records often distinguished between recensions of Chinese novels as well, and it is clear that Japanese readers were keenly aware of the differences between various commentarial editions of *Shuihu zhuan* and other novels. The Suzhou literatus Jin Shengtan's (1608–1661) commentary was famous for his condemnation of the actions of the Liangshan outlaws and for his insistence that the second half of the novel, in which the outlaws are pardoned by the Song emperor, was a later forgery that should be excised. For Nantō, however, such considerations of literary structure and ethics were irrelevant to his primary focus. If one views *Shuihu zhuan* as a repository of information, then Jin Shengtan could be accused of throwing away half his data through abridgement of the novel. The one-hundred-twenty-chapter edition of *Shuihu zhuan*—the longest of the novel's many recensions—contained more material for analysis, and therefore, Nantō proposed, it should be considered the authoritative text. Nantō's name for this recension, the "original" or even "orthodox" edition (*shōhon*), borrowed the language of classical studies and historiography.[47] Nantō's concern was a worry shared by any other scholar of the period—the idea that the efficacy of instruction is linked to the edition used for study. What is remarkable is the fact that this bibliographic concern, typically the reserve of classical scholars, has been extended to the domain of fiction.

In outlining a cohesive course of study, Nantō wrestled with the two models preceding him: the line of empirical, practical interpretation (*tsūji*) exemplified in the reference works of Okajima Kanzan and the more theoretical, classics-centered discussion of translation (*yaku*) offered by Sorai. In his general understanding of linguistic development, Nantō was most clearly impacted by Sorai, arguing that the historical development of language was characterized by fundamental and unbridgeable gaps between both China and Japan and the present and antiquity. The short preface by Akutagawa Tankyū was followed by a far lengthier preface by Nantō himself, in which he lamented his Japanese contemporaries' inability to read Chinese texts. Nantō traced this ineptitude back to the Nara-period minister and envoy to China, Kibi no Makibi (695–775), whom Nantō credited with bringing Chinese writing to the "benighted" (*sōmai*) Japanese.[48] Nantō presented Kibi no Makibi as an ambiguous Prometheus, however, who created linguistic schism by trying to graft the Chinese script onto the agglutinative grammar of the Japanese language. The resultant development of kana and *kundoku* reading practices in Japan, the reader is told, resulted in would-be readers of Chinese who flip texts around to accord with Japanese grammar, intersperse Chinese texts with Japanese words, and ultimately gain only the roughest approximation of the original meaning. In short, Japanese students are reading Chinese texts in the same "Japanified" way that Tōgai and Sorai inveighed against forty years earlier in works like *Yōjikaku* and *Yakubun sentei*.

In the body of his text, however, Nantō was far more indebted to the lexicographic research of Okajima Kanzan, although he attempted to downplay the clear influence, ultimately dismissing Kanzan as a well-intentioned but dilettantish autodidact.[49] Like *Tōwa san'yō* forty years earlier, the body of Nantō's text centered on the precise explication of specific institutions and material objects, objects he claimed could not be apprehended without direct contact with continental culture. In contrast to classical scholars who derived their understanding of China purely through texts, Nantō argued that the only way in which such a culture could be studied was through the direct apprehension (*mokugeki*) of its constituent parts. In a set of reading precepts at the beginning of the text, Nantō warned his readers,

In terms of the weapons, clothes, and other items [described in *Shuihu zhuan*], it is impossible to have a sense of what they are unless you view them with your own eyes. In the past, those who claimed to understand *Shuihu zhuan* were boasters. How base of them to be ashamed to admit what they do not know. By not acknowledging their ignorance, they have bequeathed further misunderstanding to later generations. Their transgression is not slight! I, however, am different. If I am not familiar with a term, I do not dare to hazard a guess based on intuition. I simply say, "I am not familiar with this" and await the judgment of later scholars.[50]

What ultimately emerges from Nantō's guide to *Shuihu zhuan* is an attempt at establishing a new methodology for the study of contemporary language and culture that combined the empirical focus of professional interpretation with the systematic exegetical rigor of classical studies. Drawing on the rhetorical positioning of Kanzan's earlier reference works, Nantō took pains to depict himself as an outsider vis-à-vis traditional academic lineages. Denigration of the "learned of this age" (*kono yo no gakusha*) is a recurrent theme in *Chūgi Suikodenkai*, and Nantō was eager to establish a niche for contemporary Chinese studies through the aggressive denunciation of his peers. Kanzan's disciples lamented their master's exclusion from Edo's privileged scholastic circles, but Nantō wore this alienation as a badge of honor. A combative attitude is evident throughout the text, in which Nantō interspersed his explication of key terms with attacks on two groups of *Shuihu zhuan* readers: well-meaning but clumsy dilettantes like Kanzan, whose lack of erudition led to sloppy scholarship, and classical scholars who presumed to discuss the vernacular despite their ignorance of contemporary Chinese language and material culture. To purport to discuss *Shuihu zhuan* without immersing oneself in the study of contemporary Chinese culture was to be guilty of "guesswork explication" (*okkai*), the term used to describe the process of inferring new meanings from classical usage. The curious term Nantō coined for such scholars is "vernacular inferentialists" (*suiryō zokugo no hai*), referring to the act of induction that occurs when the older usage of a term is pushed back to approximate a new and potentially incorrect definition. Like Sorai in the composition of his many treatises on language and linguistic change, Nantō was eager to deconstruct any ideas of a monolithic and unchanging Chinese language, as he illustrated through a gloss of the Chinese term *cankui*:

慚愧 (pronounced *zangui*[51])—both these characters are glossed *haji* [shame, to be ashamed] when they stand by themselves. However, in the Chinese colloquial, when these characters are put together in a compound, they do not mean *haji* at all. Rather, they signify a sense of gratitude or unworthiness [*katajikenai*]. It is the same as the expression "to express thanks to Heaven and Earth." The "vulgar inferentialists" of this age come up with "shame" based upon the root meaning of the first character and learn the compound in this way. How preposterous! As a general rule, there are many instances where the use of contemporary language involves a transformation in meaning. If you do not understand this and go on basing your translation on guesswork, then your "command" over the colloquial will be laughable. Again, as a general rule, if you really wish to master the colloquial, then you must be fluent in Chinese pronunciation, and you must read broadly among the novels—chewing over their meaning and considering them one by one. You must also be up on general scholarship. If you are deficient in even one of these three categories, it will be very difficult for you to make progress. Okajima Kanzan, the monk Kunjo,[52] and the like are excellent in their spoken Chinese, but they are unlettered, so there are things that stretch their ability to the breaking point. However, the same is the case with people who rely purely on their scholastic ability and attempt to make inferences despite their ignorance of pronunciation.[53]

The lengthy and polemic explanation is a succinct encapsulation of both the style of *Chūgi Suikodenkai* and Nantō's expectations toward the would-be reader of Chinese fiction. Here, Nantō attempted to distance himself from two groups of scholars: the educated elite who make names for themselves through the explication and annotation of the Chinese classics and the professional interpreters who attempt to gain reputations through their ability with more contemporary materials. The first group includes the "vulgar inferentialists" who ignore historical and linguistic change and insist upon approaching popular texts as an extension of classical scholarship. The second, newly emergent group is made up of the Chinese instructors and professional interpreters exemplified by Okajima Kanzan and his coterie. The path Nantō charts for contemporary Chinese studies navigates between the rigid classics-centered methods of elite scholarship and the flexible but "unlearned" world of the professional interpreter. That Nantō borrows conceptual tools from both Sorai and Kanzan, however, should not hide the fact that his ultimate goal differs remarkably from both predecessors. In contrast to Sorai and Kanzan, whose engagement with the colloquial was connected to its utility in classical, historiographical, and legal scholarship, Nantō stubbornly refused to acknowledge the existence of such an application. His only goal is the precise exegesis of the term *cankui*, and short of comprehending the term, no higher utility is suggested for a study of the colloquial. By divorcing his study of contemporary Chinese language from larger political or ethical considerations, Nantō divests China of its scriptural and symbolic significance and reimagines it in a far more neutral way—presenting China as simply another space to be potentially known through firsthand contact with its textual, linguistic, and material artifacts. Ultimately, Chinese culture, as instantiated in *Shuihu zhuan*, is a research focus determined less by any potential universal philosophical significance than by the remarkable sense of cultural and linguistic difference apparent in its texts.

CODA

Of the works examined in this chapter, Nantō's study in particular may be interpreted as both a culmination of trends in contemporary Chinese studies and a transitional text in a larger history of Japanese engagement with Chinese literary texts. When Nantō used *Chūgi Suikodenkai* to inveigh against the "vulgar inferentialists" who discussed contemporary language on the basis of classical texts, we see a unique call to scholastic authority, one that sought to carve out a distinct niche for contemporary Chinese studies as a discipline and resented attempts to subsume them under traditional taxonomies. In terms of charting a broader history of Japanese sinology, Nantō's text is both emblematic and constitutive of a shift from classical scholarship of the seventeenth and early eighteenth centuries to later lineages of Chinese studies that downplayed the significance of China as a source of political or ethical truths. Though clearly indebted to conceptual models provided by Ogyū Sorai and Okajima Kanzan, Nantō's project of linguistic defamiliarization and contextualization ignores the question of larger, universal structures of meaning in favor of an interrogation of language as a discrete field of study. China as a locus of normative authority and universal meaning has been replaced with a China that is decentered, culturally and geographically unique, and irreducibly Other with respect to Japan. Such a conceptualization would have important effects on later lineages of sinological study. Scholars of Meiji-period *kangaku* such as Watanabe Kazuyasu, Miura Kanō, and Machida Saburō have argued that Meiji-period *kangaku* was characterized most by its shift from universalized moral inquiry to a more geographically bounded focus on Chinese material and textual culture.[54] I agree that such a transition took place, but rather than seeing this transition as unique to the Meiji period, I would argue that it had its roots in earlier discourse from the eighteenth century.

Certainly it is relatively simple to establish a textual link between Edo- and Meiji-period scholarship on contemporary Chinese language. Throughout the Edo period, Kanzan's dictionaries and Nantō's guide to *Shuihu zhuan* served as base texts for similar lexicographic projects. Kanzan's *Tōwa san'yō*, in particular, was quoted in the reference list of numerous works, including the *Goroku yakugi* (Translations of lecture records, preface dated 1744) of Rusu Kisai and Morishima Chūryō's *Zokugokai* (Lexicon of the vernacular, preface dated 1809), which also included Suyama Nantō's *Chūgi Suikodenkai* in its list of references. Recent scholarship by Okada Kesao, Murakami Masataka, and William Fleming has described the cumulative nature of these reference projects by demonstrating the degree to which mid-eighteenth and nineteenth-century lexicographic research was enabled by pioneering reference works by Kanzan and Nantō. In turn, Edo-period reference guides served as a basis for Meiji-period lexicographic research, a prominent example being Ichikawa Seiryū's seminal *Gazoku kango yakkai* of 1878.[55]

We can also see conceptual continuity in terms of this transition from the Edo to the Meiji period. In its emphasis upon describing China solely in terms of the direct apprehension (*mokugeki*) of particular objects and artifacts, *Tōwagaku* possessed certain conceptual affinities with later traditions of Chinese studies similarly structured around the acquisition of verifiable information about contemporary Chinese language and material culture. When Japanese literati began traveling to China in the second half of the nineteenth century, the writing of Ogyū Sorai and his coterie enjoyed a resurgence of interest among Meiji-period intellectuals, who made frequent reference to the Edo-period philosopher in their arguments for updated scholastic methodologies. In an 1879 polemic, for instance, the historian Shigeno Yasutsugu (1827–1910) criticized would-be reformers who deemed *kangaku* an anachronistic mode of study and maintained that classical studies had a great deal to offer in the modern era, provided that its scope was enlarged. Decrying the fact that Japanese intellectuals spent their entire careers studying China but could not exchange a single word of conversation with Chinese peers, Shigeno stressed the need for a "professional *kangakusha*" (*senmon kangakusha*), who in Shigeno's formulation would be "half scholar" and "half Nagasaki interpreter."[56] Shigeno explicitly pointed to Ogyū Sorai as the source of his inspiration and praised his willingness to incorporate new perspectives and methodologies into his curriculum.

Shigeno's discussion of Nagasaki interpretation also singled out Okajima Kanzan by name, and although Kanzan would fail in his attempt at making a name for himself as a scholar of the Chinese classics in his own lifetime, his reputation underwent a posthumous rehabilitation in the century and a half after his death. As early as the first half of the nineteenth century, Kanzan was elevated to an elite position in a text called *Sentetsu sōdan kōhen* (Collected tales of former worthies, part 2), Tōjō Kindai's (1795–1878) continuation of the historian Hara Nensai's (1774–1820) collection of biographies of Confucian scholars. Although Kanzan did not make it into Nensai's original collection, he would likely have been delighted by the biography presented in Kindai's continuation, which substituted the workmanlike title of interpreter (*tsūji*) with the more refined "scholar of translation" (*yakushi*). In describing Kanzan's accomplishments against a larger backdrop of sinological studies, Kindai argued,

When Kanzan would lecture on the classics and histories to his students, his method was considerably different from that of the established scholars of the day. They inevitably discoursed on the morality of righteousness and duty, or the principles underlying good and bad governance, and in doing so fell into prolixity and error. Kanzan, on the other hand, would lecture only on substantive recent events and things that could be witnessed in person [*jisei mokugeki no jijitsu*]. . . . He himself said, "If you don't make this your focus, then how far removed you will be from understanding human feeling!"[57]

In his assessment of Kanzan's accomplishments, Tōjō Kindai situates the translator squarely within the rhetoric of contemporaneity and eyewitness that connect the reference works discussed in this chapter. This representation of Kanzan as an unhailed forerunner of a new scholastic zeitgeist continued into the Meiji period, when Kindai's capsule biography was incorporated almost verbatim into a work called *Nihon risshihen* (Tales of ambition from our nation), a collection of biographies compiled in clear imitation of Nakamura Masanao's famous translation of Samuel Smiles's *Self Help*.[58] In an era characterized by the elevation of fiction and the novel as the pinnacle of literary expression, Kanzan was again singled out for his precocious attention to the form, as well as his ability to break free of the "clichés" that had enmeshed earlier scholars:

Ever since the beginning of the Tokugawa period, Confucian ideals were widespread and popular. However, they took as their focus only the classics, histories, and poetry and occasionally works of military strategy. But never have I heard of someone making a name through the study of fiction. Only Kanzan proclaimed the virtues of fiction and, through his explication of passages, assisted those who could not read it well. It's said that this was because of his facility with Chinese pronunciation [*Ka'on*], but I think it's also that he refused to adhere to the clichéd stereotypes of earlier scholars and established his own school.[59]

If Kanzan's colleagues at the Ken'en academy had voiced his lack of affiliation with reference to geographical difference ("a Chinese guest wandering among the Japanese," as Hattori Nankaku described him), here it is suggested that Kanzan was a modern progressive wandering among a temporal cohort unable to appreciate his accomplishments.

One of the most interesting passages in the posthumous accounts of Kanzan is his attributed declaration that contemporary Chinese language and texts allow for a clearer appreciation of "sentiment" (*ninjō*). It is immediately clear why such a statement (genuine or not) would find favor during the Meiji, when fiction was increasingly presented as a point of direct access into the emotions and interiority of an individual author and society alike. What the writing of Kanzan, Nantō, and others does *not* tell us is what first compelled them to pick up a novel like *Shuihu zhuan*. What did they make of the controversial actions of its protagonists, and did they condemn or condone the often muddy morality of the text? Would they have sided with the "sentiments" of a critic like Li Zhuowu, who read the novel as a tale of unappreciated virtue and slandered gallantry, or would they have been more sympathetic to the emotional appeals of Jin Shengtan, who interpreted *Shuihu zhuan* as a narrative of iniquity chastened? The writing of Kanzan and his contemporaries tells us little about the ways in which early modern Japanese readers interpreted the narratological structure and moral themes of the novel. The next chapter examines what happened when

Japanese critics turned their attention to the literal margins surrounding the printed text of the novel, where Chinese writers penned their critical commentary and offered their suggestions for finding what Nantō's contemporary, the Kyoto historian Seita Tansō, termed "the real *Water Margin* beyond the surface of the text."

Chapter Two

HISTORIES OF READING AND NONREADING

Shuihu zhuan as Text and
Touchstone in Early Modern Japan

This book deals with those in the middle, the men and women who do not write
literature, but rewrite it. It does so because they are, at present, responsible for the
general reception and survival of works of literature among non-professional readers, who constitute the great majority of readers in our global culture, to at least
the same, if not a greater extent than the writers themselves.

—ANDRÉ LEFEVERE, "PREWRITE"

When we think of *Shuihu zhuan*, we think of Jin Shengtan.

—KŌDA ROHAN, "KIN SEITAN" [JIN SHENGTAN]

From a certain vantage point, the Chinese novel *Shuihu zhuan* is a ubiquitous presence in the literary and visual culture of early modern Japan.
Indeed, Japanese engagement with *Shuihu zhuan* is nearly coeval with the
establishment of Tokugawa hegemony itself, as evidenced by the presence
of a 1594 edition of the novel in the library of the Tendai abbot and adviser
to the fledgling Tokugawa regime, Tenkai. Tenkai's death in 1643 provides
us with a lower limit for dating the novel's importation into Japan, demonstrating the remarkable rapidity with which certain Chinese texts found
their way into Japanese libraries. The trickle of sporadic references to *Shuihu
zhuan* in the seventeenth century becomes a steady stream by the end of
the Genroku period, and by 1705 we find the Kyoto publisher Hayashi Gitan
hatching plans to commission the Nagasaki interpreter Okajima Kanzan
to undertake a translation. The previous chapter attested to widespread
awareness of *Shuihu zhuan* in the first half of the eighteenth century, especially among the intellectual circles of scholars like Ogyū Sorai and Itō
Tōgai, and it is this period that witnessed the first two tentative attempts at
making the text accessible to a wider range of Japanese readers. A 1728 Japanese reprinting (*wakokubon*) of the novel, mentioned in the previous chapter, reproduced the first ten chapters of the original Chinese text. Reading
marks (*kunten*), affixed to both sides of each line of text, indicated verb

and adjective inflections and demonstrated how the text should be read in accordance with Japanese syntax. Thirty years later witnessed the publication of the so-called popularization (*tsūzokubon*), which went an additional step by rewriting the text in a mixture of Sinographs and kana— obviating the need for the mental operations necessary to read the *wakoku-bon*.[1] Takashima Toshio has identified the publication of the *tsūzokubon* translation—published in four installments between 1757 and 1790—as a watershed event in the Japanese reception of the novel, and it is true that the middle of the eighteenth century marks the beginning of a century-plus-long epoch of protracted fascination with *Shuihu zhuan*.[2] Kyokutei Bakin's use of the novel in the composition of *Nansō Satomi hakkenden* (Eight dogs of the Satomi clan of southern Fusa) is perhaps the most famous and well-studied example of Edo-period interest in the work, but Bakin's *yomihon* was but one of innumerable other adaptations, digests, sequels, illustrated prints, and parodies produced in the years between 1760 and 1860. The list of authors, publishers, and artists involved with *Shuihu zhuan* at some point in their careers reads like a veritable Who's Who of Edo-period cultural production, and a number of canonical authors established both their reputations and templates for emergent literary genres through creative engagement with the novel.[3] Even a cursory survey of literature from the final century of Tokugawa rule reveals innumerable *Shuihu zhuan*–based works in nearly all major written and visual genres: from *yomihon*, *kibyōshi*, *haikai*, and *senryū*; to woodblock illustrations and *surimono* prints; to material artifacts like the *Shuihu zhuan*–themed *sugoroku* board by Utagawa Kuniyoshi, preserved in the National Diet Library, in which players gradually work their way toward the center of the board, where a stern-faced Song Jiang presides over the Liangshan marshes.[4] The features of many of these adaptations and rewritings have been discussed in detail in the painstaking and thorough bibliographic research of scholars such as Takashima, Nakamura Yukihiko, and most recently Inada Atsunobu, whose panoptic view of Japanese engagement with *Shuihu zhuan* and other Chinese novels suggests a continuous narrative of encounter, naturalization, and assimilation: a narrative that neatly spans the establishment of the Tokugawa regime in the early seventeenth century and the activities of artistic virtuosi like Bakin, Santō Kyōden, and Utagawa Kuniyoshi more than two centuries later.

Step back and look at the situation through the other eye, however, and the view changes dramatically. In addition to presenting the novel as a perennial springboard for translation, adaptation, and pastiche, it would be equally easy to structure an account of *Shuihu zhuan* in early modern Japan around the themes of frustration, false starts, and incomprehensibility. Despite the panoply of *Shuihu zhuan* texts and paraphernalia available to Japanese readers of the period, the novel is a singularly elusive presence in other key respects. Yes, the novel was imported into Japan as early as the first decades of the seventeenth century, but it remained largely inert for nearly a century after that—a spectral presence found only in the catalogues of elite libraries like Tenkai's or a few desultory mentions by frustrated literati unable to procure a copy. The Nichiren monk Gensei (1623–1668), for instance, attempted to follow in the footsteps of his idol, the Ming poet Yuan Hongdao (1568–1610), by reading *Shuihu zhuan*, only to encounter the bibliophile's nightmare of being told the bookseller's copy had been sold.[5] And although the title is frequently mentioned in the early eighteenth century, it would be misleading to describe it as popular reading. While Hayashi Gitan claimed to have commissioned Kanzan in 1705 to do a translation of *Shuihu zhuan*, nothing resulted from the charge,[6] and the 1728 publication of the *wakokubon* appears to have had very little immediate effect on the novel's visibility or accessibility. Finally, as demonstrated in the previous chapter, the extant lecture records of readers like Suyama Nantō attest to the continued difficulty even highly educated Japanese intellectuals experienced with the novel.

Although the situation changes in later periods, there is a certain sense of déjà vu in terms of the problems encountered by Japanese readers of *Shuihu zhuan* throughout the early modern era. The forlorn Gensei, for example, might have found comfort in the fact that his literary descendants continued to struggle to obtain their own copies of the novel. The relative scarcity of imported Chinese editions of *Shuihu zhuan* is evinced by the Kyoto scholar Minagawa Kien's (1735–1807) peevish recollections of a friend who carried off his beloved copy, and Kanda Masayuki has chronicled the extreme difficulties that Bakin—the universally acknowledged heavyweight of Chinese fiction scholarship in Edo-period Japan—encountered in his search for particular editions.[7] Similarly, while we are accustomed to thinking of literary translation as a teleological process of gradually increasing accessibility, eighteenth- and nineteenth-century materials related to *Shuihu zhuan* tell a somewhat different story. In an 1820 miscellany, Bakin catalogued the translations and reference works available to would-be read-ers of *Shuihu zhuan*—including the *wakokubon* edition, the *tsūzokubon* translation, and Suyama Nantō's *Chūgi Suikodenkai*—but finished by describing many of the materials as "difficult to obtain" (*e-yasukarazu*) in the present because of printing-house fires and publishers' neglect.[8] Bakin was dismissive of the quality of the *tsūzokubon* and embarked on a new translation as a corrective. However, despite his snide appraisal of the earlier work, Bakin's *Shinpen Suiko gaden* (A new illustrated translation of *The Water Margin*)—a collaboration with the artist Katsushika Hokusai (1760–1849)—ended in relative failure as well. He abandoned the project after a single installment, and the work was finished only twenty years later by his collaborator Takai Ranzan (1762–1838), who struggled mightily with the language of the novel and relied extensively on the earlier *tsūzokubon* to complete the project.[9] The important point is this: throughout the early modern era, there are numerous complaints about the challenges of acquir-ing an edition of *Shuihu zhuan*; there are laments about the linguistic dif-ficulties encountered in reading *Shuihu zhuan*; and there is a cantanker-ous tradition of denigration of earlier efforts at translation and scholarship. What we lack is extensive evidence of readers' sitting down and reading *Shuihu zhuan* from start to finish—at least prior to the mass publication of commercial editions of Chinese fiction in translation during the Meiji period. It is possible, then, to think of *Shuihu zhuan* as a "classic" in both the traditional understanding of a widely praised and recognized work and in Mark Twain's more cynical sense of a work that is widely praised but rarely read.

Although Twain's quip is a familiar presence in contemporary literary scholarship, it is rare to find scholars who treat it as anything more than a resigned comment on readerly indolence. Yet what Twain is suggesting is that in accounting for *Shuihu zhuan*'s dizzying rise to prominence in the early modern era, the self-evident importance of the act of reading *Shuihu zhuan* might not be that self-evident, after all. Although there were undoubt-edly many readers who painstakingly worked their way through the origi-nal text (i.e., Suyama Nantō), others encountered *Shuihu zhuan* in the form of adaptations and visual representations that had only tenuous links to the original text. Going one step further, the very idea of an "original text" itself needs to be complicated, since *Shuihu zhuan* circulated in Japan in a variety of recensions and commentarial editions, whose narratives, prefaces, and paratextual features conditioned wildly divergent reading experiences. If anything, tracking the trajectory of a novel like *Shuihu zhuan* in early modern Japan demands that we first relinquish the idea of a stable text being transmitted intact from one reader to the next.

This is a point made with tremendous sophistication in Michael Emmerich's recent study of the *Genji monogatari*, in which Emmerich emphasizes the role of what he terms replacements in the process of literary canonization. Emmerich defines replacements as all translations, adaptations, and material artifacts that, in some way, "hold out the promise, however tenuous, of an indirect connection to *Genji monogatari* and its canonical prestige."[10] As he argues,

Vastly more important than "the text" and its reception are its replacements: translations, broadly defined to encompass all the varieties of books just mentioned and more, that *literally take the place of Genji monogatari, texts that are read instead of the (unknown and unknowable) original.* This is what I mean, first of all, by "replacing" a text: canonization as the continual replacement of canonical texts by new, different versions of themselves that answer to the needs not only of authoritative institutions intent on preserving and propagating their own values and ideologies, but also of their consumers; the literary canon as an enormous gallery of look-alikes, a string of placeholders.[11]

Emmerich's pioneering study was inspired in part by the 2008 "millennial" celebrations of the composition of the *Genji*, a nationwide campaign that resulted in the production of a wide range of *Genji*-related events and paraphernalia, including limited edition stamps and postcards, *Genji*-themed incense, lottery tickets, special radio and television programming, and advertising campaigns by companies like "Black Cat" Yamato Transport. All of these, Emmerich argues, allowed consumers (not necessarily readers) to "participate in the communal act of valuing the story it was made to represent." From a classical understanding of literary reception, the unveiling of a *Genji monogatari* Millennial Anniversary Matcha Baumkuchen is a gimmicky sideshow at best, and an act of literary lèse-majesté at worst. However, Emmerich argues—correctly, I believe—that we should take this production seriously as an example of the ways in which a wide range of replacements, from "derivative" secondary works to outright kitsch, "nevertheless participate in a world of textual transmission and presume a particular understanding of what the canonical text is like."[12] While I have some reservations about the claim that replacements are "vastly more important" than their referents, Emmerich's argument provides two pathways for advancing our understanding of Japanese engagement with late imperial Chinese fiction. First, it establishes a certain degree of ontological parity between a Chinese edition of *Shuihu zhuan* and replacements like the later translations, Santō Kyōden's adaptation *Chūshin Suikoden*, and the aforementioned *Water Margin*–themed *sugoroku* board. Rather than reading the latter items in the series as derivative and secondary, the notion of literary replacements allows us to explore the canonization of a work like *Shuihu zhuan* without necessarily worrying about how familiar early modern readers were with an original work. Such an approach is consonant with the arguments of scholars such as Linda Hutcheon, who advocates "treating adaptations like adaptations," without exclusive concern for questions of fidelity and significatory reference to a so-called parent text.[13] Second, Emmerich's shift away from supposedly stable texts allows us to appreciate not only how the canon functions as a way of replicating a set of values or ideologies (as, for instance, in classic discussions by John Guillory and Terry Eagleton)[14] but also how the texts that constitute the canon often resist the ideologies that are imposed upon them. Although *Shuihu zhuan* was a title that would have been recognizable to nearly all Japanese readers of the late eighteenth and nineteenth centuries, the message of the text was subject to vociferous debate at all times.

In many ways, the questions that motivate this chapter are perfectly embodied in the oldest extant evidence of *Shuihu zhuan* in Japan: the aforementioned edition of the text formerly in the possession of the long-lived abbot Tenkai. The full and literal title of the Tenkai edition is the *Expanded, Collated, and Fully Illustrated Capital Edition of the Loyal and Righteous Chronicle of the Water Margin with a Forest of Commentary* (*Jingben zengbu xiaozheng quanxiang Zhongyi shuihu zhizhuan pinglin*): an impressive moniker that belies the edition's rather hasty and utilitarian production. The edition is an example of the self-explanatory "picture on top, text on the bottom" (*shangtu xiawen*) printing format, in which the top of each page is occupied by a simple illustration, with densely packed text below it. Each illustration is labeled with a caption, which is helpful to the modern reader, considering the minimalist nature of the illustrations themselves. In contrast to later editions of *Shuihu zhuan*, which included detailed representations of individual figures, it is difficult to distinguish characters like Song Jiang from Wu Song from Li Kui without a hint from the caption.

The fact that this relatively plain production eventually found its way into the library of one of the most powerful political figures in early modern Japan demonstrates the often vertiginous rise in prestige experienced by many Chinese novels in their transplanted context. As the extant catalogue of Tenkai's bibliographic holdings demonstrates, *Shuihu zhuan* was one of several works of Chinese fiction in his possession. Other holdings include works that are well known to readers today (like *Romance of the Three Kingdoms*, *Plum in the Golden Vase*, and *Journey to the West*), as well as titles that have faded into relative obscurity.[15] On its surface, the presence of so many titles suggests exposure to a wide range of Chinese texts, and Jonathan Zwicker has argued that by the end of the Edo period, "virtually the entire literary imagination of late imperial China" was available to Japanese readers.[16] While I agree with Zwicker that this vast tradition was at least technically accessible to *certain* Japanese readers, I am equally persuaded by William Fleming's caution that the presence of a text should not be conflated with its consumption.[17] As initially anticlimactic as it might sound, what stands out most about the early history of *Shuihu zhuan* and other Chinese novels in Japan is the length of time many of them sat in private libraries before becoming catalysts for the translations, adaptations, and parodies familiar to scholars of early modern Japanese literature. As the preceding chapter indicates, the scattered handful of references to *Shuihu zhuan* in the early eighteenth century suggests that reading the novel was a slow and labor-intensive affair, even for the most educated readers. Suyama Nantō, in his guide to *Shuihu zhuan*, used the word *konomi* (hobby, passion) to describe his experience with the text, an attitude that accords with our contemporary association of the novel with leisure, pleasure, and disposable capital. Compare, however, Nantō's self-description with a slightly earlier discussion of Okajima Kanzan's engagement with another work, the pornographic novel *Carnal Prayer Mat* (*Rouputuan*): "Okajima Kanzan possesses only a copy of *The Carnal Prayer Mat*. He intones it [*nenju*] morning and night, without pausing to rest for even an instant. His knowledge of contemporary Chinese is all culled from the pages of this book. . . . Thus, one sees that the secret to reading lies in thoroughness and not in volume."[18] In contrast to the pleasure reading suggested by Nantō, the use of *nenju* to describe Kanzan is more reminiscent of the concentrated, sustained respect one would bring to a Buddhist sutra or a work of history. Was Tenkai's reading of the edition of *Shuihu zhuan* in his possession an example of *nenju* or *konomi*? Did he even read it at all, and if not, what did the possession of such a text signify?

It is equally important to emphasize that Tenkai's edition of *Shuihu zhuan* was a commentarial edition, as evidenced by the "forest of comments" (*pinglin*) mentioned in the full title of the work. The commentary in the Tenkai edition—probably done by the edition's publisher, the Fujian printer Yu Xiangdou (fl. 1590–1609)—is not nearly as extensive as that found in certain later recensions like Jin Shengtan's edition, in which the volume of critical commentary rivals that of the narrative itself. Nevertheless, the commentator in the Tenkai edition is an active presence in the text. Nearly all pages feature a comment of some kind, from a guide whose persona ranges from moral exemplar to formalist critic to chatty friend at the movies. When, for instance, the imperial arms instructor "Panther Head" Lin Chong is falsely arraigned and forced into exile in the eighth chapter of the novel, the commentator reminds the reader how lucky he is to encounter his soon-to-be protector "Small Whirlwind" Chai Jin on the road.[19] When the tiger killer Wu Song meets his lascivious sister-in-law Pan Jinlian in a later section, the commentator gets a bit ahead of himself by telling the reader that a poem foreshadows Pan's eventual murder of Wu's older brother. The reader is thus reminded to pay close attention to foreshadowing and seemingly inconsequential details.[20] Taken one by one, these comments don't add up to much, and twentieth-century editors excised them on the grounds that they were an antiquated distraction from the narrative itself. However, as I demonstrate in this chapter, these commentaries profoundly affected the ways in which Chinese readers approached novels like *Shuihu zhuan*, and later Japanese readers engaged them in their exegeses of a complex and morally problematic work. If Tenkai did peruse the copy of the novel in his possession, he would have been hard-pressed to avoid the commentary, and it is probable that his interpretation of the novel was affected by the editor's constant nudges.

Finally, by virtue of its very existence, the Tenkai edition illustrates the transregional dimensions of the circulation, interpretation, and, ultimately, canonization of Chinese narrative. Readers interested in this particular edition of *Shuihu zhuan* no longer need to make a pilgrimage to Nikko, where much of Tenkai's former library is housed. At present, any reader with a functioning library card can easily peruse the photo facsimile of the volume preserved in the monumental *Guben xiaoshuo jicheng* (Collectanea of classic fiction) series, printed by the Shanghai Classic Works Publishing House (Shanghai guji chubanshe). The series, which provides high-resolution photo facsimiles of rare and inaccessible works of Chinese fiction, includes numerous recensions of *Shuihu zhuan*, and like the Tenkai edition, several of the works included in the series are reproductions of texts preserved in Japan. But Japanese libraries did not act simply as stagnant repositories where works of fiction could be discovered, dusted off, and reinjected into the literary bloodstream. In the course of—and as a direct result of—its peregrinations abroad, the Tenkai edition of *Shuihu zhuan* underwent a dramatic taxonomic reclassification. A closer look at the full title of the Tenkai edition (*Jingben zengbu xiaozheng quanxiang Zhongyi shuihu zhizhuan pinglin*) reveals that it does not match the title of the series produced in Shanghai. While the modern Chinese editors present their project as a collection of classic *fiction* (*xiaoshuo*), Yu Xiangdou himself termed his work a chronicle or account (*zhizhuan*). Yu's deliberate use of the term "chronicle" positions the *Shuihu zhuan* narrative within a flourishing tradition of late-Ming unofficial historiography, a tradition that included works rooted solidly in historically verifiable fact as well as texts that bolstered the historical record with extrapolation, legend, and outright invention.[21] Regardless of the compositional ratio of fact to fancy in individual works, it is crucial to point out that *zhizhuan* and the term *xiaoshuo* as it is understood at present are overlapping but not purely isometric categories. Yu Xiangdou would have been extremely loath to describe his undertaking as "fiction" in the modern sense, and he and other publishers of *zhizhuan*, "historical explications" (*yanyi*), and similar handmaidens to official historiography (*zhengshi*) justified their enterprises as attempts at making conventional history more accessible to less-educated readers.[22] The rhetoric of these works is couched not in the language of imagination and authorial creation but in terms of educational and moral imperatives. We can (and in most cases, I think, should) take these claims with a grain of salt, but the fact remains that the equation fiction = *xiaoshuo* = *shōsetsu* is a relatively recent phenomenon, dating in my estimation to the third decade of the Meiji period, and the product of extensive and long-standing contact between Chinese and Japanese (and later, Western) conceptions of writing.[23] That in the twenty-first century scholars can describe *Shuihu zhuan* as "fiction" or a "novel" and be instantly understood by Chinese-, Japanese-, and English-speaking peers invites the question: when did *Shuihu zhuan* become a "novel," and how precisely did the term "novel" itself acquire its associations and standing within a more broadly constituted network of literature?

We know that Japanese readers of the Edo period were deeply interested in Chinese fiction; we know far less about the forms that interest took. The goal of this chapter is to qualify the common characterization of *Shuihu zhuan* (and by extension other Chinese narratives as well) as popular fiction by demonstrating the tremendous hermeneutic obstacles these allegedly "popular" works presented to even the most sophisticated Japanese readers. In contemporary discussions of the Japanese reception of late imperial Chinese fiction, research has been conducted chiefly within the framework of an impact-response paradigm, characterized by almost exclusive focus on the starting and end points of engagement—namely, the Chinese parent work and the final Japanese product. This discussion shifts emphasis to the messy and conflicted systems of hermeneutics underlying Japanese engagement with Chinese fiction. By reading imported Chinese texts as contested sites of literary contact, where Japanese commentators alternately appropriated and rejected arguments made by Chinese critics, we gain a better understanding of the processes by which a text like *Shuihu zhuan* entered Japan in the early seventeenth century as a *zhizhuan* and emerged two centuries later as a "novel"—the recently consecrated pinnacle of literature itself.

SHUIHU ZHUAN AS TEXT AND PARATEXT

When we ask an illusorily simple question like, were Edo-period readers reading *Shuihu zhuan*? the answer is both yes and no. As I suggested in the previous chapter and argued explicitly in the introduction, there is no such thing as a late imperial Chinese novel called *Shuihu zhuan*, strictly speaking. Any edition of the novel imported into Japan during the early modern era would have been what is now known as a commentarial edition: an edition of the text in which the narrative itself was published along with punctuation and critical evaluation by Chinese commentators, whose remarks appeared most commonly between the vertical lines (*hang*) and in the upper margins (*lan*) of the printed page. This criticism, known as *pingdian* (literally, "evaluations and punctuation"), served such disparate functions as providing glosses and definitions for difficult terms; drawing the reader's attention to symbolism, foreshadowing, and other literary techniques; and passing moral judgment on the actions of the characters in the text. David Rolston, a leading expert on traditional *pingdian* criticism, has argued that "the appearance of hard and soft boundaries between text and commentary is quite deceiving" and conclusively demonstrates the variety of ways in which authors and commentators engaged in a mutually productive dialogue that affected the narratological structure of later works.[24] As Rolston has noted, commentaries are "usually reserved for the kinds of texts that civilizations anchor themselves to and consider most worth fighting for."[25] Fiction was a relative latecomer to this hallowed designation, and the practice of applying evaluative commentary (*piping*) and emphatic punctuation (*quandian*) to novels like *Shuihu zhuan* and *Romance of the Three Kingdoms* built on a long-standing tradition of critical evaluation in more established genres like classical scholarship and historiography. Fiction commentary of the type discussed in this chapter appears to have begun in the late Ming, and although there are examples of published works of fiction without commentary, these recensions often went out of circulation because of a lack of consumer interest.

This vibrant critical tradition was overwhelmingly effaced in the twentieth century by the publication of modern editions whose editors expunged commentaries to focus exclusively on the "text proper." Seminal literary reformers such as Hu Shi (1891–1962) objected to the fact that these commentaries were written in literary Chinese (*wenyan*) rather than the "unadorned speech" (*baihua*) he advocated, and other critics found fault with their allegedly conservative, feudal, and retrograde sentiments. As scholars of East Asian literary culture, however, we ignore the historical importance of these commentaries at our hermeneutic peril—not only in the case of China but also, as I argue in this chapter, in that of Japan. As late as 1894, the Tokyo-based Matsugyokudō publishing house republished a typeset edition of Jin Shengtan's edition of *Shuihu zhuan* (a project in which Meiji-period cultural luminaries like Narushima Ryūhoku and Shigeno Yasutsugu were involved), and in 1923, we find Kōda Rohan announcing in the pages of *Bungei shunjū* that "the fact that there is someone named Jin Shengtan among the commentators on novels like *Shuihu zhuan*,

Romance of the Three Kingdoms, and *Journey to the West* is something that everyone knows."[26] There is considerable evidence in both China and Japan that commentary by celebrity commentators was as prized as the text of the novels themselves, and as Rolston points out, even if readers desired to read only the narrative proper, they would be hard-pressed to ignore the "assault" presented by the paratextual features.[27] In addition to the inclusion of prefaces, punctuation, illustrations, interlineal and marginal commentary, commentarial editions of Chinese novels might include any combination of "statements of principle" (*fanli*); general essays on the theme of the book (*dufa, zongping*); question-and-answer dialogues (*huowen*); essays on specific topics (*zhuanlun*); quotation of documents and historical sources; charts and lists of characters; commemorative poems; concluding remarks; postfaces; and so forth. Although this copious body of paratextual material was intended to fix or determine a particular interpretation of the work under scrutiny, it often had the opposite effect. If a text was subject to commentary by more than one commentator, the reader could easily be led into a thicket of debates and disagreements—as is the case in the famous Zhiyanzhai commentary to *Dream of the Red Chamber* (*Hongloumeng*). Even editions with commentary by only *one* critic—such as the Jin Shengtan edition of *Shuihu zhuan*—contained conflicting and paradoxical interpretations. To read late imperial Chinese fiction in its original context is to be made keenly aware that tension, textual contradiction, and polyvocality existed well before their discovery at the hands of twentieth-century post-structuralists.

To repeat: Edo-period readers did not read a novel called *Shuihu zhuan*. They read *The Fifth Book for Men of Genius: Shi Nai'an's "The Water Margin"* (*Diwu caizishu Shi Nai'an Shuihu zhuan*) with commentary by Jin Shengtan; or they read *The Loyal and Righteous Water Margin with Commentary by Mr. Li Zhuowu* (*Li Zhuowu xiansheng piping Zhongyi shuihu zhuan*),[28] whose preface and comments were attributed to the iconoclast philosopher Li Zhuowu. Scholars of Chinese fiction have increasingly noted the centrality of *pingdian* commentary to the late imperial reading experience, and this chapter demonstrates that instead of being seen as an optional supplement to the text, Chinese critical commentary was equally important to Japanese engagement with traditional Chinese fiction.

Even a cursory look at the *Hakusai shomoku* reveals that different commentarial editions of particular novels were distinguished from one another in importation records, and as the previous example of Suyama Nantō shows, Japanese connoisseurs of Chinese fiction were highly partisan in their selection and endorsement of editions. A 1741 entry in the *Hakusai shomoku*, for instance, notes the importation of a Jin Shengtan edition of *Shuihu zhuan* "with annotations included" (*chū ari*), and the writing of Edo-period literati demonstrates an easy familiarity with the names of Chinese commentators like Jin, Mao Zonggang, and Zhang Zhupo.[29] When, as a young boy, the historian Seita Tansō sent a selection of his writing to his mentor, the Akashi poet Yanada Zeigan (1672–1757), Zeigan responded, "I received your work, and it is clear that half a lifetime's worth of energy went into it. Even before I was finished reading, I knew that it was the harbinger of a long-lasting literary elegance. Later, I'll draw up a commentary—sweeping aside everything else on the desk and lighting incense to summon Jin Shengtan and Wang Wangru."[30] Zeigan's playful promise to act as Tansō's personal Jin Shengtan illustrates the high regard in which the Chinese commentator was held and presumes that his young correspondent would know who Jin was. Later, Tansō befriended the aforementioned Minagawa Kien, who shared his passion for Jin Shengtan's writing and ruefully recalled editions of *Shuihu zhuan* that he had lost to fellow aficionados: "When I was young, I loved the Jin Shengtan–edited *Shuihu zhuan* because of its marvelous commentary. Even after I grew up, I still read it without ever growing bored. Later, I loaned my copy to a friend, who admired it so much that he refused to return it! I bought another copy, which I loaned to Seita Tansō to read. He also loved it—perhaps too much—and carried it off as well."[31]

In order to better understand the ways in which Japanese readers of *Shuihu zhuan* engaged Chinese commentarial traditions, it is necessary to at least briefly outline the features of the commentaries themselves. As the praise of Minagawa Kien and the denigration of Suyama Nantō suggest, Jin Shengtan was by far the most familiar paratextual presence in the copies of *Shuihu zhuan* imported into Japan. A native of Suzhou, Jin is best known in the present for his intense devotion to traditional fiction and drama. *Shuihu zhuan* was a work of particular importance to Jin, and he signaled his attachment to the novel by listing it alongside five other "genius works" (*caizishu*): the poet Qu Yuan's (ca. 340–278 BCE) poem "Li sao" (Encountering sorrow), the *Zhuangzi*, Sima Qian's (ca. 145–86 BCE) *Shiji* (*Records of the Grand Historian*), the poetry of the Tang poet Du Fu (712–770 CE), and the thirteenth-century dramatic work *Xixiang ji* (*Romance of the Western Chamber*). As a young man, Jin attained the lowest of the three degrees in the imperial examination system, but he does not appear to have sat for more advanced degrees.[32] The absence of official responsibilities freed up time for Jin's preferred pastime of reading and explicating a wide range of literary texts. His annotated edition of *Shuihu zhuan*, the third preface of which is dated 1641, can fairly be considered his magnum opus. The edition he prepared contained five fascicles of introductory material, including three prefaces by Jin himself, a selection of excerpts from historical texts, a general "reading guide" to the novel (*dufa*), and a clearly spurious preface attributed to the novel's putative author, Shi Nai'an. The bulk of Jin's textual analysis appeared in the body of the novel itself, where Jin copiously annotated each chapter through interlineal, marginal, and prechapter comments.

Additionally, Jin excised the vast majority of the text's poetry and parallel prose and rewrote a number of passages in ways that accorded with the arguments raised in his commentary. He justified these emendations by claiming that his edition of the novel was an "ancient edition" (*guben*) faithfully preserving the authorial intention of Shi Nai'an. He named his edition the Guanhuatang edition after the studio in which it was allegedly discovered. This discovery of an ancient edition of *Shuihu zhuan* was patently untrue, but Jin stuck to his story: throughout his commentary, he elevated his ancient edition through the castigation of various other "vulgar editions" (*suben*) in circulation. Jin's largest innovation was the excision of the second half of the novel. In the longer recensions of *Shuihu zhuan*, the first seventy-one chapters chronicle the individual adventures of the 108 bandit-heroes and describe their gradual assemblage in the Liangshan marshes. In the second half of the novel, the outlaws are pardoned by the Song emperor and make amends for their crimes by going to war with other groups of rebels and invaders. Jin's edition removed this second half and ended the novel on a note of suspense, in an ending clearly written by Jin himself. One of the bandits, the newly arrived "Jade Unicorn" Lu Junyi, has a portentous dream in which the Liangshan gang is put to death in a grisly execution scene—an ending meant to suggest that the outlaws would ultimately be punished for their crimes. Jin claimed that this dramatic ending was the conclusion Shi Nai'an had originally written. The longer narrative, in which the outlaws were pardoned by the Song court, Jin told his readers, was nothing more than an inferior "dog's tail" (*gouwei*) by the Yuan-dynasty playwright Luo Guanzhong (ca. 1330–1400). By excising the chapters in which the bandits are pardoned, Jin insisted that he was restoring the text to a pristine condition.

Jin's excision of the second half of the novel was rooted in both aesthetic and moral concerns. Of the many aspects of earlier editions he found objectionable, nothing sparked his ire more than the worry that readers might find the outlaws sympathetic, and he was highly critical of readers who read *Shuihu zhuan* as a tale of unappreciated valor. The Guanhuatang edition's full title, *The Fifth Book for Men of Genius: Shi Nai'an's "The Water Margin,"* was itself a polemical attempt at rebuking publishers who included the terms "loyal" (*zhong*) and "righteous" (*yi*) in the title of the text. One such edition was an earlier, 1610 edition of the novel prepared by the Rongyutang publishing house in Hangzhou. The text's full title was *The Loyal and Righteous Water Margin with Commentary by Mr. Li Zhuowu*. As promised, the edition included a preface by Li Zhuowu, who discoursed at length on the meaning of the novel's title:

The Grand Historian Sima Qian wrote, "[The Warring States philosopher Han Feizi's] 'The Difficulties of Persuasion' and 'Solitary Frustration' were composed by a virtuous man who sought to express his righteous anger." Looking at this, we see that in antiquity, men of virtue did not compose literary works unless they were overcome by indignation and frustration. If they did not feel ill at ease but still composed something, then this was like shivering without being cold, or groaning without being sick. You can do it, but who would ever watch such a thing! *Shuihu zhuan* is also a work produced by the author's indignation. The Song imperial line's decline meant that honors were given indiscriminately. Men of great virtue were forced to the bottom, and the unworthy rose to the top. Soon, barbarian invaders were in control, and the residents of the Central Plains were under their yoke. . . . Who were the ones venting their grief? The gallants who banded together in the water margins in former days. It is impossible not to call them men of loyalty and righteousness. For this reason, the authors Shi Nai'an and Luo Guanzhong called their work *Chronicle of the Water Margin* and capped it off with the words "loyal" and "righteous."[33]

By cutting off the narrative after the assemblage of the outlaws and subjecting them to oneiric execution, Jin Shengtan denied the Liangshan rebels a chance at redemption. In the second preface to the Guanhuatang edition, Jin made his intentions explicit by directly attacking the proposals raised in Li Zhuowu's essay:

Shi Nai'an chronicled the exploits of the bandit Song Jiang and titled his work *The Water Margin*. This is because he hated Song Jiang in the extreme, dismissed him, and did not want him sharing the Middle Kingdom. Later generations didn't understand that Song Jiang was a sower of discord and mistakenly affixed "loyal and righteous" to the title of the tale. Alas! Can there ever be such a thing as loyalty and righteousness in a place like the water margin? . . . What Shi Nai'an means by "the water margin" is this: the fringes of the empire are bounded by water, and what is beyond the water is called the "margin." It is a term of distance. Those who are distanced in such ways are the loathsome creatures of the world: what everyone in the realm should attack! They are the nauseating creatures of the world: what everyone in the realm should forsake! If we say that loyalty and righteousness are in the water margin, then we are saying that loyalty and righteousness are loathsome, nauseating things. Moreover, if loyalty and righteousness are in the margins, then does that mean that the realm has none?[34]

Jin objected equally strenuously to Li Zhuowu's claim that *Shuihu zhuan* was a work created out of the author's righteous indignation and presented a very different portrait of the author in his preface, famously describing Shi Nai'an as "well fed, warm, idle, and carefree," in contrast to the image of a tortured artist presented by Li Zhuowu.[35]

Jin Shengtan's claims about the origin of the Guanhuatang *Shuihu zhuan* strained the credulity of even many premodern readers, but he was a perceptive critic whose edition established a new standard for fiction criticism in late imperial China. Despite his professed distaste toward the outlaws' actions, Jin frequently distinguished between *wen* (the style of writing) and *shi* (the events related in the text), separating the author's description of a particular event from his endorsement. For instance, in a grotesque scene in chapter 54, the bandit "Black Whirlwind" Li Kui murders a small child in order to convince his ward, Zhu Tong, to join the gang. Jin shifted attention away from Li's shameful action by rebuking sentimental readers who conflated text and authorial intention: "Those who read to this point and sigh in consternation are fools. This is nothing more than a remarkable piece of writing by Shi Nai'an; how could something like this really happen?"[36] In truth, Jin's most profound innovations in the field of narratology were necessitated by the radical nature of his claims. In crafting a new ending that unambiguously condemned the actions of the Liangshan outlaws, Jin was left with the task of justifying the preceding sixty-nine chapters, a narrative in which many of the outlaws are presented in a positive light. Some members of the group are clearly the victims of government malfeasance, and as the Li Zhuowu preface suggests, readers sympathized with their actions. An alternative to acknowledging the subversive expectations of the reading public was the assertion of subtly elucidated messages by the author, discernible only to an educated few. The best example of this interpretation was Jin's treatment of the outlaw chief, Song Jiang. In contrast to his predecessors' fulsome praise of the rebel leader, Jin heaped abuse on Song with a ferocity bordering on the self-parodic. It was true, Jin acknowledged in his commentary, that Song Jiang was frequently presented as a well-liked and heroic leader. By paying close attention to the language and structural principles of the novel as a whole, however, a perceptive reader would see that Shi Nai'an in fact detested Song Jiang and expressed his dislike through subtle clues. The fact that Song Jiang was often praised by his fellow outlaws (and, by extension, the implied author as well) was nothing more than a red herring:

In this novel, it was simple to write about 107 of the heroes. It was writing about Song Jiang that was the most difficult. Therefore, when reading the novel, it is a simple matter to read about 107 of the heroes. Again, it is interpreting Song Jiang that is the most difficult. This is because Shi Nai'an uses "direct brushwork" to flesh out 107 of the heroes. If they are good, then he represents them as being good; if they are inferior, then he represents them as such. But when he came to Song Jiang, this isn't the case. If you rush through the text, then it seems like he's entirely good. Read it a second time, and it seems like he's about half good and half bad. Read it one more time, and the bad aspects outweigh the good. And the last time you read it, you see that he's entirely rotten with nothing to redeem him. And so, if someone reads Song Jiang's biography once, twice, three times, and once more again—finally realizing that he's all bad and no good at all—we can call this person a good reader![37]

This desire to train sensitive readers permeated the interlineal commentary and prefatorial essays in Jin's edition of the text. The rhetorical justification for the annotation stemmed from traditional concerns (the punishment of vice and allotment of historical blame), but the end result of Jin's labors was the enunciation of a sophisticated set of critical concepts and terminology, a complex mode of literary analysis focused on the recovery of authorial intention through close attention to textual detail.

WRITING IN THE MARGINS OF THE MARGINS: TWO EARLY MODERN TAKES ON JIN SHENGTAN

Seita Tansō (1719-1785)

A largely overlooked contributor to the dissemination and popularization of Chinese narrative in eighteenth-century Japan, the historian and classical scholar Seita Tansō hailed from a prestigious line of literati. His father, Itō Ryūshū (1683–1755), served as a scholar in the service of the daimyo of Echizen, and his older brother is better known under his adopted name, Emura Hokkai (1713–1788), author of *Nihon shishi* (A history of Japanese Sinitic poetry) and a noted poet and arbiter of literary taste.[38] Despite his lifelong interest in Chinese fiction, Tansō made it clear in his writing that his paramount concern was history and historiography. Like many scholars of his generation, he was deeply interested in postclassical Chinese history, and in 1769 he published a Japanese-language translation of the Korean scholar Ch'oe Pu's (1454–1504) castaway narrative *Kŭmnam p'yohae rok* (Record of my time adrift), a text that remains an important source of information about Ming society and culture. The publication of Ch'oe Pu's account was indicative of a widespread desire to learn more about a China less removed in time than the archaic texts constituting a classical education. One source of information was the ever-increasing number of Chinese novels and short stories available in either Japanese translation or *kundoku* editions. Tansō appears to have assisted in the preparation of a *kundoku* edition of the short-story collection *Zhaoshi bei* (A cup for reflecting the world, Jp. *Shōseihai*) in 1765. Although Tansō's name did not appear on the text itself, his involvement has been assumed on the basis of his nom de plume Kujaku Dōjin (The Peacock Adept) in the collection's preface: a remarkable essay titled "The Three Precepts for Reading the Colloquial" (Doku zokubun sanjō). Although the text under scrutiny was ostensibly *Zhaoshi bei*, Tansō's preface centered instead on the far better-known *Shuihu zhuan* to argue that, when reading works of Chinese fiction, deeper meaning might be concealed beneath the surface of the text:

It is true that there are many works written in the colloquial, but if you truly become conversant with *Shuihu zhuan*, then approaching the others is as easy as crushing bamboo. The reason for this is that, in the case of *Shuihu zhuan*, there is a "real water margin" beyond the surface of the text. In fact, the entire history of the Song dynasty is folded into the novel. [The outlaw leader] Chao Gai is really [the Song emperor] Taizu. [Chao Gai's successor] Song Jiang is really emperor Song Taizong. [The outlaw strategist] Wu Yong is really [the Song minister] Zhao Pu, Guan Sheng is [the southern Song general] Wei Sheng . . . and so on. Thus, we see that *Shuihu zhuan* can be a great help in reading the official histories.[39]

While an uninitiated reader will see the novel *Shuihu zhuan* merely as an exciting tale of heroes and bandits, Tansō claimed, a sophisticated reader recognizes that the story is actually an extended allegory describing the foundation and history of the Northern Song dynasty. Tansō's interest in the "real" water margin to be glimpsed through a close reading of the novel provided a bedrock for his extended discussions of *Shuihu zhuan*, which took the form mainly of protracted engagement with the novel's most prolific commentator, Jin Shengtan. As I demonstrate in the following, Tansō disagreed with Jin on many issues, but he took a cue from his Chinese predecessor by emphasizing the need to account for hidden themes and symbols not immediately apparent to superficial readers. Although a contemporary of vernacular philologists like Suyama Nantō, Tansō's conception of *Shuihu zhuan* substituted earlier Japanese interest in fiction as fodder for linguistic study with a far more literary focus on the language, imagery, and narrative themes of Chinese fiction.

Tansō's understanding of *Shuihu zhuan* can be reconstructed through an analysis of three main sources: entries in his occasional notes *Kujakurō hikki* (Notes from the Peacock Tower); the marginal comments inscribed in his personal copy of *Shuihu zhuan* (preserved in the library of Tokyo University's Institute for Advanced Studies on Asia); and most important, a set of lecture notes titled *Suikoden hihyōkai* (Explication of *The Water Margin* and its commentary). *Suikoden hihyōkai* is a lengthy, three-hundred-page manuscript dealing with the terminology, structure, and proper interpretation of Jin Shengtan's Guanhuatang edition of the novel. The manuscript is a student's transcription of Tansō's comments, and like many other dictionaries and reading guides compiled during the Edo period, the explication was never published. Two of the comments are dated to the middle of the Meiwa period—1768 and 1769, respectively—providing a general idea of when Tansō's discussion of *Shuihu zhuan* took place. *Suikoden hihyōkai* is structured as a tripartite analysis made up of direct quotations from the Guanhuatang *Shuihu zhuan* (both the novel and Jin's comments), Tansō's original analysis, and clarification of that analysis by Tansō's transcriber, a certain Takada Jun from Hizen. Short phrases from the Guanhuatang *Shuihu zhuan* and Jin's commentary are quoted at the top of each page. Tansō's comments, written in *kanbun*, are provided next, indented below the level of the quoted text. These comments are generally terse and rarely exceed ten characters or so in length. Takada Jun fleshes out these brief remarks in glosses that provide context for Tansō's remarks and clarify his pronouncements.

Although he was skeptical of many of Jin's arguments, Tansō appears to have accepted the Chinese commentator's claims about the authenticity of the Guanhuatang edition. In *Kujakurō hikki*, for example, Tansō presented Shi Nai'an as the sole author of the original text: "The seventy chapters of *Shuihu zhuan* were written by Shi Nai'an. Luo Guanzhong wrote a continuation of fifty chapters, which brings the novel up to a total of one hundred twenty chapters."[40] Similarly, throughout *Suikoden hihyōkai*, Tansō adopted Jin's custom of referring to the seventy-chapter Guanhuatang edition as the "ancient edition" distinct from other "vulgar editions" (Jin's *guben* and *suben*, respectively) in circulation. Tansō also agreed with Jin's fundamental moral orientation toward the novel. Despite his considerable enthusiasm toward the novel's writing and structure, Jin had declared *Shuihu zhuan* unworthy of use for instruction,[41] and Tansō imported this comment directly in his first remark in *Suikoden hihyōkai*: "*Shuihu zhuan* is a popular novel. However, it speaks only of deception, treachery, and ruthless scheming. It is not a work that can be used for [moral] instruction."[42] Demonstrating Tansō's awareness of the Rongyutang edition and critics who mistook the Liangshan outlaws for loyal vassals, Takada Jun explained, "[Tansō's comment] was in response to Mr. Li [Zhuowu]'s titling the novel *The Loyal and Righteous Water Margin*."[43]

With lip service to the dangers of reading *Shuihu zhuan* out of the way, both critics were free to engage in precisely that activity. Despite commonalities in their general rhetorical orientation toward the novel, Tansō immediately departed from Jin's analysis by firmly connecting the novel to his own interests in historiography. In his earlier preface to *Zhaoshi bei*, Tansō had described Chinese fiction as a complement (*tasuke*) to official historiography, and in a marginal note inscribed in his personal copy of *Shuihu zhuan*, he criticized less-educated readers for lacking the historical training necessary for its proper interpretation: "The text *Shuihu zhuan* is of enormous scope. It gathers together three hundred years of the history of the Song, its lords, and its ministers without letting anything slip by. If one is not deeply conversant with the principles of historiography, however, then he will be unable to understand its outline."[44] In *Suikoden hihyōkai*, Tansō built on his earlier assertion that *Shuihu zhuan* was a work of historical allegory in which different characters in the novel should be taken to represent figures at the Song court. This professed interest in the historical narrative embedded in the novel functioned as Tansō's central hermeneutic principle and justified his interest in the unorthodox and marginal field of Chinese fiction. For instance, Tansō insisted throughout his commentary that perceptive and well-trained readers would recognize the bandit leader Chao Gai and his successor Song Jiang as fictional stand-ins for the Song emperors Taizu (r. 960–976) and Taizong (r. 976–997). Lest the identification appear far-fetched to the reader, Tansō showed how close attention to textual details uncovered a key to the hidden narrative:

SEITA TANSŌ: Chao Gai is [Song] Taizu.

TAKADA JUN: Song Taizu's surname was Zhao. The surname Chao is pronounced the same as the character for "wave" [*chao*]. "Zhao" is pronounced with ascending tone, and thus it is different from "Chao," but the sound is absolutely identical. The term *gai* [蓋] refers to something that covers over the realm. Taizu was the first lord of the Song dynasty, and so he was on top and akin to the lid on a vessel. Thus, the character Chao Gai is a veiled reference to Taizu.

TANSŌ: Song Jiang is Taizong.

TAKADA JUN: Song Taizu established the great Song. [The next emperor] Taizong assassinated him and usurped the realm. Chao Gai made his abode in the marshes of Mount Liangshan and was murdered by Song Jiang, who assumed his position.[45] Thus, we see that the two instances are very similar.[46]

A number of other characters are listed and identified as fictional avatars of figures at the Song court, before Tansō breaks off by writing that "the rest may be inferred" through close reading.

This allegorical interpretation departed dramatically from Jin Shengtan's own interpretation, but Tansō did not specify whether his reading was original or based on Chinese precedent. In his *dufa* essay, Jin Shengtan pointed to Chao Gai's name to demonstrate how Chao "covered up" (*gai*) Song Jiang until Song assumed leadership of the outlaws, but he did not make Tansō's final leap into extended allegory.[47] One possibility is that the interpretation was suggested by the characters of the novel themselves. In chapter 40, for example, during a gathering of the outlaws, Li Kui exclaims, "With all our cavalry and armaments, why should we be afraid of rebelling? Our brother Chao Gai will be 'Senior Emperor of the Song,' and our brother Song Jiang can be 'Junior Emperor of the Song'"![48] Jin Shengtan merely chuckled at the irrepressible Li's comment, but the passage was dotted (the premodern equivalent of underlining) in Tansō's personal copy of the novel. It is tempting to see a particularly Edo-period fascination with historical camouflage at work in Tansō's analysis. The interpretation of fiction and drama as a masked reference to historical events would have been second nature to Tansō and his peers—all of whom faced prohibitions on the representation of contemporaneous events and would have been skilled at encoding and decoding subtle references. At roughly the same time Tansō was commenting on *Shuihu zhuan*, for instance, the *jōruri* play *Kana dehon Chūshingura* (A treasury of loyal retainers) was being viewed and appreciated with similar double vision. With the large number of extant Chinese *Shuihu zhuan* glosses, it is highly possible that Tansō was building on earlier Chinese interpretations, but without information about these sources, this must remain speculative.[49]

Jin Shengtan and Li Zhuowu were perhaps the most famous commentators on *Shuihu zhuan*, but they were by no means the only ones. In the opening pages of *Suikoden hihyōkai*, Tansō bolstered his interpretive credentials by demonstrating his familiarity with other critics who had written on *Shuihu zhuan* in recent years: "Hu Yuanrui and Xie Zaihang have also touched on *Shuihu zhuan* in their writing many times. Yuanrui writes that in recent years there was a gentleman who kept two books on his study table: on the right, a copy of the *Zhuangzi*, and on the left, a copy of *Shuihu zhuan.*"[50] The figures mentioned are the famous late-Ming literati Hu Yinglin (1551–1602) and Xie Zhaozhe (1567–1624). Both Hu and Xie are known for championing the creative merit of fiction and classical tales, and in the words of Allan H. Barr, "for challenging the conventional assumption that narrative should record only what is known or believed to have happened."[51] The anecdote Tansō recounts comes from Hu's miscellany *Sha-oshi shanfang bicong* (Collected jottings from the Shaoshi Retreat), in which Hu tells the story as an example of *Shuihu* mania in sixteenth-century China.[52] In the original text, Hu makes it clear that the tale was recounted "in jest" (*huaji*), but Tansō does not, or refuses to, get the joke. Takada Jun's explication—"This anecdote demonstrates the degree to which *Shuihu zhuan* is valued [in China]"—suggests that Tansō has misunderstood or misrepresented the novel's prestige in contemporaneous China.

Tansō's allegorical interpretation of *Shuihu zhuan* further contradicted the other influential Chinese theorist named. Xie Zhaozhe's *Wu za zu* (Five assorted offerings) provided support for fiction writers who wished to liberate their craft from the strictures of historical accuracy. As a connoisseur of Chinese-language fiction, Tansō was certainly aware of the following passage by Xie:

Now, in writing fiction and drama, historical truth and imaginative fancy should be equally present before a work can be called truly entertaining. . . . There's no need to inquire as to whether such and such an event really occurred. . . . [When plays are written,] authors feel compelled to go through each and every event so that dates and names accord to the dynastic histories. If they don't match up, they won't write it. If we approach drama like this, then just reading the dynastic histories should be enough—why even call it a "play"?[53]

Xie's text was well known in eighteenth-century Japan, and his discussion of narrative's relation to the "actual" and "fictional" (Ch. *shi, xu*; Jp. *jitsu, kyo*) found its way into Japanese critical writing on fiction and drama.[54] Although Tansō was clearly aware of Xie's corpus, there is no deeper analysis of his arguments about the nature of fiction in *Suikoden hihyōkai*. Indeed, Tansō seemed more interested in borrowing the names of Hu Yinglin and Xie Zhaozhe to promote *Shuihu zhuan* as cultural capital than engaging their theories of narrative in any depth. What is important for the purposes of this study, however, is Tansō's clear awareness of multiple commentaries to *Shuihu zhuan*—an indication of the degree to which eighteenth-century Japanese readers considered Chinese criticism in their own readings.

Although his allegorical reading provided a frame for analysis, the bulk of *Suikoden hihyōkai* focused on the aesthetic and literary structure of the novel itself by noting, often in critical terms very much indebted to Jin Shengtan, passages that were particularly well written, turns of phrase that demonstrated the structural principles at work in Shi Nai'an's composition, and deceptively complex sections that even Jin had misinterpreted. The anxiety of influence played a large role in Tansō's commentary, and Tansō alternated between enthusiastic endorsement and withering disdain for his predecessor. At many points, Tansō appeared to be trying to channel Jin's own unique commentarial voice. We see Jin's brash self-confidence reflected in the Japanese text when Tansō voices his approval by writing "Jin's comment hits the mark!" "Jin is absolutely correct!" or even applying Jin's trademark adjective "Marvelous!" (Ch. *miao*, Jp. *myō*) back to Jin's own remarks. When Jin insisted that prospective readers must read the novel four times before realizing the author's hatred of Song Jiang, Tansō indicated his support by remarking, "Jin Shengtan's comments on *Shuihu zhuan* are all refined and marvelous!"[55] Moments later, he undercut this embrace by showing how even Jin could be led astray in his readings. He was perennially troubled that Jin remained unaware of the historical allegory encoded in the narrative, complaining that "Jin Shengtan was a man of great talent, but even he missed things among the details."[56] Tansō often accused Jin of overreading or forcing an interpretation, and a number of the Chinese critic's more fanciful flights were dismissed as exaggerated or extraneous. For example, Jin praised *Shuihu zhuan*'s use of "the unfinished clause method" (*buwan jufa*), in which the author creates a sense of conversational verisimilitude by having one character interrupt the other midsentence. When Jin claimed that the use of this technique was "unprecedented" (*conggu weiyou*), Tansō quickly accused him of hyperbole by noting that "recent playwrights have all used this technique, and it's not remarkable in the least."

Structurally, *Shuihu zhuan* consists of a number of discrete story cycles focusing on the adventures of individual outlaws, and one of the most ambitious assertions Jin Shengtan made about *Shuihu zhuan* was that the episodic novel could be analyzed as a coherent whole. Rather than seeing the transference of narrative focus from one character to another as disjointed,

Jin argued that the novel was ordered by means of recurrent motifs that surfaced at regular intervals throughout the text. Where the untrained eye would see chaos in *Shuihu zhuan*, the educated reader realized that a complex narrative scheme existed. As Jin claimed in a prefatorial essay, "In *Shuihu zhuan*, every passage has its method, every phrase has its method, and every character has its method. Children should be made to pore over it closely as soon as they can recognize characters. If you get a grasp on *Shuihu zhuan*, then understanding other works of literature will be as easy as crushing bamboo."[57] This passage from Jin's essay was vigorously dotted in Tansō's personal copy of the novel, and throughout his commentary Tansō followed Jin's example by alerting the reader to the variety of means by which the author sculpted the episodic plotline into a cohesive whole. Although he refused to follow Jin's lead by elevating the novel to the level of the Confucian classics and histories, he agreed that *Shuihu zhuan* demonstrated the same attention to method (Ch. *fa*; Jp. *hō, nori*) and structure (Ch. *zhang*, Jp. *shō*) expected in more elevated genres.[58]

An example is provided by Tansō's interest in "narrative structuring" (*shōhō*): the author's use of a particular motif to tie together passages or create seamless links between episodes. In the twenty-first chapter of the novel, for instance, Song Jiang—newly on the lam for the murder of his wife—takes shelter in the residence of the rebel patron "Small Whirlwind" Chai Jin. When Song Jiang tipsily makes his way to bed after an evening of feasting, he upsets a charcoal brazier and burns a yet unseen invalid convalescing beside it. The singed sleeper turns out to be the soon-to-be-famous tiger killer Wu Song, who will take the leading role in the next cycle of chapters. The furious and malarial Wu Song breaks into a sweat, at which point Tansō tells the reader, "This [having Wu Song break out in a sweat] is structural." His student Takada Jun explains, "The sweating brings together Wu Song's fever with his killing of the tiger [in the next chapter]."[59] Though seemingly a mundane detail, the sweat acts as a linking motif by connecting the twenty-first chapter with the next, in which Wu Song will break into a cold sweat before dispatching a man-eating tiger with his bare hands. Similar instances, Tansō claimed, were scattered throughout the text, and he often criticized Jin for failing to live up to his own high interpretive standards. Often, Tansō claimed, Jin allowed something to "slip by" (*rōshitsu*) on the level of formal analysis. When the imperial executioner prepares to chop off the head of expert swimmer "White Streak in the Water" Zhang Shun in the thirty-ninth chapter of the novel, for instance, Tansō chided Jin Shengtan for not realizing that the reader had been prepared for this moment in an earlier scene: "[The execution] resonates with the earlier scene in which Zhang Shun was [chopping up and] selling fish in the marketplace. Jin Shengtan let this slip by!"[60] Or again, when Song Jiang meets a seller of medicine en route to murdering his adulterous wife, the commentator chortles over the irony that Song meets a vendor of salubrious and life-extending elixirs only moments before ending the life of his spouse: "Medicine is something that keeps people alive, but in this section of the text the meeting with the medicine vendor segues into Song Jiang's murder of his wife!"[61]

Although Tansō's interpretations often seem somewhat stretched to the modern reader, the important aspect to note is the similarity between his style of reading and Jin Shengtan's theories. Even in upbraiding his Chinese predecessor, Tansō demonstrates the degree to which he has been influenced by Jin's method of careful attention to detail. Compared with the cautious interpretive stabs at *Shuihu zhuan* made by the generation preceding him, Tansō's *Suikoden hihyōkai* is a confident and systematic attempt at using an earlier critic's method to produce an original reading.

Kyokutei Bakin (1767-1848)

Tansō's *Suikoden hihyōkai* was unique in terms of both its length and its exclusive focus on the literary criticism of Jin Shengtan, but it was not the only work that examined the pronouncements of Chinese critics in detail. Although he remained perennially distrustful toward many of Jin's central claims, for example, the prolific fiction writer Kyokutei Bakin spent much of his lengthy career addressing Jin's hermeneutic agenda—namely, the question of how the ethically troubling actions of the Liangshan outlaws might be reconciled with the bewitchingly compelling narrative itself. Throughout his lifetime, Bakin lauded *Shuihu zhuan* as a "great work" (*kohaku*), but qualified his praise by arguing that it muddied distinctions between right and wrong. As scholars such as Hamada Keisuke, Itasaka Noriko, and most recently Glynne Walley have demonstrated, Bakin's desire to rectify these distinctions was the underlying motivation behind original compositions like *Keisei Suikoden* (A *Water Margin* of beautiful ladies) and, especially, *Hakkenden*.

Traditionally, scholars have approached Bakin's engagement with Chinese texts like *Shuihu zhuan* from the standpoint of a polarized tension between art and morality, a hermeneutic inheritance from Meiji-period critics, who objected to Bakin's subservience of fiction to the conveyance of "didactic" messages. Recently, this approach to Bakin's oeuvre has come under criticism by Glynne Walley, who argues that a distinction between art and ethics is an anachronistic reification that distorts Bakin's understanding of the form of *shōsetsu* itself.[62] As Walley convincingly demonstrates, narrative structure and moral edification were inextricably linked for Bakin: a tightly and effectively constructed narrative should be and would be, by definition, morally edifying as well. It was precisely in this respect that *Shuihu zhuan* presented a problem for the Japanese critic. A central contention running throughout Bakin's decades-long commentary on *Shuihu zhuan* was the belief that the work's hazy morality was indissolubly linked to the fact that, on a structural level, it was an unnecessarily complex, or even unfinished, work—particularly in the form of the truncated Jin Shengtan edition.[63] In contrast to Seita Tansō writing forty years earlier, Bakin came to believe that Luo Guanzhong, not Shi Nai'an, was the original author of the text, and he presented the longer one-hundred- and one-hundred-twenty-chapter recensions of the novel as the authentic versions of the narrative. In the "Disquisition on Translating *Shuihu zhuan*" (Yaku *Suiko* ben) that capped his own abortive attempt at translating the novel, Bakin cited readers' surprise that he had elected to translate the longer hundred-chapter edition of the novel rather than the truncated Jin Shengtan version.[64] Bakin used the preface to enumerate his objections to the Guanhuatang edition. His complaints included Jin's favorable comparison of the subversive novel to the Confucian classics, Jin's demonstrably false claim that *Shuihu zhuan* eschewed the supernatural elements found in novels like *Journey to the West*, and Jin's inability to decide whether *Shuihu zhuan* was a work born of authorial "indignation" (*fafen*) or the "free and easy mind-set" he posited in his preface.[65] The uniting feature of these somewhat desultory complaints was a sense of inconsistency and self-contradiction that Bakin claimed permeated Jin's exegesis.

Recovery of Luo Guanzhong's authorial intention required negation of the interpretive principles advanced by Jin Shengtan and detailed analysis of the many "subtleties" (*inbi*) that allowed the reconstruction of an original text. Although he would have been loath to admit it, there was a clear parallel between Bakin's project and Jin Shengtan's quest to enter the mind of Shi Nai'an two centuries earlier. Like Jin, Bakin claimed that proper interpretation of *Shuihu zhuan* depended on identifying the innumerable overlooked details that enabled the apprehension of "esoteric meanings" (*shingi*). In an essay titled "Rebuking Jin Shengtan" (Kin Seitan o najiru), Bakin echoed Seita Tansō's earlier accusation that Jin had allowed significant clues to "slip by" (*rōshitsu*) in his analysis. Whereas Tansō had limited his examination to minor examples of foreshadowing and praised Jin's overall acumen, Bakin claimed that Jin's carelessness had compromised the fundamental integrity of the novel itself. By eliminating the second half of *Shuihu zhuan*, Bakin argued, Jin had failed to account for the many subtle structural resonances that connected both halves of the work. Like Tansō, Bakin centered his analysis on the allegorical dimensions of the characters' names. Tansō had drawn attention to Chao Gai's role as a "lid" (*gai*) covering the empire and Song Jiang's aspirations to become a "junior Song emperor." Bakin turned instead to the figure of "Jade Unicorn" Lu Junyi—a relative latecomer to the Liangshan confederacy, who eventually becomes Song Jiang's second-in-command. In the longer recensions of the novel, Lu serves both Song Jiang and the emperor faithfully as a commander in the campaigns against the Khitans and Fang La. In the final chapter of the novel, however, Lu is poisoned by the emperor's distrustful ministers, and after falling victim to a slow-acting dose of mercury, he topples into the Huai River and drowns. The Jin Shengtan edition of *Shuihu zhuan* excised this episode, but Lu Junyi retained central focus at the end of the work as the character who experiences the nightmare that concludes the novel. Bakin criticized Jin for letting Lu and his associates off the hook with a mere scary dream and justified his objection by pointing to a minor clue the author had provided. What Jin had failed to realize, Bakin claimed, was that from the moment Lu Junyi appeared onstage, perceptive readers would realize that he was marked for a preordained demise:

Take the number-two commander in the novel, the Jade Unicorn Lu Junyi, who's described as a dashing gallant of the first order. At the end of the novel, Lu Junyi falls into the river and drowns, but this happens *after* the seventieth chapter of the novel [where Jin's version cuts off]. Now, there happens to be a type of mountain pheasant called a *junyi* [Jp. *shungi*].[66] The name "Junyi" appears to be derived by removing the "bird" radicals from the characters and adding a "person" radical [to the character *jun*].[67] Thus, from the name he's given in the novel, you know that the author is going to have this character drown. The reason for this is that the mountain pheasant loves its reflection to such an extent that it often [falls into the water and] drowns. In his *Treatise on Curiosities* [*Bowuzhi*], Zhang Hua of the Jin dynasty wrote, "The mountain pheasant has beautiful plumage and prides itself on its color. It spends all day looking at its reflection in the water, to the extent that it can grow bedazzled and drown"—this is what I'm referring to.[68]

By ending the novel at the seventieth chapter, Bakin argued, Jin Shengtan had blithely disregarded the author's deliberate clue: discerning readers would recognize from Lu's name and their presumed awareness of the homophonous avian *junyi* that he was destined to meet his end by drowning.[69] Like his predecessor Seita Tansō, Bakin concluded, "When you look at the text closely, you see that the plot of the novel [*shukō*] is derived from the names of the characters, and the names of the characters accord perfectly [*tsuke-taru*] with the plot of the novel. By lifting up one corner of the rug, I make the author's profound intention perfectly clear for the reader."[70] In other words, analysis of minute detail can be deployed in the "uncovering" (*satorashimu*) of larger structures of meaning.

The ending of the truncated edition was an unmitigated disaster for Bakin, who read the one-hundred- and one-hundred-twenty-chapter editions of the novel as a narrative of transgression and ultimate redemption. By subjecting the outlaws to oneiric execution at the precise moment their assemblage is complete, Bakin argued, Jin Shengtan denied them a chance to atone for their earlier transgressions. As he wrote in the same essay,

Even Jin Shengtan cannot be said to be a good reader. Take a look at the seventieth chapter of [his version of] the novel, which is titled "The Stone Stele in the Hall of Virtue Is Engraved with Heavenly Script / The Heroes of the Marsh Are Surprised by a Terrible Dream." It goes against the message of the novel as a whole. In the beginning of the novel, Marshal Hong opens the stone stele and thereby releases the evil spirits. The 108 bandits appear, and much later the stele appears again, taking them in and returning Song Jiang and the rest to their original good natures [*honzen no zen ni kaerite*]. Afterward, they campaign against other groups of bandits on behalf of the emperor and root out iniquity. Jin's truncation cuts things off at the halfway mark, so that even if the stone stele comes back down, the novel remains unfinished.[71]

In other words, the second half of the longer recensions of the novel, in which Song Jiang and his coterie are pardoned by the emperor, dispatched against other groups of rebels and invaders, and ultimately betrayed and poisoned, was integral for Bakin to the meaning of the novel. This was not to say, however, that it was a fully satisfactory ending. In a preface to the ninth volume of *Hakkenden*, Bakin demonstrated his sensitivity toward his audience's affective responses to the text by making two important concessions: that readers were legitimately troubled by the seemingly duplicitous way in which Song Jiang, Lu Junyi, and Li Kui are tricked into drinking poison and that the second half of the novel appeared "significantly inferior" (*sukoburu otoreru*) in quality to the first.[72] As Glynne Walley demonstrates, Bakin argued that the two issues were intertwined, and he patiently explained that the deaths of Song Jiang and the relatively dull and repetitive second half of the novel were both necessary in light of the *shōsetsu's* requisite focus on the encouragement of virtue and chastisement of vice.[73] Luo Guanzhong, the putative author of the novel, *had* to write the second half so that Song Jiang and his peers might make reparations for their earlier behavior. Luo's primary shortcoming as an author was in writing a narrative that required him to create extra plotlines for the sake of the outlaws' redemption. A superior writer (like Bakin himself, for instance) would have made the protagonists good from the outset so that they would not have to engage in superfluous adventures to redeem themselves. In the same preface, Bakin chastised would-be critics who "twisted theories to make them accord with their favorite parts," and he pointed to Jin's truncation as an example of this practice. As Bakin, imagining himself in the role of Luo Guanzhong claimed, "If I ever have my own Jin Shengtan, do not make this kind of mistake in reading my own ninth volume [of *Hakkenden*]."[74]

The aforementioned issue of the outlaws' "original good natures" (*honzen no zen*) was a question that was taken up in the preface to another rewriting of the novel, *Keisei Suikoden*, the eighth fascicle of which was published in 1829. In the preface, Bakin responded to an imaginary interlocutor who asked about chapter 39 of *Shuihu zhuan*, in which a drunken Song Jiang pens a rebellious poem on the wall of a tavern at Xunyang Pavilion in

Jiangzhou. The poem is a clear proclamation of revolt, and Bakin's interlocutor asks how the Song Jiang who penned the bloodthirsty poem might be reconciled with the Song Jiang who docilely submits to the emperor's offer of amnesty. In his characteristically patronizing way, Bakin chided the imaginary reader for "seeing the meat of *Shuihu zhuan* but failing to penetrate to its bones and marrow" (*Suiko no hiniku o mite, imada kossui o shirazaru*).[75] What the reader had failed to notice is that, on an ontological level, the Song Jiang who penned the poem was not the Song Jiang who attacked the Khitans and Fang La on behalf of the emperor:

Song Jiang, as depicted in the novel, begins as a clerk, follows by being a bandit, and in the end becomes a loyal subject. The section in which Song writes the rebellious poem is during the section in which the Heavenly and Earthly Stars are running amok, and therefore Song Jiang's nature [*menmoku*] during that interval is truly evil. When the stone stele descends from Heaven and takes in the evil spirits for a second time, not only Song but also all the 108 bandits become loyal retainers of the empire. Therefore, the parts when praise and chastisement, good and evil are all mixed up all come in the middle third of the text, where the characters are different from Song Jiang and the other bandits at the end of the novel.

In other words, the questions of good and evil that so obsessed Jin Shengtan in his lengthy exegesis were fundamentally misconceived. The answer to the question of whether Song Jiang and his cohorts were good or evil was a resounding yes: they were in effect different characters at different points in the novel.

What Kanda Masayuki has called the tripartite interpretation of *Shuihu zhuan* was an idea that Bakin developed elsewhere, in an 1833 letter to the writer Tonomura Yasumori (1779–1847).[76] Though brief, the letter combined a sense of Bakin's larger understanding of the novel with the type of close attention to narrative details that enabled it. Continuing the discussion of names that he had advanced in earlier essays, Bakin suggested a complementary relationship between the martial arts instructor Wang Jin, who plays a minor role in the first chapters of the novel, and the hapless Marshal Hong Xin, who sets the plot of the novel into motion by releasing the spirits:

Hong Xin and Wang Jin are concurrent incarnations of the same figure [*zengo shin*]. In the beginning of the novel, Marshal Hong is the one who initially releases the spirits by opening the stone stele. Similarly, Instructor Wang instructs Shi Jin in martial arts, at which point the various incarnations of the spirits first appear. . . . Now, the names Hong and Wang are very close in sound, and the same can be said for Xin and Jin. What's interesting is that the author calls an untrustworthy [*fushin*] person trustworthy [*shin*] and a reclusive person outgoing [*jin*].[77] This narrative technique has been analyzed by Hu Yinglin, who writes about the use of inverted [*tentō*] names in drama. For instance, women are associated with night, but in Chinese drama the female role is called a "sunrise" [Ch. *dan*]. The play starts with the opening curtain, but the character who performs that role is called the "ending" [Ch. *mo*]. The clown—the most filthy and lewd character—is called the "pure" [Ch. *jing*], and so on.[78] Ultimately, the author of *Shuihu zhuan* places all the real bandits in court clothes and makes the "bandits" themselves loyal. All of this plays on the reversal of names, which is something that Jin Shengtan—for all his thousands and thousands of words—never realized! Instead, he simply relied on his own guesswork and puffed-up estimation of his own abilities, which aren't even worth mentioning.[79]

Decrying Jin Shengtan as another reader who knew only the flesh of *Shuihu zhuan* and never tasted its marrow, Bakin described himself—and not Jin Shengtan and Li Zhuowu—as the "one who understands the sound" (*chiin*) of the novel's author. Like Seita Tansō before him, Bakin internalized the principles elucidated by Jin Shengtan and other Chinese critics and used them to topple the master from his position of authority.

MORAL *MITATE* IN EARLY MODERN JAPAN— SANTŌ KYŌDEN'S *CHŪSHIN SUIKODEN*

Bakin's attempts to rewrite *Shuihu zhuan* in a way that balanced moral and narrative imperatives have received copious scholarly attention, but he was certainly not the only writer of the Edo period to attempt this feat. A decade and a half prior to the publication of the inaugural volume of *Hakkenden*, Bakin's erstwhile mentor, Santō Kyōden (1761–1816), had utilized the Chinese novel as a springboard for a lesser-known but brilliant work titled *Chūshin Suikoden* (A treasury of loyal retainers from *The Water Margin*). As the title suggests, *Chūshin Suikoden* combines the plot of *Shuihu zhuan* with the enormously popular *jōruri* and kabuki play *Kanadehon Chūshingura* by Takeda Izumo, Miyoshi Shōraku, and Namiki Senryū.

Kyōden's text, published in two installments in 1799 and 1801, is now widely regarded as an inaugural example of the later *yomihon*, and it exhibits a number of qualities that would become hallmarks of the nascent genre: for example, the plot's clear reliance on Chinese source texts, the hybrid language of the text, and the deployment of vocabulary and turns of phrase culled from works of imported fiction.[80] In terms of Kyōden's overall career, *Chūshin Suikoden* represented a narratological and thematic volte-face for its author, who had recently abandoned the satiric *kibyōshi* after falling afoul of newly instituted censorship laws.[81] That Kyōden, at such a delicate stage in his career, would consider the overtly subversive *Shuihu zhuan* to be an attractive springboard for adaptation can be explained only by the profound changes to the moral structure he effected in the course of his rewriting.

In the preface to the first volume of *Chūshin Suikoden*, Kyōden claimed that he was inspired to write the work after noticing similarities between episodes in the respective stories: in particular, the third act of *Chūshingura*, in which Enya Hangan is finally goaded into attacking the villain Kō no Moronao after he makes advances on Enya's wife, and the story of "Panther Head" Lin Chong in the seventh chapter of *Shuihu zhuan*, where Lin's comely wife becomes the object of similarly unwanted amorous attention from the wastrel son of the novel's archvillain, the minister Gao Qiu.[82] To rid themselves of the formidable Lin, the son and his cronies devise a scheme in which Lin Chong is tricked into buying an antique sword and led unwittingly into the palace's White Tiger Hall, where possession of arms is a capital offense. Kyōden cleverly blended the two narratives in such a way that the major contours of the plot (the villain's lecherous advances on the wife, the drawing of a sword in a sacred space, and the heroes' respective punishments by the authorities) are mirrored by an array of minor resonances and correspondences. For example, in *Chūshingura*, Enya's retainer Hayano Kanpei offends his fellow retainers by being absent during Enya Hangan's attack on Kō no Moronao, and in Kyōden's adaptation he plays an analogously guilty role by fecklessly purchasing the antique sword from one of Moronao's disguised henchmen. These resonances continue even on the level of diction: an attentive reader of the two narratives would certainly notice that both Kō no Moronao's and the dissolute Young Master Gao's surnames are written with the same character (高).

Needless to say, much of the pleasure of reading Kyōden's *yomihon* rests in the recognition of details from both narratives and appreciation of the ways in which they are repositioned in new contexts. Readers intimately familiar with the plotline of *Shuihu zhuan*—via either imported Chinese copies or the *tsūzokubon* translation that Kyōden himself appears to have relied upon extensively[83]—would find much amusing ground to traverse. For instance, many of the characters from the original puppet play have been granted the powers and attributes of the Chinese heroes found in *Shuihu zhuan*. The rather unremarkable foot soldier Teraoka Heiemon, for instance, has been given the ability to swiftly travel long distances like his *Shuihu zhuan* counterpart, the divine-footed courier Dai Zong. These parallels and superimpositions in characterization are mirrored at the level of plot. In the sixth chapter of *Chūshin Suikoden*, when Hayano Kanpei bludgeons a marauding boar to death—first with a club and then with his bare hands—few readers would fail to recognize the story of Wu Song the tiger killer, who accomplishes an analogous feat in chapter 22 of *Shuihu zhuan*. Throughout the *yomihon*, Kyōden is careful to preserve details that commentators like Jin Shengtan singled out in their commentary. In the original *Shuihu zhuan*, for example, Wu Song is horrified when, after dispatching his adversary, two more tigers emerge from the brush. Fortunately for the exhausted Wu, the tigers turn out to be pelt-clad hunters, leaving Jin sputtering, "Unbelievable!" (*qiwen*) no fewer than four times and effusively praising the ripple effect that gradually brings the reader off an adrenaline high. Kyōden was either similarly entranced by the effect or aware of Jin's comment, and in *Chūshin Suikoden* the exhausted Kanpei is also startled by the appearance of a second boar that turns out to be a disguised hunter.

Unsurprisingly, *Chūshin Suikoden* is a highly metafictional work, in which the characters themselves are aware of their own literary predecessors. At numerous points in the narrative, they helpfully point out that the situations befalling them are exactly like what happens in "that book *Shuihu zhuan*" (*kano Suikoden*), an observation that draws attention to Kyōden's simultaneous invocation and subversion of the earlier text.[84] Often, the narrative of *Chūshin Suikoden* takes back seat to the cerebral and ludic, and Kyōden embedded a variety of puzzles and games into the text as early as its unremarkable-seeming opening lines: "The story goes that while Emperor Kōmyō of the Northern lineage was on the throne, at the fifth watch of the third day of the third month of the third year of the Ryakuō reign period, the hundred officials made their obeisance in the Imperial Hall."[85] The scene is, of course, immediately reminiscent of both the original *Chūshingura* and

Shuihu zhuan, whose respective stages open by depicting court audiences with the shogun Takauji and the Chinese emperor Renzong. A beginning reader might be temporarily thrown by Kyōden's deployment of exotic Chinese vocabulary—for example, "the story goes," the same term glossed by Suyama Nantō in his *Chūgi Suikodenkai* thirty years earlier. A slightly more advanced reader would take pleasure in the ways in which the action of the first chapter alternates between narratives. Emperor Kōmyō's court is interrupted by a minister's report of a plague in the Hokuriku region (*Shuihu zhuan*), which the reader learns is caused by the restless spirits of the warriors Kusunoki Masashige and Nitta Yoshisada (*Chūshingura*). Enya Hangan and Kō no Moronao are dispatched to Hachiman Shrine at Tsurugaoka to enshrine Nitta's helmet (*Chūshingura*), and in the course of performing his duties, Moronao (whose surname in Japanese is homophonous with that of Marshal Hong Xin) impulsively opens a stone casket and releases an array of malevolent spirits into the ether (*Shuihu zhuan*). A sense of Kyōden's attention to minute detail is provided by the sentence quoted above, which echoes *Chūshingura* by setting the narrative in the Ryakuō reign period but borrows the "fifth watch of the third day of the third month of the third year" from Renzong's audience at the beginning of *Shuihu zhuan*. Thus, on the level of plot, characterization, and topos alike, *Chūshin Suikoden* is a perfect illustration of Edo-period *mitate*: a mode of literary appreciation in which signifiers from different periods, texts, or cultures are superimposed upon one another and viewed as one.

Kyōden was, however, rarely constrained by the original narrative. Throughout *Chūshin Suikoden*, the author radically remaps the moral topography of the narrative in such a way that the poetics of *mitate* reinscribe the framework of "loyalty and righteousness" (Ch. *zhongyi*, Jp. *chūgi*) interrogated by Bakin, Tansō, and Jin Shengtan. In the context of the Chinese *Shuihu zhuan*, to adopt the posture of an outlaw-gallant (*haohan*) is to subscribe to an alternative code of morality. Bakin's perceptive comment about the normative "reversal" (*tentō*) in which the true bandits wear the caps and gowns of officials at court draws attention to the imperial center's spatial counterpart: the "greenwoods" (Ch. *lülin*, Jp. *ryokurin*) that are physically and ethically cordoned off from the world of the imperial court. Although the rituals and conventions governing outlaw behavior bear little resemblance to those of their urban counterparts, they are every bit as coded and precise. As scholars such as Keith McMahon and Martin Huang have demonstrated, even the most shocking episodes in *Shuihu zhuan*—Li Kui's murder of a child as a means of acquiring a new member for the gang, Song Jiang's consumption of a defeated enemy's liver, and so on—are consistent with a larger "*haohan* ideology" stressing honor, duty, and androcentric comradeship above all other considerations.[86]

By contrast, in *Chūshin Suikoden*, these normative distinctions are leveled by the author's subjection of all characters and regions to a common ethical standard. Kyōden's narrative represents, above all else, a taming of the *haohan* ideology, in which the most morally problematic (and by virtue of this, often most interesting) episodes of the original novel are reencoded along clear moral binaries. In the fifth chapter of *Chūshin Suikoden*, for example, the virtuous retainer Kakogawa Honzō is charged with delivering a shipment of gifts to the capital to celebrate the ascension of the Ashikaga shogun, Takauji. The situation is instantly reminiscent of chapter 15 of *Shuihu zhuan*, in which the soon-to-be outlaw "Blue-Faced Beast" Yang Zhi is entrusted with the leadership of a convoy delivering birthday presents to the corrupt official Cai Jing. En route, Yang and the members of his company are duped by a confederacy of outlaws led by Chao Gai, who offers the convoy drugged wine and absconds with the gifts. Chao Gai's exploits not only lead to the hapless Yang Zhi's forfeiting his government position and "dropping into the grasses" (*luocao*) of banditry but also ultimately ensnare Song Jiang when he covers for Chao's transgressions. In *Shuihu zhuan*, the theft of the birthday gifts is justified—however tenuously—by the fact that they are "tainted treasures" (*buyi zhi cai*) bound for the rapacious minister Cai Jing.[87] (The very necessity of a defense, of course, reveals an element of moral uncertainty surrounding the heist.) In *Chūshin Suikoden*, however, moral dilemmas are effaced through Kyōden's imposition of the shogun Takauji on the figure of Cai Jing and the assigning of a clear villain to the role played by Chao Gai and his associates: in *Chūshin Suikoden*, it is Ono Sadakurō, the solitary treacherous retainer in Enya's employ, who dupes Honzō's men and steals the birthday presents.

The *yomihon* contains numerous other instances of the domestication of key characters. The shopkeeper Amakawaya Gihei, for example, is an important ally to the assembled retainers in the *jōruri* play but unremarkable in terms of his individual representation—save for the fact that as a merchant townsman (*chōnin*) whose valor is depicted favorably vis-à-vis his samurai conspirators, he would have been well received by the merchant audiences of kabuki and *jōruri* theater. In Kyōden's hands, however, Gihei becomes a crystallization of *haohan* ideology, a hard-drinking and hard-living warrior who excels in archery, riding, the use of staff and spear and values matters of duty and honor far over material gain. Illustrations in the first volume of *Chūshin Suikoden* depict Gihei as muscular and shirtless, with an elaborate dragon tattoo winding around his right arm. The celebratory poem that acts as a caption reads,

> Born amid the humble alleys and byways,
> His intentions ever loyal and pure,
> Who could compete with a man of his sense of duty,
> A fleck of gold amid silt; a lotus growing from the mud?[88]

In the tenth chapter of *Chūshin Suikoden*, Gihei is given an elaborate backstory (absent in the original play) involving the rescue of a delicate entertainer girl and her aged father from a loutish and brutal suitor. In one of the novel's most humorous interludes, Gihei disguises himself as the suitor's betrothed and is carried away to the groom's abode in her palanquin. When the lustful suitor comes in search of consummation, Gihei grinds him into the dust. The episode clearly identifies Gihei with "The Tattooed Monk" Lu Zhishen, who adopts an identical stratagem to rescue an oppressed village girl in chapter 5 of *Shuihu zhuan*. Unlike Lu, however, who becomes an outlaw after failing to conform to an incognito life as a Buddhist monk, Gihei has little difficulty adapting to a comfortable lifestyle as a member of the *chōnin* bourgeoisie. After marrying the young girl he rescued, we find the once-vulgar Gihei abandoning his *haohan* lifestyle and settling down into the comfortable domesticity of *chōnin* life as a successful and well-remunerated merchant. The sublimation of Gihei's outlaw impulses into normative domesticity is mirrored on a political level, as evidenced when Gihei eventually sacrifices his beloved wife and child to save Enya Hangan's persecuted widow and orphaned son. Thus, even when he reverts to form, his actions contribute to a solidification of the same hierarchy that *Shuihu zhuan* deconstructs. Whereas the Chinese novel interrogates clearly delineated social hierarchies and warily circles the question of service to a corrupt regime, Kyōden's adaptation climaxes in an assertion of devotion to precisely that same system.

CODA

An exhaustive catalogue of allusions to *Shuihu zhuan* in *Chūshin Suikoden* would serve little purpose other than demonstrating the author's creativity and literary virtuosity. There is no question that Kyōden's mash-up was intended primarily for readers with knowledge of the Chinese novel, and a reader as intimately familiar with *Shuihu zhuan* as Suyama Nantō, Seita Tansō, or Kyokutei Bakin would find much exegetical ground to explore. And yet I would argue that knowledge of the source text is not a prerequisite for reading *Chūshin Suikoden*, a rewriting that, in a manner comparable to Seita Tansō's and Kyokutei Bakin's respective engagements with Chinese critical precedent, calls into question the authority of an original text at the same time it attempts to resolve its thorny thicket of moral issues.

In this respect, *Chūshin Suikoden* is similar to the final work I discuss in this coda: the magisterial and deservedly famous set of *musha-e* warrior prints prepared by Utagawa Kuniyoshi between 1827 and 1830. Even more than the *tsūzokubon* translation and adaptations by authors like Kyōden and Bakin, Kuniyoshi's prints are credited with sparking a surge of interest in *Shuihu zhuan* in the final decades of the Edo period that manifested itself in an array of new cultural practices and adaptations of the novel. As Inge Klompmakers, one of the leading scholars of Kuniyoshi's corpus, has demonstrated, Kuniyoshi's prints were piggybacking on the popularity of earlier engagements with the text, most notably Bakin's abandoned translation *Suiko gaden*, which had been languishing in incomplete form since the inaugural installment two decades earlier.[89] In turn, the popularity of Kuniyoshi's series in the late 1820s created an impetus for the creation of additional adaptations and retellings, not least among them the resumption of the *Suiko gaden* translation, which would be continued by Takai Ranzan in place of Bakin in 1828.

What does it mean to talk about Japanese engagement with Chinese fiction when distinctions between original and adaptation, author and critic are consistently blurred and reversed in this way? What would the title *Shuihu zhuan* signify to a consumer who lacked the linguistic and exegetical skills of Kyokutei Bakin and encountered the narrative in the form of Kyōden's adaptation? How would the experience of "reading" *Shuihu zhuan* through the *musha-e* prints of Kuniyoshi differ from the more traditional modes of engagement discussed in the earlier sections of this chapter? In contrast to the processes of moral and cultural domestication apparent in works like Bakin's *Hakkenden* and Kyōden's *Chūshin Suikoden*, the intricate portraits play up the exoticism of the foreign novel by highlighting the Chinese settings and clothing of the characters, and by making use of imported Western visual techniques.[90] Among the most famous features of Kuniyoshi's series are the intricate tattoos sported by several members of the group: the outlaw Zhu Gui, for instance, stands with his muscular back to the viewer so that his elaborate panther tattoo can be better appreciated. As scholars such as Klompmakers and Sarah Thompson have noted, the presence of these tattoos represents a departure from the Chinese narrative, since many of the tattooed heroes in Kuniyoshi's series are not described as having tattoos in the book.[91] The fact that Kuniyoshi's illustrations led to a craze for *Shuihu zhuan* tattoos in nineteenth-century Japan demonstrates once again the process by which adaptations assume the authority we usually associate with original texts.

The series includes a number of iconic scenes from the novel: among the first prints Kuniyoshi prepared were those depicting "Nine Tattooed Dragons" Shi Jin's defeat of the Shaohuashan bandits and a potbellied Wu Song's bludgeoning of a roiling tiger with his bare hands. And yet the series is not simply a greatest-hits collection, and a new story and set of relations emerge from Kuniyoshi's own idiosyncratic selection, prioritization, and even invention of details. Kuniyoshi's focus on individual characters, for example, conditions a leveling of the complex social structure of the Liangshan outlaws. In contrast to the rigid hierarchy depicted in the novel—a hierarchy cemented by the stone stele that lists the names and respective ranks of the assembled 108 heroes—Kuniyoshi's outlaws emerge on equal ontological footing. Second-tier heroes like "Flea on the Drum" Shi Qian and "Featherless Arrow" Zhang Qing are granted the same amount of physical space, focus, and visual detail as far better-known and developed characters like Wu Song, Shi Jin, and Li Kui. The captions to the text reinforce this leveling by adopting a consistent format, beginning by explaining where the hero comes from and summarizing his unique talents in a few terse lines. That a viewer would care very much that the outlaw Yang Lin hailed from Zhangde commandery, or that Shi Jin was from Gaotang prefecture is doubtful; rather, the effect of the captions is to create a basis for the comparison and contrast of individual characters. If the original novel centers on hierarchies and rankings, Kuniyoshi's detailed portraits focus instead on individual distinctions to be compared laterally.

As readers work through the collection, they become aware of a remarkable lacuna: that of the bandit chief, "Timely Rain" Song Jiang, whose actions and moral standing kept critics like Jin Shengtan, Seita Tansō, and Kyokutei Bakin busy for generations on both sides of the East China Sea. Song Jiang, of course, plays a central role in the narrative from his first appearance in the eighteenth chapter of the novel to his poignant death in the final installment, and he is not only the most significant character by far to be left out of Kuniyoshi's series but also one of the extremely few to be excluded at all.[92] Considering the near-encyclopedic scope of Kuniyoshi's series, accounting for Song's absence is puzzling, to say the least.[93] While it is true that Song is consistently described as short, swarthy, and visually unimpressive, this would not seem to be disqualifying—especially considering the liberties Kuniyoshi felt comfortable taking with the other outlaws. Certainly, it is hard to argue that Song Jiang is less notable than minor characters like Shi Qian and Zhang Qing, or less physically imposing than the elderly physician An Daoquan, whose only claim to fame in *Shuihu zhuan* is treating a boil on Song Jiang's back. Was Kuniyoshi swayed by Jin Shengtan's argument that Song was a hypocritical deviant and left him out as punishment? Did he intend to paint Song at a later time, or was he simply uninterested in the character?

Barring a remarkable bibliographic discovery, these are unanswerable questions, but they allow us to make a simple but important point. The *Shuihu zhuan* presented in the form of Kuniyoshi's prints cannot and should not be assumed to be equivalent to the *Shuihu zhuan* imported into Japan via the customhouse at Nagasaki, in the same way that *The Fifth Book for Men of Genius* with annotations by Jin Shengtan cannot and should not be taken as equivalent to the Rongyutang edition with commentary by Li Zhuowu. Far too often studies of early modern Japanese engagement with Chinese literature have adopted the paradigm of impact and response, in which we begin with an original Chinese text, genre, and motif and explore the process by which it is reworked into something quintessentially Japanese. In this chapter, I have attempted to destabilize the very idea of an original text and explore some of the ways in which Japanese interest in Chinese narrative was characterized not by passive reception but by creative redaction and invention. In his discussion of "world literature" as an analytic category, scholar David Damrosch has argued that the study of literary circulation is potentially hobbled by exclusive focus on propriety questions of origins and source texts. Damrosch proposes that we give equal attention to developing a "phenomenology of the work of art," an orientation toward border-crossing texts that stresses their movement and transformation in new cultural contexts.[94] The trajectory of *Shuihu zhuan* in early modern Japan suggests that for many Japanese literati interested in Chinese fiction, texts like *Shuihu zhuan* were always engaged phenomenologically: concomitant with the obsessive search for original authorial intentions by critics like Seita Tansō and Kyokutei Bakin, we find creative engagements that advanced radically new narratives and moral schemas with varying degrees of interest in the existence or authority of an original text.

Chapter Three

JUSTIFYING THE MARGINS

Nation, Canon, and Chinese Fiction in Meiji and Taishō Chinese-Literature Historiography (*Shina bungakushi*)

Historians of literature come only after the artist has passed; they hold measuring rods, they take measurements and construct useful laws for their science, but these are useless for the creator because he has the right and the strength—this is what creation means—to break them by creating new ones. When a vital soul feels, without previous aesthetic theories, the necessity to create, then whatever shape his creations take cannot help but be alive.

—NIKOS KAZANTZAKIS, PREFACE TO *THE ODYSSEY: A MODERN SEQUEL*

Chinese literature should be called the second national literature of Japan.

—PREFACE TO *COMPENDIUM OF CHINESE LITERATURE*

In 1908, an anonymous Chinese writer calling himself Yannan Shangsheng published an inflammatory polemic regarding recent attitudes toward China's literary past. The editorial was appended to a newly printed edition of *Shuihu zhuan*, a novel that had maintained its status as a pillar of the Chinese fiction canon but come under intense scrutiny and repeated attack in the twilight of the Qing. The author began his defense by noting a sea change in the reception of earlier novels like *Shuihu zhuan*. Writing in an era that had recently witnessed the conceptual birth of the "New Novel" (*xin xiaoshuo*) as a possible panacea for Chinese social woes, Yannan Shangsheng lamented a corresponding decline in status for works that would shortly be relegated to the status of "ancestral" relics:

Everyone agrees that novels have become "tools of enlightenment," and there's no use adding anything further to that. But ever since the influx of translated [Western and Japanese] novels into China, there has been a concomitant tendency to look down on the fiction of our own country. Mr. X says, "China doesn't have any good novels," and Mr. Y echoes, "China doesn't have any good novels." He goes on: "*Dream of the Red Chamber* encourages lascivious behavior, and *Shuihu zhuan* incites banditry!" After that, everyone else starts howling along with them in the same key. What an absolute pity: has the denigration of our ancestral country really come to this?[1]

Although Yannan Shangsheng did not identify "Mr. X" and "Mr. Y," it is clear from the context of his remarks that he was referring to the revolutionary reformer, journalist, and propagator of the New Novel, Liang Qichao (1873–1929), who had indeed castigated both *Shuihu zhuan* and *Dream of the Red Chamber* as texts "offering instruction in depravity and banditry" (*huiyin huidao*). Captivated by the revolutionary potential of the Western-inspired political fiction he encountered in Japan as a refugee, Liang argued that the novel's ubiquitous popularity and linguistic accessibility could make it an ideal vehicle for social and political change. In the essays "On the Translation of the Political Novel" (Yiyin zhengzhi xiaoshuo xu, 1898) and "A Discussion of the Relationship Between the Novel and Mass Governance" (Lun xiaoshuo yu qunzhi zhi guanxi, 1902) Liang maintained that the problem was not the form of the novel itself but its content: retrograde material that exacerbated China's social decline by tending toward the sensational, superstitious, lascivious, and violent.[2]

The fact that the late Qing did witness a radical transformation in the structure and rhetorical positioning of the novel has occluded the entrenchment of earlier reading practices and canons of taste.[3] Although Liang Qichao's essays, for example, are deservedly famous for the reforms they both demanded and engendered, far less critical attention has been paid to the backlash *against* his proposals. As Liang himself acknowledged, there were innumerable aficionados of fiction who enjoyed texts like *Shuihu zhuan* or *Dream of the Red Chamber* and continued to read them blissfully unaware of their denigration at the hands of condescending elites. Other readers, however, took a more aggressive stance by arguing that the changes demanded by Liang and his coterie were unnecessary. As literary texts underwent rapid reclassification among newly emergent genres and genre hierarchies, *Shuihu zhuan*, in particular, was defended on the basis of the uncannily protomodern—even radical—qualities it was alleged to possess. For commentators such as Yannan Shangsheng, the republication of an old chestnut like *Shuihu zhuan* was not a nostalgic gesture but a revolutionary one, since *Shuihu zhuan* could be read as both a repository of ethno-national sentiment and a work possessing immediate relevance to shifting political tides in East Asia. As Yannan Shangsheng went on to say,

Can one possibly argue that there is nothing for us to take from *Shuihu zhuan*? Equality and freedom: these are the blossoming flowers of European civilization that the whole world now struggles to pluck. Rousseau, Montesquieu, Napoléon, Washington, Cromwell, Saigō Takamori, Huang Zongxi, Cha Siting: these are the great politicians and philosophers from both China and abroad. But Shi Nai'an, without availing himself of a master or any kind of instruction, was able to propagate his brilliant political thought well in advance of these various worthies. He was afraid that people would have trouble understanding him, so he couched his tale in the language of a popular novel [*tongsu zhi xiaoshuo*]. If the murder and arson [in *Shuihu zhuan*] are taken for banditry, and its opposition to government taken for lawlessness, then you would have to take luminaries like Rousseau, Montesquieu, Washington, and Huang Zongxi as sinners deserving to be put to death. For this reason, I say that *Shuihu zhuan* is the number-one novel in our ancestral country, and Shi Nai'an is the progenitor of the world's novels.[4]

In addition to being the world's "number-one novelist," Shi Nai'an, the reader is told, produced a work exhibiting the thematic and structural hallmarks of a number of *contemporary* genres, including the political novel (*zhengzhi xiaoshuo*), the social novel (*shehui xiaoshuo*), the military novel (*junshi xiaoshuo*), the detective novel (*tanzhen xiaoshuo*), the novel of morals (*lunli xiaoshuo*), and the adventure novel (*maoxian xiaoshuo*). By describing *Shuihu zhuan* as a political or social novel, the author's clear implication was that China had pioneered these genres independently of foreign guidance. In the editor's memorable phrase, "If communications had been better in the fourteenth through eighteenth centuries, then all the figures mentioned above would have made Shi Nai'an their master!"

Needless to say, this statement is not a disinterested literary taxonomy but an argument about the authority of origins. And although his argument centered on the construction of a strong Chinese nation-state, the author's placement of Shi Nai'an among the likes of Napoléon, Rousseau, and Saigō Takamori instantly betrays transnational influence. Indeed, Shi Nai'an was old friends with these luminaries by the time Yannan Shangsheng published his preface in 1908, having appeared in their company as early as 1890, in a collection of capsule biographies called *Sekai hyakketsuden* (One hundred biographies of world heroes) by the author Kitamura Saburō. Although Yannan Shangsheng did not disclose his own identity, there is every reason to believe he was familiar with Kitamura's account: *Sekai hyakketsuden* was mentioned by a number of late-Qing Chinese intellectuals, whose pride at seeing their countryman's elevation was qualified by shock at his inclusion and unease that a foreign writer had beat them to this recognition. Whereas Japanese writers presented Shi Nai'an—possessively—as an "Oriental" (Tōyō) genius capable of holding his own alongside Occidental savants like Shakespeare and Milton, Chinese writers redirected this rhetoric by grounding it in specifically national terms—focusing on the putative author's resistance to a Mongol regime that might be taken as a symbol of either Western or Japanese encroachment.

Although they disagreed about the precise meaning of the novel, readers on both sides of the East China Sea agreed that *Shuihu zhuan* offered some kind of perspective on the contemporary political situation and should not be jettisoned among the various and conflicting calls for social and literary reform. In 1908—the same year that Yannan Shangsheng made his argument about the significance of *Shuihu zhuan*—Shi Nai'an's revolutionary credentials were bolstered further in a Japanese retranslation (*shin'yaku*) of the novel. The translator of *Shin'yaku Suikoden* was one Itō Gingetsu (1871–1944), a novelist, literary critic, and journalist for the *Yorozu chōhō*, who introduced his translation with a preface in which he described the novel as a "text that nurtures a rebellious spirit and serves as a scripture of revolution; a work whose characters are written in blood and fire." Although it is unlikely that Itō and Yannan Shangsheng ever directly crossed paths, the Japanese *Shin'yaku Suikoden* made similarly expansive claims for the novel's potential as a catalyst for social change in East Asia, although the translator's ultimate aims were directly opposed to the calls for self-determination and national rejuvenation made by Chinese critics. In the preface, "On My Reason for Translating This Text Anew" (Honsho o aratani yaku shitaru riyū), Itō justified his production of yet another Japanese translation of *Shuihu zhuan* by connecting the events described in the novel to events unfolding on the world stage:

In the future, China will serve as a wedge for the peace and stability (or lack thereof) of the entire globe.[5] Any country that has faith in its status as a global power will express its ambitions with respect to China. . . . Any country that fails to appreciate the importance of solving the China problem is a powerless country, and any citizenry that fails to realize the responsibility it has to research China is a powerless people. At present, the Japanese people and our nation of Japan are bound to China by a destiny as inevitable as the flow of rivers into the sea. If we hesitate and stagnate, then the age of "Peach Blossom oaths" with our neighbor will come to an end. Whether we advance and by doing so live to take the day, or whether we retreat to guard our own deaths, every step is a true matter of life and death. Thus, we must resolve to move forward. Already, we have taken the first and second steps, into Taiwan and Korea, respectively. If we dawdle and stop here, then the sea will beat us back against our destiny. China is where our third and fourth steps lie. And China is the target [teki] of any country with capability and ambition. It will be a fight like the [Warring States–era] Battle of Yamazaki, a time in which the enlightened Chinese will gradually be extracted from the wriggling hordes of benighted masses [shunji taru kokumin]. The age is in a pressure cooker, and as members of the Japanese race that first stoked the fires of revolution and expansion, we have a deep responsibility to pay attention to and interest ourselves in the situation.[6]

On the surface, Itō's imperialist rhetoric appears to share little with the search for origins and celebration of Chinese literary primacy that we saw in the preface by Yannan Shangsheng. When Itō turned to a discussion of his interest in *Shuihu zhuan* as a target of translation, however, certain commonalities in the respective authors' rhetorical strategies become clear:

Shuihu zhuan is a text that nurtures a rebellious spirit and serves as a scripture of revolution; a work whose characters are written in blood and fire. It is like a repressed and dissatisfied child, pitted against his time, who has finally given voice to his anger. Every word is cutting and every phrase meaningful. When you touch it with your hand, it is hot enough to burn you; scratch it with your fingernail, and blood oozes forth like mist. . . . *That China would produce this book is only natural, but I would add that it is even more natural for this book to produce China.*[7]

Both this chapter and the chapter that follows take as their starting point Itō's tautological identification of the novel *Shuihu zhuan* with China the emergent nation-state: an identification that had largely been naturalized in both Chinese and Japanese writing on the work by 1908. The central contention of this chapter is that this intertwined and isometric identity of novel and nation was forged in the emergent academic discipline of Chinese-literature historiography (*Shina bungakushi*)[8]—a field that emerged from the same discursive cauldron as the study of Japanese "national literature" (*Nihon bungaku, kokubungaku*) in the second and third decades of the Meiji period and that played a complementary role in determining the contours of Japanese cultural uniqueness. As I demonstrate, the study of *Shina bungaku* shared a great deal of conceptual architecture with its Japan-centric cousin—namely, the use of a nation's literature as an index of its development, a search for unitary and unifying cultural essences, and the increasingly central position in the canon accorded popular genres such as the novel and drama.

As is well known, Meiji-period historiographers of Japanese literature such as Ueda Kazutoshi, Haga Yaichi, Ochiai Naobumi, Takatsu Kuwasaburō, and Mikami Sanji were highly indebted to contemporary European models of literary development, and in most cases these scholars were candid in admitting their influences. When Japanese historians turned their attention to Chinese literary texts in the third decade of the Meiji period, works such as Mikami and Takatsu's *Nihon bungakushi* (A history of Japanese literature, 1890) provided an equally ready model for emulation. As a result, the theories of geographic and racial determinism espoused by European critics like Hippolyte Taine (1828–1893) found their way into seminal works like Kojō Teikichi's *Shina bungakushi* (A history of Chinese literature, 1897) and Sasagawa Rinpū's *Shina shōsetsu gikyoku shōshi* (A short history of Chinese fiction and drama, 1897) as well. Japanese engagement with Western literary theory was, however, anything but direct and unmediated. When the proclamations of Western scholars like Taine were applied by Japanese scholars to Chinese texts, they came into contact with an extensive and venerable body of Chinese critical commentary—a corpus of writing that readers like Kojō and Sasagawa were intimately familiar with. The process by which Chinese critics like Liang Qichao used Japanese literary categories like the *seiji shōsetsu* to elevate Chinese works to respectability was mirrored by the Japanese use of classical Chinese fiction and drama commentary to establish the novel as a genre deserving of critical attention. Observant Chinese readers of Japanese texts noted this indebtedness to the Chinese critical tradition and used it to advance arguments about Chinese cultural primacy or superiority. The editor and publisher Di Baoxian (1872–1940), writing in Liang Qichao's *Xin Xiaoshuo* in 1903, credited an epiphany with regard to the value of the work to his contact with Japanese literary theory:

In the past, I was always shocked that scholars of literature in both the East and West would rank the novel as being the most important among literary forms. And I was equally shocked when I saw that a Japanese author had written a work called *A Hundred Biographies of World Heroes*[9] that placed Shi Nai'an among the ranks of Shakyamuni, Confucius, Washington, and Napoléon. And I was shocked most of all when I heard that there were lectures on *Shuihu zhuan* and *Romance of the Western Wing* in the literature departments of Japanese universities. But when I thought about it some more, what need was there to be surprised? The novel really is the highest conveyance of literature.[10]

Di's acceptance, via Japanese mediation, of *Shuihu zhuan*'s preeminent position in the recently constituted network of "literature" (*wenxue*) bespeaks a profound epistemological shift involving Chinese, Japanese, and Western conceptions of writing. The Japanese understanding of *bungaku*—especially in the Chinese context—triangulated between these three poles, and the relation of these traditions requires further analysis. The form or genre of literary historiography might have been a Western importation, but this fact tells us nothing about what Japanese writers used to fill this vessel. In her study of translation and national culture in modern China, Lydia Liu warns, "Serious methodological problems arise when a cross-cultural comparative theory is built upon the basis of an essential category, such as "self" or "individual," whose linguistic identity transcends the history of translation and imposes its own discursive priority on a different culture."[11] The same caveat applies to the discussion of "literary history" and its Japanese offspring, *bungakushi*. Following Liu's analysis of "translated modernity" in the context of late-Qing and Republican-era China, I am interested in not only the qualities of *Shina bungakushi* itself but also the discursive maneuvers necessary to equate *bungakushi* with the Western genre of "literary history."

The categorization and cataloguing of China's literary past was an enterprise inextricably linked to Meiji-period quests for self-knowledge and self-definition. The emergent field of *Shina bungakushi* was but one of several academic divisions that concerned itself with the description and explication of China in the Meiji and Taishō periods. The nascent field of *Shina bungakushi* had a tortured relationship to sister disciplines like Oriental philosophy (*tetsugaku*), ethics (*rinrigaku*), history and historiography (*shigaku*), and a revitalized and revamped study of the classics (*kangaku*). On the one hand, the development of Chinese-literature historiography illustrates Watanabe Kazuyasu's observation that Meiji-period *kangaku* was marked by a shift away from universal metaphysical inquiry to a more narrowly constituted focus on China, a contraction that allowed for the analysis of new topics that had been previously excluded from scholarly analysis.[12] However, although they voiced the same rhetoric of "scientific" (*kagakuka*) methodologies and objective inquiry embraced by peers in other fields, literary historians attempted to distinguish their methodology from these disciplines from the outset. Early works of Chinese-literature historiography are largely united, for instance, by the claim that the study of literature provided a privileged point of access into the voices and lived experience of a putative national people (*Shina kokumin*) that had been effaced in more elite disciplines like philosophy, ethics, and history. If there is one theme uniting the myriad works of *Shina bungakushi*, it is the idea that the body of texts, government institutions, and cultural practices labeled "Confucian ideology" (*jukyō shugi*) hindered or interfered with the natural development of Chinese literature. Even in histories focusing overwhelmingly on texts from the pre-Qin period, the utilitarian (*jitsuyōteki*), despotic (*kunshu sensei*), ideological (*shisō*) and antiquarian (*shōko*) tendencies supposedly observable in Chinese culture were used to explain how China could be both a historical font for writing and civilization and a place with a frustratingly uneven tradition of literary development. The denigration of Confucian interference created queer paradoxes and aporias in these works of historiography. Enormous epochs of Chinese literary history were deemed less authentically Chinese by the historian, even as he often took loving care to describe the texts themselves in painstaking detail. The example par excellence of this tendency was Kōjō Teikichi's pioneering *Shina bungakushi* of 1897. This magisterial seven-hundred-plus-page work spanned mythical antiquity to the contemporaneous Qing dynasty but nonetheless began by extolling the direct simplicity of Shang and Western Zhou literature over the effete and artificial output of later epochs: a statement that at least rhetorically discounted more than 90 percent of the works under consideration in his own study! While they accused the Chinese of being obsessed with the past, it is often in the works of Japanese literary historians that we observe an antiquarian purism at its zenith.

In spite of its almost fanatical extremism, Kojō's statement is the logical conclusion of an obsessive search for origins and a valorization of the "people" and their perceived imprints in the textual record. If Confucian ideology had interfered with or suppressed the development of authentic or "pure" literature (*junbungaku*), then it made sense to search for this allegedly authentic literature either in prelapsarian antiquity or else in moments of disruption or revolution (*kakumei*) when the Confucian social structure was forced into abeyance. Fujita Toyohachi, whose *Sen-Shin bungaku* (Pre-Qin literature) appeared in the same month as Kojō's history,[13] similarly characterized Chinese literature as "utilitarian, imitative, emotional, and dismissive of outside influences" and argued that it was not until the influx of Buddhism in the medieval period that the "lack of imagination" (*risō ketsubō*) in Chinese belles lettres was "remedied" (*i suru*).[14] Fujita's classmate and frequent collaborator Sasagawa Rinpū employed similar reasoning when he undertook his seminal *Shina shōsetsu gikyoku shōshi* (also published in 1897), a work that stated it was only under the auspices of the Mongol Yuan, when Confucian orthodoxy was allegedly overthrown, that the voices of the people could be clearly discerned and recorded in the form of fiction and drama. In an academic environment obsessed with the location and identification of various types of cultural, psychological, and above all national essences, Chinese-literature historiography was united by its insistence that the "real" China could be found only by searching the margins of orthodox Confucian culture.

This direct connection to China and the palpable (if often patronizing and naive) sense of cultural identification with Chinese literary texts complicates arguments about the scientification of literary history. Indeed, Sasagawa defined his subject as "the hidden profundities of human feeling," and other historians espoused similarly sentimental attachments to the topic of their research. Kojima Kenkichirō, a graduate of Tokyo University's Classics Training Course (Koten Kōshūka), argued that the study of literature was superior to other Sinocentric disciplines in its ability to allow one to both objectively observe history and subjectively investigate people's feelings.[15] Although *shi* poetry had previously been the primary vehicle of such direct expression, scholars would increasingly argue that fiction (*shōsetsu*) and drama (*gikyoku*) had usurped its place.

When the familiar and culturally unifying trappings of Confucian culture were stripped away, many a literary historian found himself surprised by the unfamiliar Other grinning back. This sense of difference and shock is indicated by the nomenclature adopted by the first wave of literary historians: Shina—a term that, as scholars such as Joshua Fogel, Stefan Tanaka, and Saitō Mareshi have argued, indicates a radically different way of conceptualizing Japan's place in a larger world order vis-à-vis China.[16] Although Shina had not yet acquired the pejorative overtones it would be associated with later (and indeed, numerous Chinese writers adopted it in its Chinese pronunciation, *Zhina*, after their exposure to Japanese texts), it is clear from the writing of Meiji-period intellectuals that their embrace of the term was related to a desire to reimagine status relations between China and Japan. In an essay titled "On the Value of Chinese Literature" (Shina bungaku no kachi), the critic and aesthetician Takayama Chogyū (1871–1902) made a point of reminding his readers that the Chinese empire (*Shina teikoku*) was situated "in the eastern part of the continent of Asia" and complained that designations like Chūgoku or Chūka "denigrated" (*keibu*) China's neighbors to the east by implying that they were barbaric.[17] Even for writers who continued to feel that China *was* a cultural center, the toponym Shina provided a way of conducting the kind of scientific, objectively neutral, and above all *comparative* research that defined the newly constituted study of literature. Saitō Mareshi has analyzed the deployment of this term with reference to what he calls an intellectual and epistemological "externalization" (*gaizaika*) and "excision" (*gaishutsu*) of China during the first half of the Meiji period. In contrast to the familiar dyad *wakan*, the toponym Shina was, for Saitō, a way of throwing Japanese culture into relief by emphasizing those elements of Chinese culture that could not be subsumed or absorbed into Japan.[18] As discussed in chapter 1, the word Tō had similarly emphasized those elements of Chinese civilization that were irreducibly foreign to Japan during the Edo period, but Tō was inevitably tied to a particular temporal moment; namely, the contemporary China that could be experienced, albeit indirectly, through the flow of texts, material objects, and Chinese sailors and émigrés enabled by the establishment of official trade facilities at Nagasaki. In contrast, I believe that the term Shina should be understood and distinguished from earlier formulations in terms of its unique intersection of geographic specificity and temporal indeterminacy. In contrast to *wakan*, Shina fits China (and, by extension, Japan) into an equalized cartographic schematic whose basic unit is the clearly demarcated, ontologically equal nation-state, a unit that allows one to posit the unique qualities of a particular nation but also positions them in a geographic schema in which they are subject to the same material forces. Similarly, in contrast to Tō, which emphasized a rupture between the China of antiquity and contemporaneous China, the function of Shina was to create a sense of continuity and linkage that bridged the gap between contemporary China and its past—implicitly providing an intellectual framework for explaining how China "got where it is today." Shina might be unique and culturally distinct—and indeed it was the mission statement of scholars to enumerate and elucidate these differences—but it was only one nation among the ten thousand (*bankoku*) of the world.[19] In his discussion of the linear "Enlightenment histories" that often served as an inspiration for Japanese literary historians, Prasenjit Duara has argued that,

the subject of History is a metaphysical unity devised to address the aporias in the experience of linear time: the disjuncture between past and present as well as the non-meeting between time as flux and time as eternal. . . . The nation as the subject of History is never able to completely bridge the aporia between the past and the present. . . . Little noticed by analysts, the nation actually both lives in History and also at the end of it.[20]

The adoption of the toponym Shina was a way of resolving this aporia between the past and present. As a concept, Shina is both timeless and temporally specific, resting on the assumption of a reified essence spanning antiquity and the present. It could be (and was) used to refer to the contemporary and "young" (*atarashiki*) nation-state described in the current-events section of Japanese newspapers or in travel accounts by Japanese abroad in Shanghai or Beijing. At the same time, the China of classical antiquity was Shina, too—as evidenced in the titles of this first wave of Chinese-literature historiography, or Taguchi Ukichi's declaration that "half of the literature of our land belongs to the realm of *kanbun*, and *kanbun* of course has its roots in Shina."[21] Such a conceptualization explained how China could be represented as ancient and venerable by some writers and immature and childish by others. Or, to conclude with an arresting image from Takayama Chogyū's essay on Chinese literature,

Why is it that Chinese literature has stagnated and failed to advance? China is an ancient land, and yet it's still immature. Or better yet: China is old and broken-down but has the appearance of a child. Legend has it that [the founder of Daoism] Laozi was in his mother's womb for eighty years, and when he finally came out, his hair was white as snow. If that's so, then Laozi is a perfect embodiment of China's national character.[22]

The following discussion centers on Japanese historians' responses to this uncannily aged and immature literary progeny, as well as on their attempts to locate an authentic and unitary Chinese character along the margins of an increasingly decentered civilization.

THE FIRST WAVE OF JAPANESE-LITERATURE HISTORIOGRAPHY: IMPOSING ORDER ON A "PERFECT FARRAGO OF SUBJECTS"

Like many of the academic disciplines that emerged in the wake of Meiji-period educational reform, the study of *bungaku* was characterized by an attempt to strike a delicate balance between the universal and particular. Di Baoxian's "profound shock" (*yihai*) that novels were counted among the ranks of literature in Japan can be adequately understood only when one takes into consideration how recently the term "literature" (Ch. *wenxue*, Jp. *bungaku*) had been recalibrated in East Asia to include works of fiction and drama alongside more broadly humanistic works. The explosion in publication of Chinese-literature histories in the mid to late 1890s followed on the heels of a better-studied wave of interest in Japanese-literature historiography. In the preface to their works, authors like Kojō Teikichi and Fujita Toyohachi made frequent reference to recent interest in "literary history" (*bungakushi*), and it is clear from the structure and contents of these works that earlier histories of Japanese literature were employed as models. Like Chinese-literature historiography, the first wave of modern Japanese-literature historiography was disproportionately represented by graduates of Tokyo University—in particular, the Department of Japanese Literature (Wabun Gakka; after 1889, Kokubun Gakka) and the short-lived Classics Training Course (Koten Kōshūka) established as an ad hoc field of study from 1882 to 1888.[23] As scholars such as Michael C. Brownstein have demonstrated, the recently established and consolidated Tōdai provided a fertile environment for works like Mikami Sanji and Takatsu Kuwasaburō's *Nihon bungakushi* (1890), Ueda Kazutoshi's *Kokubungaku* (1890), Haga

Yaichi and Tachibana Sensaburō's *Kokubungaku tokuhon* (1890), and the *Nihon bungaku zensho* edited by Ochiai Naobumi, Ikebe Yoshikata, and Hagino Yoshiyuki (1890–1892).

Despite the diversity of this corpus, there are a number of similarities observable in these histories. Most obviously, the works were united by an interest in redefining the scope of *bungaku*, a term with a lengthy history in East Asia and, as Tomi Suzuki has argued, one whose association with a more broadly humanistic *gakumon* was never entirely effaced from consideration.[24] This redefinition involved conceptual expansions and contractions. Brownstein demonstrates that Japanese-literature historiographers differentiated their field from earlier *kokugaku* traditions by claiming that *kokugakusha* had been too narrowly focused on the earliest epochs of Japanese textual culture. Although many of these historians would praise the "purity" and uniqueness of Nara- and Heian-period classics such as the *Man'yōshū* and *Genji monogatari*, analysis was certainly not limited to these texts. The Tokugawa period, in particular, was consistently hailed as a highpoint or microcosm of Japanese literary history.[25] Haga and Tachibana described the Edo period as Japan's "Renaissance," Ueda Kazutoshi's unfinished series *Kokubungaku* included *only* material from the Edo period, and the preface to Mikami and Takatsu's text urged the reader to read the chronological history backward, so that the reader might "progress from the easy to the difficult."[26] The inclusion of later epochs allowed the authors to examine texts and genres that had previously been excluded from scholarly consideration—from Mikami and Takatsu's *Nihon bungakushi*, which included popular authors like Bakin, Chikamatsu Monzaemon, and Ihara Saikaku alongside the *wabun* classics, to the first volume of Ochiai Naobumi's *Nihon bungaku zensho*, which presented the Heian-period *Taketori monogatari* as Japan's most ancient "work of fiction" (*shōsetsu*).[27]

Unlike their *kokugaku* forebears, these works also attempted to emplot individual texts and authors within a larger narrative of development (*hattatsu*), transformation (*hensen*), and progress (*shinpo*). Although Japan had a rich tradition of textual criticism and could boast of writers like Ki no Tsurayuki, Fujiwara Teika, and Motoori Norinaga, literary historians complained of an unwillingness to systematize this criticism and look beyond the borders of Japan. As Mikami Sanji and Takatsu Kuwasaburō stated, further distancing themselves from earlier *kokugaku* traditions of commentary,

Looking at the present situation, we're in the same boat with China: really quite rich in terms of literature. But critical judgments like "rich," "poor," "strong," "deficient," and so forth make sense only in the context of a comparison. When the *kokugaku* scholars of our time celebrated Japanese writing [*wabun*], then they were taking only the ancient writing of Japan and comparing it with China. The comparison was much too narrow. Now, more than two thousand years of our history are being brought out, put together, and put next to the countries of Europe for a comparison. True, there is no end of shortcomings in the literature of our country, but you can also see our many unique strongpoints.[28]

An understanding of chronological development was held up as the central feature of the nascent discipline, as evidenced by Mikami and Takatsu's statement that *bungakushi* could be defined as the branch of history that "records the origin, development, and transformation of *bungaku*" (*bungaku no kigen, hattatsu, hensen o shirusu mono nari*).[29] Haga and Tachibana's *Kokubungaku tokuhon* similarly informed the reader that its goal was to illustrate the "developmental transformation" (*hattatsu hensen*) of literature from its beginnings in antiquity, when literature was "purely and essentially Japanese" (*junsui no Nihonteki nari*), through the complex florescence following the importation of Chinese learning in the middle ages, and culminating in the "Renaissance" (*runeitsūsanzu*) of the Edo period.[30]

Finally, the first wave of Japanese-literature historiography established a synecdochal relationship between texts, authors, and the nation-state. Even when the definition of *bungaku* itself remained unclear, it was still presented as a privileged point of entry into the thoughts and psyches of not only the individual author who produced it but also of the nation to which he or she belonged. From its inception, there was a perennial obsession with isolating the distinct qualities of Japanese literature and placing them in a comparative framework with both Western and Chinese literature. This comparison ranged from the mutually complimentary formulation of Haga and Tachibana, who contrasted the gracious elegance (*yūbi*) of Japanese literature with the expansive strength (*gōitsu*) of Chinese literature, to the far more aggressive preface to *Nihon bungaku zensho*, which compared the "classics-rooted" (*keishi ni motozashi*) Chinese corpus unfavorably to the "distinct beauty" (*koyū no bi*) of a *wabun*-centric Japanese canon.[31] The Darwinian emphasis on evolution and adaptation was supported by other organic metaphors, such as Haga and Tachibana's elevation of literature to a paramount and nurturing "soil" (*dojō*) that provided a space in which all other specialized disciplines (*senmongaku*) could grow.[32]

In contrast to "specialized disciplines" like science and technology, however, the realm of literature held out promise as a potential space of compromise between Westernizing and anti-Westernizing impulses. It navigated the difficult balance between the potentially homogenizing implications of universal development and the fear that Japanese culture might be found somehow lacking in its particularities. Literature was not only necessary to the presence or absence of civilization, as the soil metaphor suggests; rather, it was one of the few spaces in which a particular nation could continue to define and assert its cultural uniqueness. As conceptual spaces, the nation-state and its literature constituted a clear homology. Both offered entry into a theoretically egalitarian schema of relationships (all nations produce literature, which can be compared and evaluated laterally), while at the same time guaranteeing a sealed space in which to define, express, and safeguard cultural uniqueness. Like the nation-state itself, the nation's literature was ontologically equal and internally unique. Or, as Mikami and Takatsu expressed it, "Literature is universal for all nations, whereas national literature is particular to a nation."[33] At the same time they sought to identify the essential hallmarks of Japanese literature in general, Japanese-literature historiographers fit the resulting "package" back into a comparative and global framework. From Haga and Tachibana's *Kokubun-gaku tokuhon*:

Ultimately, a single passage of prose or a single poem expresses an aspect of its author. And the work of a single author expresses an aspect of all the literature of its era. The literature of any era directly expresses an aspect of the literature of the entire nation, and the literature of the nation directly expresses an aspect of the entire world and humanity as a whole. It's just like individual pearls that are linked into a chain, which are then linked into a band.[34]

Properly investigated, classical Japanese texts could serve as a repository for the values and themes increasingly identified with the "national polity" (*kokutai*) or "national essence" (*kokusui*).

The central problem in Japan, as presented by these authors, was a problem of recognition. It was not that Japan had no written texts that could be favorably compared with those of the West; rather, its people lacked the capacities to discern their tradition of literature for what it was—in terms of both the value of individual works and the underlying narrative of development obscured by the profusion of discrete texts. This lack of discernment was understandable, perhaps, in light of the fact that Japanese literature's first wave of chroniclers seemed similarly unsure of how to define *bungaku*. Whatever it was, they agreed that it was necessary to the preservation and development of the Japanese state, increasingly so in the atmosphere of competition inaugurated by contact with the West. In an 1889 essay titled "The Necessity of Japanese Literature" (Nihon bungaku no hitsuyō), Ochiai Naobumi took issue with what he imagined to be the "general opinion" (*sejin no yoron*) regarding the status of textual exegesis:

This thing called "Japanese literature" may have had value in the past before culture was developed. However, in an age of contact and competition with the West, if you ask if it is still necessary, most people would say no, save for a handful of scholars who have made it their livelihood. . . . They would go on to say that our country lags far behind the West in terms of its culture, and that government, law, even language and customs should be exchanged along Western lines, in order to more quickly reach their level.[35]

Though he credited these sentiments to an "excess of patriotism" (*aikoku no yu*) and a laudable urge to reform and strengthen the Japanese state, Ochiai criticized lack of interest in Japanese texts as ultimately myopic. Describing the rapid transformations in Japan's political and technological landscape as "nothing more than cosmetic civilization" (*yūyōjō no bunmei ni sugizaru nomi*) or external (*hisōteki*), Ochiai argued that literature could be the basis for a more permanent sense of *national* affiliation. Indeed, what separated Ochiai most from even the generation directly preceding him was his argument against the idea of a monolithic "West" (*Ō-Bei shokoku*) positioned in a binary struggle against Japan. Instead, he regrounded his discussion of Western literature along the contours of the nation-state, pointing out that each nation has its own strengths (*chōzuru tokoro*) that are manifested in distinct ways. Although civilization was still presented in terms of universal standards of evaluation, Ochiai argued that its manifestations would differ from nation to nation:

For this reason, this thing called "civilization" is different from place to place. English civilization cannot be applied to France, just as French civilization is incompatible with German. This is a natural and inescapable principle. . . . Thus, when assessing the culture of our nation of Japan, it is absolutely essential that our polity, our customs, and our manners are thoroughly investigated and established as a base.[36]

Quoting the antique Chinese military classic *Sunzi* approvingly, Ochiai concluded, "I have heard it said that if one knows oneself and knows the other, he will be victorious in one hundred battles."[37] The most expedient and effective means of knowing oneself as a national body was, he argued, through literature, where the "polity, history, geography, feelings, teachings, and customs" of Japan were most clearly manifested.

But without a clearer understanding of precisely how scholars such as Ochiai understood the term *bungaku*, we are dealing with a floating signifier, an elusive aporia that continues to be debated in present-day scholarship on Japanese-literature historiography.[38] Nowhere was the attempt to identity and consecrate a focus of study more visible than in Mikami and Takatsu's *Nihon bungakushi*—a work that centered on the attempt to properly delimit the scope and range of the Japanese term *bungaku* and clearly demonstrated the ways in which Japanese historians engaged, challenged, and creatively adapted Western models of literary historiography. The question of Western influence on this work is undeniable. Michael Brownstein singles out for special attention Hippolyte Taine's *History of English Literature* and the Irish–New Zealand scholar Hutcheson Macaulay Posnett's (1855–1927) *Comparative Literature*.[39] Taine's influence is easy to ascertain: his history is mentioned by name in the study (and in most Japanese histories of the period). As is well known, Taine espoused a crude "psychology" of literature, elucidating the qualities of a given work of literature through a thorough study of the "race, surroundings, and epoch" underlying the text.[40] In a maneuver that would have profound effects on Meiji-period literary historiography, Taine began his epochal survey of English literature not with the glories of Shakespeare, Milton, and Spenser but with a far more prosaic exegesis of the geography, weather, and tidal patterns of the North Sea.[41] Taine's argument that the text both "explains and is explained by"[42] the racial, environmental, and temporal circumstances of composition would be developed at great length in Meiji-era studies of both Japanese and Chinese literature.

The influence on Mikami and Takatsu of Taine's emphasis on psychology is clear from the opening paragraph of *Nihon bungakushi*, where the authors presented literary historiography as a privileged point of entry into the "thought, emotions, and imaginaries" (*shisō, kanjō, sōzō*) of individual author and nation alike. In making this argument, the authors of *Nihon bungakushi* suggested that *bungaku* superseded other manifestations of civilization:

History, and especially the history of culture [*bunmeishi*], broadly examines transformations in things like politics, religion, scholarship, aesthetics, emotion, and customs. It labors to clarify the causes and consequences of events and presents the development of learning and morality. Needless to say, *bungakushi* is one branch of this endeavor. However, polished writing [*bunshō*] and poetry are the most ideal way of manifesting thought, emotions, and imagination, and for this reason literature is the best material for knowing the progress of man. Literature is created on behalf of politics; it receives the influence of religion. It transforms along with people's feelings and customs, so that the more it progresses, the more it stores up some kind of primal spirit. In the end, it's able to *control* politics, religion, feelings, and customs.[43]

In this way, then, *bungaku* was not merely a manifestation of external developments in politics, religion, and so on but a force that ultimately exerted control over these entities.

Mikami and Takatsu were still left with the task of defining a term that "although easy to use is much more difficult to define" (*bungaku naru go no mochiiyasuku shite, teigi no kudashigataki*),[44] and in this respect they were far more indebted to the work of Hutcheson Macaulay Posnett. What has perhaps been underemphasized in recent scholarship on Japanese-literature historiography is the fact that the Westerners who were invoked as models were often themselves similarly confounded by the task of defining literature. Self-confident pronouncements by Taine aside, the "Western" conception of literature was as nebulous and unfixed as the Japanese translation *bungaku*. In his *Comparative Literature* of 1886, Posnett described the history of literary studies as a tradition of exegesis without a clearly constituted object, criticizing nineteenth-century scholarship by Charles

Augustin Sainte-Beuve, Jean-Jacques Ampère, Jean-Charles-Léonard Si-
monde de Sismondi, Henry Hallam, Charles Lamb, and especially his contemporary Taine for undertaking the study of literary historiography
without first adequately defining the term "literature" itself:

The unfortunate word [literature] has indeed been sadly abused. In popular usage
it has come to resemble an old bag stuffed out and burst in a hundred places by all
kinds of contents, so that we hardly know whether it could not be made to hold
anything "written," from to-day's newspapers or the latest law reports, to Assyr-
ian inscriptions, the picture-writing of the Aztecs, or the hieroglyphics of Egypt.
Even professed scholars have contributed little toward the prevention of this cruelty to words. For example, Sismondi, one of the pioneers of literary history, though
starting in his *Littérature du Midi de l'Europe* (1813) with the suggestive promise
that he intended "above all to illustrate the reciprocal influence of the peoples' history, political and religious, or their literature, and of their literature on their
character," vitiates from the outset any scientific treatment of his subject by leaving its nature unexplained. It is the same with Hallam. Shirking any effort to define
the meaning of "literature," or even indicate the necessary difficulties in such a definition, Hallam uses the word (as he tells us in the preface to his *Literature of
Europe*) "in the most general sense for the knowledge imparted through books;"
and so treats it as a common, and apparently useless, label for a perfect farrago of
subjects—logic, astronomy, the drama, philology, political economy, jurispru-
dence, theology, medicine. . . . No doubt we would not now, with Hallam, apolo-
gize for neglecting such "departments of *literature*" as books on agriculture or
English law; still we have by no means reached any settled idea of "literature" such
as Hallam himself obscurely outlined by excluding history, save where it "had
been written with peculiar beauty of language or philosophical spirit," from his
Literature of Europe. Must we, then, surrender the word to the abuse alike of the
learned and unlearned at the peril of some such caprice as that of Lamb—
caprice not to be enjoyed as a freak of humour, but rather despised as the miscar-
riage of sober, possibly prosaic, inquiry?[45]

In contrast to Taine, who treated the literature of England as an a priori
corpus that could be used to reconstruct and understand the intellectual
and geographic forces that produced it, Posnett divorced the term "literature" from considerations of form and content and viewed it instead as an
index of social and cultural progress:

The word *literatura* even among the Romans had no settled meaning. Tacitus uses the phrase *literatura Græca* to express "the shapes of the Greek alphabet;" Quintilian calls grammar *literatura*; and Cicero uses the word in the general sense of "learning" or "erudition." Accordingly, when scholars of the Renaissance began to use the word they did not intend to convey ideas which it now readily suggests. They did not intend to convey the idea of a body of writings representing the life of a given people; much less did they purpose by using the word to draw distinctions between one class of such writings and another. Borrowing the word in its Latin significations, they did not stop to dream of days when modern nations would possess their own bodies of writings, just as they did not stop to inquire whether Greek or Latin ideas of the lyric, the epic, the drama, were suited or unsuited to the new life of Europe they saw around them. Greece and Rome, though rich in terms for special branches of poetry, oratory, or philosophy, had not in fact needed a word to express the general body of their writing as representing a *national* development. Greece had not needed such a word because she never was at one with herself, never attained to permanent national unity. Rome had not needed such a word partially because she passed, as if at one bound, from municipality to world-empire without halting to become a nation, partially because the cultured few who were the makers of her writings worked day and night upon Greek models. It was only when bodies of national writings, such as those of England and France, had been long enough in existence to attract reflection, it was only when the spread of democratic ideas in the eighteenth century began to make men regard the writings of their countrymen as something more than elegant copies of antique models made under the patronage of courts and princes, as in truth the fruits of the nation's historic past, that the word "literature" became useful to mark an idea peculiar to the nations of modern Europe. But the word in which the new idea was embodied served rather to conceal than to disclose any conceptions of national authorship. "Literature," long a mere generalization for letters or the knowledge of letters, classical or modern, was ill adapted to express the idea of a definite national growth.[46]

Whereas Taine had confined his discussion to a specific geographic area, Posnett included writing from the Middle East, India, and China as a way of reminding the reader that expectations toward writing varied dramatically from culture to culture.[47] Posnett's own study largely eschewed the primacy accorded to race and geography in Taine's account in favor of an approach centered on the analysis of different stages of social development.

In Posnett's hands, literature was conceived of less as a material object with clearly demarcated boundaries than as an index of social development that begins with the clan, progresses to "city commonwealths" like Athens, and ends in a modern configuration of nation-states. As Posnett pointed out, earlier cultures like Greece and Rome, for all their cultural sophistication, could not have conceived of their written works as "literature" in the modern sense. While any social body might produce works that could be deemed "literature," it was only the modern nation-state that possessed the self-reflexive need and capacity to constitute and study it under this rubric.

This was an idea that hit hard with Mikami and Takatsu, who labored valiantly to prove that their nation's assorted writing could be assembled in the discursive frameworks presented by European writers like Taine and Posnett:

When the two of us were at the university, we often read Western literary histories and admired their marvelous order. We took joy in the fact that there was such a thing called literary history, that allowed the reader to understand the development of literature with such precision and order. At the same time, we had neither works designated "literature" nor literary histories, which made studying the literature of our own realm even more difficult than studying that of foreign countries. How often we found ourselves being jealous and resentful. We vowed that in our country, too, we would have a tradition of literature and literary history that was in no way inferior to that of the West.[48]

The dilemma, clearly inherited from Posnett, was not that Japan has no literary texts per se but rather that Japan is in a state like that of ancient Greece or Rome, in which there has not yet been an epistemological revolution that would "make men regard the writings of their countrymen . . . as in truth the fruits of the nation's historic past." This lack would be remedied by Mikami and Takatsu's "first literary history in Japan" (*waga kuni bungakushi no kōshi*), which would reconstitute a heterogeneous body of texts by "considering divisions according to period, making clear the nature of different types of writing, and searching for traces of development."[49]

The crucial theoretical kernel of *Nihon bungakushi* was the section called "On the Difficulties in Defining 'Literature' / A Definition of 'Literature'" (Bungaku no teigi o kudasu no konnan naru koto / Bungaku no teigi), much of which was taken almost exclusively (and without attribution) from

Posnett's study. Like Posnett, the authors noted that Rome had no fixed meaning for the term *bungaku* and that Tacitus had used it to refer to the Greek alphabet. Quintilian and Cicero are both mentioned, along with Cicero's equation of *bungaku* with general learning (*gakumon*). What began as a direct regurgitation of Posnett changed, however, when the authors of *Nihon bungakushi* undertook a similar investigation of the uses of the term *bungaku* in China: a monumental presence whose millennia-long literary legacy most European historians did not factor into their theorization. Mikami and Takatsu noted that China had a strong tradition of learning since antiquity and located the earliest use of the term *bun* in Confucius's references to the culture of the Zhou kings. Over time, they argued, the term *bun* became increasingly associated with the act of writing, as immortalized in the eleventh-century neo-Confucian philosopher Zhou Dunyi's argument that "writing is a vehicle for the Way" (*wen yi zai dao*). The authors concluded, "When you look into utterances like these, it becomes clear that in China, writing [*bunshō*] and morality [*dōgi*] were inseparable."[50] Turning to Japan, Mikami and Takatsu argued that this understanding of *bun* had been institutionalized at the government level by the Tokugawa *bakufu*, where learning (*gakumon*) was isometric with Chinese learning (*kangaku*), and the term *bungaku* was best understood as "that which makes morality clear" (*dōgi o akiraka ni suru*).[51] Coming at last to their conclusion, the authors provided a definition of "pure literature" (*pūa riterachūa*)[52] that both acknowledged *bun*'s long history and addressed contemporary needs: "Literature is writing that uses a particular form to skillfully express the thought, emotions, and imaginative capacities of its author. It combines utility and pleasure and imparts general knowledge to the greatest number of people."[53] At first glance, the definition by Mikami and Takatsu appears almost identical to that proffered by Hutcheson Macaulay Posnett, who, after much squirming, had finally provisionally defined literature as "consisting of works which, whether in verse or prose, are the handicraft of imagination rather than reflection, aim at the pleasure of the greatest possible number of the nation rather than instruction and practical effects, and appeal to general rather than specialized knowledge."[54] Despite the clear similarities here, however, the millennia-old tradition of writing in East Asia affected the way in which this term was explicated by Mikami and Takatsu. Whereas Posnett had consciously excluded issues of utility from his definition of literature ("aim at the pleasure of the greatest possible number of the nation *rather* than instruction and practical effects"), Mikami and Takatsu gave issues of utility (*jitsuyō*) equal weight alongside the clear inheritance from Posnett: pleasure (*kairaku*). In fact, as their argument progresses, it becomes clear that pleasure is consistently subordinated to utility in the authors' schema. Having earlier argued that literature supersedes and incorporates endeavors such as politics, religion, customs, and so on, *bungaku* has also assumed their functions—foremost among them, the inculcation of morality:

By "utility" [*jitsuyō*], we refer to the passing down of teachings and the conveyance of information. Pleasure [*kairaku*] refers entirely to psychological pleasure. In this way, *bungaku* is not purely concerned with the teachings of the Sages like the classics are; nor is it concerned entirely with the conveyance of information like history. Neither, however, is it purely a vehicle for pleasure. In combining both [utility and pleasure], it doesn't offer direct instruction like other branches of specialized learning. Instead, it acts as a medium for introducing it indirectly. . . . In ancient China, poetry was seen as a means of effecting civilized transformation [*kyōka*], and the rationale for incorporating songs and music into the current educational curriculum is exactly the same. Even the best medicine tastes bitter, and talk of loyalty goes against what the ear likes to hear. No matter how earnestly you attempt to talk of morality, duty, loyalty, and the like, you'll never be as appealing to the common person's ear as military tales and comic recitation.[55]

Noting that today even rickshaw pullers stand around on street corners with novels in hand,[56] Mikami and Takatsu advanced to the final stage of their argument that a nation's literature might be used not only to reflect its "thought, emotions, and imagination" but also to inculcate a set of specific virtues. Just as they argued literature both reflected and controlled politics, so, too, does literature act as both a repository of a nation's virtue and a mode of moral suasion. Clear inheritances from Taine and Posnett aside, there was little in this understanding of literature that Zhou Dunyi or Confucius would find objectionable. Although the field of *bungakushi* was presented as an objective and scientific mode of inquiry—one that broke clearly from earlier modes of impressionistic criticism like *kokugaku* exegesis—it retained links to the less easily quantified. In fact, it was the alleged ability of *bungakushi* to apprehend and catalogue the interiority of its subjects—their "thought, emotions, and imaginaries" (*shisō, kanjō, sōzō*)—that was held up as a hermeneutic advantage over other branches of *bunmei* like politics and religion. When the arguments espoused by critics like Mikami and Takatsu were applied to Chinese texts, a similar emphasis was made on *bungakushi*'s ability to chart the interiority of its subjects—an interiority increasingly defined along national lines.

LITERATURE HISTORIOGRAPHY MOVES TO CHINA
WITH SWORD IN HAND

Like many of their European counterparts, the authors of the first wave of Japanese-literature historiography presented their pronouncements on literature as applicable to the literature of both a particular nation and the world as a whole. In *Nihon bungakushi*, Mikami and Takatsu compared the pleasures of literature to a glass of sake that "dispels all cares from the highest echelons of the aristocracy to farmers and laborers in the fields,"[57] and this image of literature's efficacy in cementing national unity across class lines was advanced in other works of Japanese-literature historiography. Echoing Hippolyte Taine's trinity of race, surroundings, and epoch, Mikami and Takatsu argued that the literature of any given nation takes shape from three factors: the fixed and unique characteristics of a *national* people (*kokumin koyū no tokusei*), external phenomena (*shingai no genshō*), and temporal momentum (*jiun*).[58] The genre of literary historiography would by its very nature address the second and third items in this triad, so many authors of Japanese-literature historiography used the prefaces to their work to elucidate the qualities of a putative Japanese national character. Tomi Suzuki, Lee Yeounsuk, Tomiko Yoda, and Michael C. Brownstein have analyzed the effect of this discourse on the construction of a Japanese canon increasingly defined by phonocentrism, the usage of kana over Sinitic scripts, and an emphasis upon "elegance and grace" as a putative hallmark of Japan's textual corpus. As mentioned earlier, the qualities of *kokubungaku* were often placed in a comparative framework with China and the West. Haga Yaichi and Tachibana Sensaburō's *Kokubungaku tokuhon*, for example, compared the gracious elegance (*yūbi*) of Japanese literature to the expansive strength (*gōitsu*) of Chinese literature and the subtle thoroughness (*seichi*) of Western literature.[59] Mikami and Takatsu made distinctions between a Japanese national canon characterized by its "reverence for the gods and loyalty to one's liege" (*keishin chūkun*), a Chinese literature devoted to "decorum and order" (*reigi chitsujo*), and a Western tradition emphasizing people's rights and the treatment of women.[60] The fact that these sweeping generalizations did not always match the authors' detailed analyses of the texts themselves suggests that the act of reifying and comparing was more important than the content of the comparison itself.

Generalizations or not, these comparisons had important consequences for the parameters of *kokubungaku*. Like Mikami and Takatsu, Ochiai Naobumi focused on reverence to the emperor (*kin'ō*) as the unifying theme of Japanese literature, and he used this characterization to effect an exclusion. Noting that the Japanese literary corpus also included a large body of writing in literary Sinitic, Ochiai argued that these works differed from *wabun* texts in their lack of this imperial reverence. Of Japan's staggeringly vast corpus of Sinitic writing, Ochiai singled out only the Mito philosophers for praise, approvingly noting their emphasis on imperial rule and their ability to "avoid the trap of paying homage to the [Chinese] Other and denigrating the [Japanese] Self."[61] As Matthew Fraleigh has recently demonstrated, Japanese Sinitic texts were among the first casualties of Meiji-period literary historiography, and genres such as *kanshi* (itself a new way of describing what were previously simply *shifu*)[62] were edged into the ambiguous ontological terrain that, in many ways, they continue to occupy today.[63] Even Mikami and Takatsu, who had relied extensively on classical Chinese thought to determine a definition of literature, excluded *kanshibun* from their scope. The authors acknowledged the clear importance of Chinese culture and texts to Japan, but they also provided a somewhat ambivalent disclaimer: "If we follow our definition of literature, then we will not treat works written in *kanbun*."[64] This exclusion was justified by a hierarchy placing script below national "psychology":

Bungakushi is a way of investigating the hearts and minds of a nation's people. Our country has, since the Middle Ages, imitated Chinese institutions and learned from the literature and culture of China. But the natures of our countries are fundamentally different, and the minds of the people are also different. Therefore, what is manifested in our respective literatures is also fundamentally different. Even in works that are written in Chinese [*kango*] and follow Chinese principles of composition, the spirit exhibited in works from Japan will be fundamentally different from those in China.[65]

Sinitic writing may have fallen through the taxonomic cracks in the reification of *kokubungaku*, but that does not mean that questions of the significance and value of China and Chinese writing to Japan's literary corpus were effaced from historiographical consideration. Rather, they were *displaced* to the emergent genre of Chinese-literature historiography (*Shina bungakushi*): a discursive body that presented Chinese literature as both "a foreign literature" (*gaikoku no bungaku*) and "the second *national* literature of Japan" (*daini no kokubungaku*)—often within the same paragraph.[66] The rhetorical maneuvers by which Chinese texts were simultaneously incorporated into and excluded from Japan's literary canon must be studied against the backdrop of a larger changing episteme. In his discussion of Meiji-period historiography, Stefan Tanaka has demonstrated how historians like Shiratori Kurakichi (1865–1942) used the concept of the "Orient" (Tōyō) as both an inclusive and exclusionary hermeneutic, one that could be used either to elevate China and Japan vis-à-vis an equally reified West or to posit radical cultural difference between China and Japan.[67] In the emergent field of Chinese-literature historiography—as with the developments in *Tōyōshi* studied by Tanaka—China was both the source of a culture of writing that far predated comparable developments in the West and an index of development that might be used to favorably reflect upon Japan's emergent "civilization." In this way, China as denoted by Shina functioned as an archive of potential narratives of Oriental development and stagnation that Japanese writers could strategically select to make a particular point.

The importation of Western literary theory had allowed theorists like Mikami and Takatsu to assemble their nation's assorted writing into a cohesive narrative of development and progress, and the same intellectual scaffolding permitted Japanese historiographers to impose order on China's written past. However, clear Western influences notwithstanding, it is crucial to note that earlier ties with *kangaku* traditions remained strong among the first wave of Chinese-literature historiographers. In an 1897 discussion of Chinese-literature historiography, Takayama Chogyū wrote that the new field was being established by "young *kangaku* scholars" (*seinen kangaku-sha*),[68] and this observation is borne out by even the most cursory examination of the authors' resumes.[69] Similarities in interest and rhetorical structure between writers like Haga Yaichi, Ueda Kazutoshi, and Mikami Sanji and their China-focused colleagues are not surprising in light of the

121

fact that the first wave of Chinese-literature historiography was also over-whelmingly represented by graduates of Tōdai's Department of Chinese Literature (Kanbun Gakka) and the Classics Training Course that had produced *kokubungaku* scholars Ochiai Naobumi, Ikebe Yoshikata, and Hagino Yoshiyuki. Aside from a few outliers like the largely self-educated Kojō Teikichi, as well as Sasagawa Rinpū and Ōmachi Keigetsu (graduates of Tōdai's Japanese History and Japanese Literature programs, respectively), the Kanbun Gakka and Koten Kōshūka were the main scholar-producing channels. Key figures in Chinese-literature historiography included Kojima Kenkichirō (a Classics Training Course graduate), as well as Fujita Toyo-hachi, Shirakawa Riyō, Takase Takejirō, Shionoya On, Kubo Tenzui, and Kano Naoki (Chinese Literature).[70] In addition to their backgrounds in traditional *kangaku* scholarship and coursework in their programs at the university, many of the scholars of the first wave of Chinese-literature historiography availed themselves of opportunities to gain exposure to new methodologies and areas of inquiry. For instance, when the Chinese-language instructor Miyajima Daihachi lectured at Tōdai, one of the students in the audience was a young Shionoya On.[71]

If Japanese-literature historiography took shape during the third decade of the Meiji period, Chinese-literature historiography followed behind only slightly. Kojō Teikichi's seminal *Shina bungakushi* was published in 1897, and the years 1897 to 1915 witnessed an explosion of other works focusing on Chinese poetry, philosophy, classical prose, historiography, "rhapsody" (*fu*), and, increasingly, fiction and drama. Although a mere half decade separated these efforts from the Japanese-literature histories penned by Mikami Sanji, Ochiai Naobumi, Ueda Kazutoshi, and others, the gap in time is significant. Writing in the immediate wake of the First Sino-Japanese War, Chinese-literature historiographers were in many ways attempting to resuscitate China's reputation as a cultural center. Nearly all histories engaged the theme of China's decline or "stagnation" (*teitai*) in some way—even if only to refute or otherwise qualify it.[72]

As in Japan-centered histories of literature, *bungaku* was more easily extolled than defined, and a survey of studies with the title *Shina bungakushi* (or some variation of it) provides a useful index of the term's fluidity as late as the third and fourth decades of the Meiji period. To the best of my knowledge, the earliest work centered on Chinese *bungaku* was the diplomat and politician Suematsu Kenchō's (1855–1920) *Shina kobungaku ryakushi* (A short history of classical Chinese culture) of 1882. The year 1882 was also the year Suematsu published his partial English-language translation of *Genji monogatari*, and his history of classical Chinese culture appears to have arisen out of the same evangelistic desire to trumpet the cultural accomplishments of Eastern civilization to domestic and foreign audiences alike.[73] By *bungaku*, however, Suematsu was not referring to belletristic genres like poetry, fiction, and drama; rather, the work was a survey of classical thought from China's Spring and Autumn (771–476 BCE) and Warring States (475–221 BCE) periods. Presaging arguments that would be incorporated into histories of more "literary" literature, Suematsu justified his project through analogy to European classical studies—arguing that "the importance of Chinese classical culture to the East is comparable to that of the study of Greece and Rome in the West."[74]

Fifteen years later, the scope of *bungaku* had enlarged considerably— seemingly through the influence of both Western-language literary history and the works of Japanese-literature historiography discussed in the previous section. By 1903, the general parameters of *bungaku* were apparently familiar enough that Kubo Tenzui could begin his *Shina bungakushi* by saying, "Having titled my work *A History of Chinese Literature*, it's only natural that the focus of inquiry is the literary texts of China" (*Shina no bungakuteki sakuhin*).[75] Nearly all histories included sections on poetry and classical prose, but whether fiction and drama belonged in this purview was not entirely settled. Kojō Teikichi's study, for example, stretched from the advent of the Chinese script in highest antiquity to poetry and prose of the contemporaneous Qing dynasty, with subchapters devoted to classical philosophy and political theory, *shi* poetry, rhapsody, history and historiography, imperial proclamations, and prose. It did not, however, include fiction and drama, a lacuna that angered at least one of his readers. In a review of *Shina bungakushi* published in the journal *Tōyō tetsugaku*, the philosopher and activist Kōtoku Shūsui (1871–1911) complained, "The thing that I regret the most in this work is that works of fiction have been completely excised. Now, the author of this work must know that in later ages of Chinese literary history there were a number of works that occupied a place of respect. But he completely ignores this."[76] Either Kōtoku's criticism struck home or Kojō received similarly negative feedback from other readers, for when *Shina bungakushi* was republished in a second edition in 1902, the author attached an appendix of "additional considerations" (*yoron*) that included, among other items, a short discussion of fiction (*shōsetsu*).[77] Kojō made it clear that he agreed with the traditional Chinese view that educated gentlemen should not "dirty their hands" (*yubi o somuru*) with the composition of fiction, but these traditional views apparently no longer found favor with his audience—the very inclusion of this apologia suggests that fiction and drama had worked their way indelibly into both the fabric of Japanese literary culture and the definition of *bungaku* itself by the early twentieth century.

Kojō's grudging inclusion of fiction might have been inspired by other Japanese historians of Chinese literature, who did not hesitate to include works of fiction and drama under the rubric *bungaku*. Sasagawa Rinpū's *Shina shōsetsu gikyoku shōshi* appeared in the same year as Kojō's study and focused exclusively on fiction and drama from the Yuan period (1279–1368) onward. In 1898, Sasagawa published an even more ambitious general *History of Chinese Literature* (*Shina bungakushi*) that legitimated these controversial genres further by situating them in a larger constellation of poetry, rhapsody, and classical prose. Despite their increasingly settled place in the canon, the position of traditionally "looked down on" (*keibetsu sareta*) genres[78] like fiction and drama within the scope of *Shina bungakushi* remained a topic of debate. As late as the middle of the Taishō period, Kano Naoki, the doyen of Chinese studies at Kyoto University, began his lectures on a slightly defensive note by declaring his intention to lecture on Chinese fiction and drama "as one pillar of Chinese literature" (*Shina bungaku no ichimon toshite*).[79]

Lack of standardization in the use of the term *bungaku* and the fact that there was already an enormous corpus of writing on China in Japan led to an unusual situation in which some authors presented their research as an unprecedented endeavor, while others claimed that Chinese-literature historiography had been flourishing for quite some time.[80] As exhaustively and scientifically as China had been chronicled in the newly emergent academy, there was a sense that certain aspects of Chinese culture had been neglected and that the nascent discipline of *bungakushi* could be used as a comprehensive (*gaikatsuteki*) way of apprehending and cataloguing those aspects of Chinese civilization overlooked in disciplines like philosophy and classical study. This was the raison d'être for Sasagawa Rinpū's history of fiction and drama, but even scholars concerned primarily with classical-language texts advanced similar claims about the transcendent position of literary historiography. As Kojima Kenkichirō wrote in the preface to his *Shina bungaku shikō* (An outline of Chinese literature),

The composition of literary history is no easy task! But this isn't because of a paucity of materials: on the contrary, it's difficult because there are so many materials in the first place. Now the Four Storehouses (Ch. *siku*, Jp. *shiko*) containing the Classics, Histories, Masters, and Anthologies are something that no student could hope to exhaust. If you're writing a political history [*seijishi*], then you'll probably rely on the Official Histories (with some reference to the Unofficial Histories), but you won't need the Classics. And if you're writing a history of philosophy [*tetsugakushi*], then you'll concern yourself with the Classics, without really needing the Histories. But if you're going to write a literary history [*bungakushi*], you'll have to go through not only tens of thousands of Anthologies from past and present but also all the Classics, all the Masters, and all the Histories with your eyes keenly attuned. That's the main reason why writing literary history is so hard.[81]

In Kojima's analysis, the Four Storehouses of Chinese texts are grafted onto modern academic disciplines like philosophy and history, which are then subsumed under the nascent discipline of literary historiography. The author argues, as did Mikami Sanji and Takatsu Kuwasaburō two decades earlier, that literature was a branch of cultural production that superseded and included all other manifestations of civilization.

Ultimately, what united the initial wave of Chinese-literature historiography more than any shared understanding of *bungaku* was a dedication to the theme of "development and transformation" (*hattatsu hensen*) as a schema for emplotting history—a conceptual framework, it was argued, that differed dramatically from past inventories of literary texts. Fujita Toyohachi's *Shina bungakushi*, based on the author's lectures at Tōkyō Senmon Gakkō (present-day Waseda) began with a youthfully brash and confident set of precepts, where he stated that "never in China has there been a history of literature" (*Shina ni wa jūrai bungakushi nashi*). When Mikami Sanji and Takatsu Kuwasaburō made an analogous statement about Japanese literature in 1890, they did not mean that Japan's literary corpus was in any way inferior to that of other countries, only that the Japanese lacked the reflexive self-awareness and conceptual vocabulary that would allow them to *recognize* these works as a potentially cohesive system. Fujita was similarly well aware that China possessed an extensive tradition of both writing and writing *about* writing, but he argued that traditional commentary lacked the sense of comprehensiveness and structure characterizing the new discipline. He continued, "Certainly there are lots of 'talks on poetry' [*shiwa*], 'talks on prose' [*bunwa*], and bibliographies, as well as various forms of explication. But since these lack an organized sense of structure and system, they should not be taken as a substitute for a history of literature."[82] The irascible Kubo Tenzui lobbed a similar accusation of lack of systematicity toward *Japanese* critics: "Yes, two or three histories of Chinese literature have come out in recent years, but what a sight they are: makeshift fakes by makeshift, shallow scholars. They're not worth the scraps of paper they're printed on! Some of the authors (who aren't necessarily scholars of literature) have no idea what literature and literary history are and just provide endless and tedious enumeration of explications and capsule biographies."[83] What was lacking in this allegedly amateurish study was an interest in the larger patterns uniting the endless explications and "capsule biographies" (*koden*) mentioned by Kubo. Kubo's criticism was likely directed at Kojō Teikichi, who did not attend Tōdai and who, in his *Shina bungakushi*, had admitted that he had no interest in passing down a general definition of literature. However, Kubo's charge against his predecessor strikes the modern reader as unfair. Indeed, no less an authority than Taguchi Ukichi (1855–1905), author of *Nihon kaika shōshi* (A brief history of Japanese civilization),[84] praised Kojō's efforts in a preface to *Shina bungakushi* precisely for emphasizing the elusive "principles" (*ri*) underlying the ebb and flow (*shōchō*) of more than three thousand years of writing:

Criticism and evaluation are difficult—especially so in the case of China. Even before the Qin and Han dynasties, there are so many outstanding works that force us to look up in awe like a great pine thrusting its dense branches into the sky. When we come to the Eight Literary Masters of the Tang and Song periods, then we find that their writings are balanced and ordered, like a precious bonsai tree. But should we think of this as "progress" or not?[85]

However one finally defined the scope of *bungaku*, Japanese historians of Chinese literature were unanimous in declaring that China had possessed it far longer than Japan. Estimates ranged from three to five millennia, but the salient point was summed up by Shionoya On, who began his *Shina bungaku gairon kōwa* (Lectures on the outlines of Chinese literature, 1919) with the simple statement, "China is an ancient nation of literature" (*Shina wa bungaku no kokoku nari*).[86] The recurrent emphasis on antiquity and primacy had important political implications—in terms of both delineating the characteristics of *Japanese* literature and making an argument about Japan's place in the world. Arguments about the antiquity of the Chinese textual tradition were consistently deployed in narratives of competition and comparison between Eastern and Western literary blocs.[87] China's position as a "wellspring of Eastern culture" (*Tōyō bunka no gensen*)[88] greatly predating the development of culture in the West implicitly placed Japan in a superior position in this contest. At the same time their narratives betrayed clear influence by scholars like Taine and Posnett, Japanese literary historiographers utilized conceptual jujitsu to subvert these narratives via the arguments they contained. The first chapter of Kojō Teikichi's *Shina bungakushi* vividly contextualized China's accomplishments within a global comparative framework by pointing out that

at this time, the people of the various countries of Europe were residing in the mountains and swamps, amid tigers, panthers, poisonous snakes, and other loathsome reptiles, still unaware of the light of civilization. Meanwhile, this grand old country [of China] had already developed palatial architecture, fine clothing, marriage and funeral rites, and distinctions between ruler and ruled. Things were not yet complete, of course, but they had certainly established a framework for society and entered onto the road of culture.[89]

This emphasis on the antiquity of Chinese writing solved one problem while giving birth Hydra-like to others. At the same time it established the temporal primacy of East Asian literary culture, the emphasis on China's role as a font or wellspring raised less-flattering questions about the original or "unique" (*tokusei*) qualities of Japanese literature that had been so fulsomely praised in Japanese-literature historiography. For Sinophilic but patriotic historians, acknowledgment of this indebtedness to China was a delicate tightrope that each historian approached differently. It was impossible of course to deny Chinese influence on Japanese literary culture, and new nomenclature like Shina notwithstanding, some authors were hesitant to deprive China of the central status it had occupied for millennia. In the aforementioned preface to Kojō Teikichi's study, for instance, Taguchi Ukichi emphasized the benefits that a literary history of China would have for Japanese efforts at self-knowledge, since "half the literature of our land belongs to the realm of *kanbun*, and *kanbun* of course has its roots in China."[90] Other writers forestalled any charges of derivativeness by emphasizing Japan's superior capacities for synthesis and advancement. Such a rhetorical strategy was observable among the editors of the monumental *Shina bungaku taikō*, who claimed that Japan's unique philosophy and culture were rooted in the synthesis of Chinese, Indian, and even Western elements—enabling "true research that could not be expected of the Chinese themselves" (*shin no kenkyū wa tōtei kore o Shinajin ni nozomu bekarazareba nari*).[91] Finally, some authors argued that Japan had eclipsed China by taking its place as a literary and civilizational beacon in Asia. In a second preface to Kojō Teikichi's history that struggled schizophrenically with the mild sentiments expressed by Taguchi, the philosopher and public intellectual Inoue Tetsujirō (1856–1944) stressed China's fallen position vis-à-vis Japanese civilization. While Chinese culture had formed the base of many Japanese institutions in the past, Inoue argued, Japan's successful incorporation of Western knowledge had allowed Japan to come out ahead of China as a cultural and military power. Despite this precipitous decline in recent years, Inoue warned that it would be a mistake to simply look down on China as a nation of "pig-tailed slaves"; rather, China might act as a source of contextualization and self-knowledge in the way that Europeans studied the culturally significant but politically irrelevant bedrock cultures of Egypt, Greece, and Rome.[92]

The assumption underlying all modes of argumentation was the idea that China was disqualified from approaching its own literary corpus and an emphasis on the unique qualifications of Japanese explicators to undertake this task. This peremptory exclusion was justified in terms of Japan's geographic and cultural proximity to China, as well as the fear that *European* sinologists might be encroaching on Japanese territory. Kojima Kenkichirō's former *senpai* Ichimura Sanjirō (another graduate of the Classics Training Course) penned a preface to Kojima's work in which he denigrated European efforts at Chinese-literature historiography and called for the emergence of a "Japanese [Hippolyte] Taine":

In the past, the Frenchman [Hippolyte] Taine secured a reputation for himself by writing *A History of English Literature*. In recent years, an Englishman named [Herbert] Giles has undertaken a history of Chinese literature.[93] However, it doesn't come up to the level of Taine's history of English literature. Why is this? It's because English is easy for a Frenchman, so it's correspondingly simple for him to write a history of English literature. For an Englishman to learn Chinese, though, is a difficult matter, and therefore it's difficult for him to capture the essence of China's literature. Outside China, only a Japanese writer is up to the task. Don't compare this text to Giles's history of Chinese literature—compare it instead to Taine's history of English literature.[94]

The close nexus between literary history and imperialism was illustrated even more explicitly in Inoue Tetsujirō's preface to Kojō's history, where he connected a surge of interest in Chinese texts to political and military developments on the mainland:

Mr. Kojō Teikichi of Kumamoto long harbored the ambition of writing a history of Chinese literature, and he often came to me to inquire about possibilities for its structure. Several years later, he sent me one section of a draft. I greatly supported him in his ambition and urged him to complete it. By then, the war between China and Japan had begun, and Mr. Kojō rushed to Seoul. A letter from him, conveyed by a friend, stated, "Now is the time for a man to be a man! I ask you to send me a Japanese sword, so that I might follow the troops to Liaodong!" After that, there was no news for a time, and I had no idea what had happened to him. One day, a note arrived from Shanghai telling me that the draft [of *Shina bungakushi*] was finished and requesting a preface from me.[95]

In Inoue's telling at least, Japan's first foray into Chinese literary historiography is voiced in a rhetoric of conquest and swashbuckling derring-do as the Japanese author's encroachment into China's literary corpus is framed by a literal incursion by Kojō Teikichi the conqueror with "Japanese sword" in hand. This imperialistic invasion was justified, Inoue suggested, since even the Chinese "lack a sense of comprehensiveness" [*gaikatsuryoku*]. They do not understand the importance of writing a history of their literature because of their ignorance of the present state of academia. Even if they did understand, they have no credentials [*shikaku*] to undertake the task. And if this is the case, then we Japanese have a responsibility to rise to the challenge."

While Japanese historiographers were unanimous in advancing their own "credentials" (*shikaku*) as custodians of China's literary past, many of them simultaneously emphasized the necessity of evaluating Chinese texts by Chinese—rather than Western—critical standards. Kubo Tenzui, who had previously rebuked his peers for their dilettantish study of literature in general, also lamented an unthinking embrace of Western literary theory among the first wave of Japanese historians, who, he admitted, were relative newcomers to the field of literary historiography: "Now it's only recently that scholars in Japan turned their attention to literary historiography. And for that reason, even the histories of our own literature remain incomplete. This is much more the case when we look at China. And yet the instant Westerners start tossing around their half-baked theories, all the phony Japanese scholars immediately accept them. How shameful and absurd this is!"[96] Rather than rely on these half-baked Western theories, Kubo recommended turning to the indigenous record: "The reader will find that I've often incorporated the poetry criticism of men like [the Qing-period literati] Shen Deqian and Zhao Yi and so on. This is because when it comes to the ancients, Chinese critics are remarkably fair and accurate in their assessments. Since they're reliable, I've borrowed their concepts when they accord with my own views (but only then)."[97]

Kubo was unique in admitting doubts about Japan's mandate in approaching China's literary past, but his sincere claim of interest in earlier *Chinese* critics' pronouncements on literature was shared by many of his coterie, who presented their work as an attempt at reconciling Western theory with Chinese content. Nowhere was the discrepancy between these two hermeneutic traditions more stark than in the case of *xiaoshuo/shōsetsu*—a mode of writing largely castigated as insignificant or morally deleterious in traditional Chinese thought but celebrated as an evolutionary pinnacle in Western criticism. In a series of "Chats on Chinese Fiction" (Shina shōsetsu no hanashi) published in *Waseda bungaku* between 1891 and 1892, the poet and classical scholar Mori Kainan (1863–1911) attempted to utilize classical Chinese thought to chart an alternative history of fiction reception. Like his colleague at Waseda, Tsubouchi Shōyō, Mori presented the development of fiction in China as a process of gradual liberation from the strictures of moralistic didacticism (*kanzen chōaku*). However, whereas Shōyō quoted English literary critics like John Morley and the Japanese *kokugaku* scholar Motoori Norinaga to advance his more morally agnostic mode of criticism, Mori turned instead to the classical Chinese canon for support—in particular, the seminal treatise *Wenxin diaolong* (The literary mind and the carving of dragons) by the Six Dynasties–period critic Liu Xie (ca. 465–522). Stephen Owen characterizes *Wenxin diaolong* as "a systematic treatise on literature, *as it was conceived around the turn of the sixth century*," and as my emphasis here suggests, Mori's enlistment of Liu Xie in his defense of Chinese *shōsetsu* involved a willful anachronism.[98] Clearly, the Six Dynasties–period Liu Xie did not and could not have had modern fiction like *Shuihu zhuan* or *Journey to the West* in mind when he penned his treatise; however, by insisting on equivalence between the term *shōsetsu* and the classical "apocrypha" (*wei*)[99] Liu Xie did discuss, Mori was able to approvingly quote the following passage from *Wenxin diaolong*: "The content of these works was marvelous and dignified, their words were rich and satisfying. Though they conferred no benefit in explicating the classics, they provided aid in refined writing in general."[100] Since the time of Liu Xie's pronouncement, Mori informed the reader, *shōsetsu* had been subject to a bifurcated reception in their native land:

When we come to the period of the Tang dynasty, tale literature flourished—to the point where there was hardly a literatus alive who was not involved in its composition. This is a result of the "aiding refined literature" mind-set. However, another type of Confucian scholar criticized this type of writing as trivial amusement [*yūgi*] and its practitioners as frivolous wastrels. This was a result of the "conferring no benefit to the classics" mind-set. Now, in my opinion, Liu Xie's remarks are eminently fair and reasonable. The deepest wish of every writer is to create a work of beauty that is rich, dignified, and marvelous—not to assist in the study of the classics.[101]

By divorcing classical texts (Ch. *jingdian*, Jp. *keiten*) from other, belletristic genres (Ch. *wenzhang*, Jp. *bunshō*)—a move that went against millennia of Chinese thought on writing—Mori was able to credit classical China not only with the development of fiction itself but also with a cohesive system of literary thought that might be used to celebrate it. Whereas by the 1890s Meiji-period critics had centered on didacticism as the defining feature (and fault) of the traditional "novel," Mori presented an alternative, and crucially *indigenous* East Asian theory of literary autonomy. Though he did not necessarily dismiss earlier critics' concern with the relation of *shōsetsu* to the classics, he attempted to point to an alternative mode of interpretation— finding in the sixth-century Liu Xie what Shōyō sought in Victorian literary criticism and late-Edo nativist thought. Claims to objectivity, scientifica-tion, and standardization notwithstanding, the pronouncements of tradi-tional critics from Liu Xie to Jin Shengtan played a major role in Meiji-period accounts of development. Taine, Sismondi, and Posnett may have provided a historiographical mold, but that mold was often filled with con-tent from traditional China.

SUPPRESSING AND FINDING AN AUTHENTIC VOICE OF THE PEOPLE

As Michael C. Brownstein argued in his seminal study of Japanese-literature historiography, Meiji-period histories were often structured as a "romance," in which a reified Japanese *kokutai* (embodied in the form of literature) progressed and developed through an agonistic relationship with an oppo-nent: in this case, the "rival *kokutai*" signified by Sinitic writing.[102] A simi-lar narrative strategy is observable in works of Chinese-literature histo-riography, where historiographers of Chinese literature traced the uneven progression of an authentic and expressive Chinese voice, locked in dialectic combat with the strictures of race, geography, and, paradoxi-cally, the idea of literature itself. As presented earlier, the hallmarks of Meiji- and Taishō-period Chinese-literature historiography might be summa-rized as follows: the incorporation of development or progress as a central interpretive axis, an emphasis on the antiquity of the Chinese literary tra-dition in comparison with that of the West, and a concomitant denigration of Chinese efforts to interpret their own literary history. Finally, as the example of Mori Kainan demonstrates, Japanese historians retained a keen interest in traditional Chinese literary thought, even as they labored to fit these "unsystematic" jottings into the mold provided by Western-style historiography.[103]

A history of the development of literature required the location of a clear point of origin and the creation of a narrative of gradual improve-ment. In the case of fiction (*shōsetsu*), many Japanese historians fol-lowed Mori Kainan's lead in "Shina shōsetsu no hanashi" by locating the origin of the novel in the myths, legends, and "fairy tales" of high antiq-uity. Just as Tsubouchi Shōyō argued that Japan had always possessed a tradition of *shōsetsu*, Mori traced the genesis of Chinese *shōsetsu* to the Western Han:

The roots of the word *shōsetsu* stretch back to the Eastern Han dynasty in Zhang Heng's *Rhapsody on the Western Capital*, where we see the line, "The nine hundred volumes of *shōsetsu* have their roots in the records of Yu Chu." Yu Chu was the name of a diviner in the service of Emperor Wu of the Han. He knew that Emperor Wu was deeply bedazzled by the lore of gods and immortals, and in order to engage with him, he sought out all manner of marvelous and bizarre tales. He edited them into a collection of nine hundred sections, with the title *Stories of the Zhou*. If this is true, then *shōsetsu* arose during the time of Emperor Wu—a period of more than two thousand years ago. Thus, it is no exaggeration to say that of all the countries of the world, China possesses the most ancient tradition of *shōsetsu*.[104]

The reign of the gullible Han emperor Wu (r. 141–87 BCE)—described in classical histories as highly susceptible to manipulation at the hands of wandering diviners and magicians—was a popular point for establishing the "beginning" of fiction, but other writers pointed toward the imaginative and often fanciful parables of the *Zhuangzi* or *Liezi* as potential points of origin. Analysis of these early "sprouts" (*hōga*) was usually followed by discussion of Six Dynasties–period "accounts of the anomalous" (*zhiguai*) and Tang-dynasty classical tales (*chuanqi*) before turning attention to the flourishing of "the type of novels we think of today,"[105] which was located variously in the Song, Yuan, or early Ming. Like Shōyō in his comparative discussion of Japanese, Chinese, and Western fiction in *Shōsetsu shinzui*, Mori's goal in his chats was twofold: first, to establish a framework that would allow stylistically disparate texts to be discussed under a common interpretive rubric, and second, to establish a line of development connecting late imperial works like *Shuihu zhuan* and *Plum in the Golden Vase* to classical-language texts from hoariest antiquity. The idea that classical anecdotes and anomaly accounts constituted the "roots" of later fiction would have a long afterlife in Japanese-, Chinese-, and Western-language scholarship on Chinese fiction.[106]

As a subset of *bunmeishi*, the existence of literary history as a genre presumed a universal model of development in which all civilizations moved along a predictable civilizational trajectory. Although China stood out among the nations of the world for its antiquity and precocity, writers like Kojō Teikichi argued that it still adhered to a familiar process:

When we come to high antiquity in any nation, then we find lots of tall tales in their histories. . . . Stories like this are found in the mythologies of all countries, and they can be used to get a glimpse of the state prior to civilization. But when writing is introduced, people's knowledge gradually develops, their modes of thought are better expressed, and their ingenuity is preserved. From simple and coarse to refined and complex, from sophomoric ditties to more complex works, *in East and West, there is never any variance from this process.*[107]

In making this argument, however, Chinese-literature historians were presented with a paradox. On the one hand, most authors used their works to emphasize the antiquity of Chinese literature, as well as the degree of Japan's indebtedness to this tradition. On the other, the assertion that China possessed the world's oldest tradition of literature was immediately undercut by the implication (or explicit assertion) that a promising beginning had been stifled early on. By focusing exclusively on pre-Qin antiquity, for instance, authors like Suematsu Kenchō and Fujita Toyohachi implicitly relegated China to the status of a dead archive like Greece or Rome. Other writers argued that certain periods in Chinese literature were either anomalous or particularly representative in terms of a presumed course of development. In the preface to his history, Kubo Tenzui claimed that the pre-Qin classics should be studied first, because they constituted "the source of culture for the Han race" (*Kanzoku bunka no engen*).[108] Be that as it may, it was precisely these classics that were often accused of inhibiting or delaying the complete florescence of a true belletristic tradition. For historians interested in the development of fiction and drama in particular, the rapid spread of Confucian ideals during the pre-Qin and Han periods was directly identified with a concomitant suppression of "imaginative" or "idealistic" (*risō*) literature. Mori Kainan had turned to Liu Xie to find a classical remedy to this alleged impediment, but many historians were far less indulgent toward the teachings of Confucius and the sage-kings. Japanese writers proudly pointed to China as the earliest culture to set out on the track but bemoaned its derailment at the hands of the "practical" or "utilitarian" (*jitsuyōteki*) hands of Confucius and the bureaucratic government established upon his thought.

Historians interested in fiction and drama found this issue particularly vexing. If China was a region synonymous with literacy and home to the oldest continuous culture of writing on earth, why had mature works of fiction and drama appeared so late in its history—particularly in comparison with Japan and Europe, where these traditions had emerged much earlier, relatively speaking? This was not only a textual quandary but also an issue of understanding the Chinese "psychology" supposedly enshrined in these works. As Sasagawa Rinpū, author of *Shōsetsu gikyoku shōshi*, noted in the introduction to his work, "When it comes to fiction and drama—the genres that shed light on the hidden profundities of human feeling and express the winding vicissitudes of fate—we find that in this land [of China], they do not have a long history of development at all."[109] The question of why fiction and drama—the genres increasingly identified in both Japan and China with the representation of quotidian life and unmediated emotional expression—appeared so late in China would keep a generation of scholars busy. Most writers pointed out that the very word for "novel" in Chinese—*xiaoshuo*—was inherently pejorative and reminded their readers that Confucius had counseled his followers to avoid talking about ghosts, spirits, and supernatural events.[110] Others, like Kojō Teikichi, explored the question of literary development by using the vocabulary of racial and geographic determinism espoused by critics like Hippolyte Taine, arguing that a tendency toward practicality was engendered by the harsh geography and cold winters of northern China, the "center of historical China" (*rekishiteki Shina no chūshin*).[111] Kojō treated China, because of its vast size, more like a confederation of nation-states than a single homogeneous entity. The harsh climate of northern and western China, Kojō argued, gave rise to a group of people whose customs were simple and honest at their best but ran the risk of descending into cruelty and violence. The warmer and more fecund climate of the south, on the other hand, produced a people who were alternately criticized by Kojō for being slothful and indolent and praised for their harmonious and peaceful dispositions. Needless to say— borrowing a page from Taine—these distinctions were manifested in the literatures of the respective regions: northern *bungaku* was characterized as "pure and resolute" (*shinkō*) while southern literature was described as "relaxed and elegant" (*yoyo waga*).

The two traditions, it is suggested, might have developed in diachronic harmony had it not been for the northern monopoly over China's political institutions. Northern practicality—personified (not created) by the worldly teachings of Confucius—engendered an autocratic and patriarchal system of government, participation in which required evidence of literary talent. With the advent of the imperial examination system, literature and government entered into a mutually parasitic and deleterious relationship. The government relied on the composition of poetry as a criterion for selecting candidates for office, and as a consequence literature became a primary means of advancing in one's career and gaining political patronage. As China became a politically unified entity, the geographic and cultural rifts distinguishing the literature of north and south were mirrored by a socio-economic gap between an effete and dilettantish "aristocratic" (*kizokuteki*) class of literati and a mass of "farmers, mulberry cultivators, and shepherds," whose voice was gradually effaced from China's literary production.[112] Since, Kojō argued, nearly all authors in the literary tradition had some stake in the government labyrinth of patronage and examination, the overwhelming majority of Chinese literary texts became gaudy, artificial, and ornamental—demoted to the role of a plaything rather than a vessel of sincere expression. The only way to discern the voice of a Chinese "people" (*kokumin*), Kojō concluded, was to comb the very earliest strata of the Chinese textual record. Kojō enthusiastically quoted the Southern Song literatus Su Zhe (1039–1112), who distinguished between the clarity, purity, and directness of Shang-period writing and the ornamentation, prolixity, and density of that of the following Zhou.[113] Although the subsequent seven hundred pages of *Shina bungakushi* lovingly elucidated the qualities of Chinese poetry and prose from antiquity to the Qing dynasty, the author dealt his subject material a near-fatal rhetorical blow in the opening pages. Having insisted that Chinese literature was worthy of consecration as a historically cohesive entity, and having gone to such pains to establish its primacy on the world stage, he proceeds to inform us that much of what we possess is not truly representative of the cultural milieu that produced it.

The idea that the harsh climate of the historically central north had engendered a tradition of utilitarian, practical literature was by no means unique to Kojō. Fujita Toyohachi's history began by noting that "Chinese culture arose from the Han race dwelling on the north bank of the Yellow River" and hypothesized that only some external force like an invasion could have driven the Han into "a land bereft of Heaven's blessings" (*tenkei naki chi*).[114] This forced migration had profound effects on all aspects of Chinese cultural production: "Because of their natural environment, they could never rest in their pursuit of simple daily necessities like food, clothing, and shelter. And as a result, the emperors and rulers they took as their Sages were all known for conferring some benefit with respect to food, clothing, and shelter."[115] Survival in this hostile environment, Fujita went on to say, left little time for the leisure necessary for imaginative literature. Instead, first consideration was given to the provision of sustenance, the creation of an inflexible and patriarchical social order, and a superstitious deference to nature. As a result, Chinese culture displayed an early tendency toward not only practicality but also autocratic forms of governance, nature worship, and a "reverence of antiquity" (shōko) antithetical to the Darwinian modes of evolutionary progression enshrined in literary historiography. Whereas scholars of Chinese philosophy, ethics, and historiography had posited a unifying schema in the thought of Confucius and its lingering influence on imperial Chinese intellectual and bureaucratic culture, now this monolith was presented as an obstacle to the type of sustained literary development observable in other nation-states. Rather than being a revolutionary or pioneer of Chinese thought, Confucius was increasingly presented as a culmination of earlier intellectual trends engendered by climate and race—intellectual trends that ultimately created an environment in which literature became little more than a formalistic game of plug and play.

If it was true that Chinese literature had gotten off to an unpromising start at the hands of climatic determinism and Confucian autocracy, then Chinese-literature historiographers were still left with the task of explaining the dazzling array of themes, styles, registers, and genres making up Chinese literature. Kojō provided one model of resolving this paradox by presenting Chinese textual variety as a result of a dialectic between a practical north and a fecund, languorous, but imaginative south. Other writers—especially those interested in Chinese fiction and drama—argued that "pure" (and representative) Chinese literature was able to thrive only at moments of invasion and historical instability, those times in the historical record when the oppressive Confucian status quo was either threatened or toppled entirely and heterodox creeds allowed to flourish. As mentioned, Fujita Toyohachi located one such moment in the "Aryan-like" migration of the Han race into the Yellow loess valley. The influx of Buddhism and Indian philosophy at the end of the Han was often cited as another moment in which an injection of fresh cultural artifacts generated a revival in literary creativity and innovation.[116] The Yuan was of particular interest to Chinese-literature historiographers for obvious reasons. Scholars of fiction and drama like Sasagawa Rinpū, Kubo Tenzui, Shionoya On, and Kano Naoki all argued that seminal masterpieces like *Shuihu zhuan*, *Romance of the Three Kingdoms*, and *Romance of the Western Wing* could only have appeared when Chinese hegemony had been overturned and "the people" were allowed to have their voices heard without the distorting filter of Confucian ideology. Kojō Tekichi's study lamented the alleged absence of the shepherds and mulberry farmers in China's textual history; projects such as Sasagawa Rinpū's *Shina shōsetsu gikyoku shōshi* sought to recover these allegedly more authentically Chinese voices.

Although Sasagawa's work was the direct inverse of Kojō's in terms of focus (Kojō included no works of fiction and drama in the first edition of *Shina bungakushi*), the two histories share a number of assumptions about the Chinese people's relation to their own literary patrimony. Like Kojō's criticizing the institutionalization of autocratic government for suppressing the development of authentic literature, Sasagawa centered his account on tensions between politics and the written word. In contrast to traditional Chinese literary thought, which presented the *shi* poem as the acme of personal expression, however, Sasagawa argued that drama and the novel had taken the place of *shi*.[117] This new focus led the author away from classical antiquity, where the seeds of Chinese literary culture had first germinated, toward the other end of the historical spectrum: the Yuan dynasty, when China had been under the political control of the Mongols. Like Mori Kainan in his "Chats on Chinese Fiction," Sasagawa believed that the tradition of fiction stretched well before the Yuan, but he was dismissive of pre-Yuan protofiction like the "fairy tales"[118] found in Han-dynasty unofficial historiography, Six Dynasties anomaly accounts, and the surviving corpus of Tang tales. For Sasagawa, like Mori, these texts were "immature works of fiction" (*yōchi naru shōsetsu*) at best and lacked the sense of comprehensiveness and development requisite for entry into the historical record.

In a series of maneuvers familiar to the point of cliché at this point, Sasagawa began his study by noting the centrality of geography (*chisei*), climate (*kikō*), and race (*jinshu*) to the trajectory of Chinese literary development. Sasagawa, like his peers, distinguished between northern China, whose colder climate and harsh, mountainous terrain had engendered an austere, valiant, and practical literary tradition, and southern China, whose warm weather, gently flowing waterways, and the indolent lifestyle these features encouraged led to a literary tradition valorized as "elegant, elevated, and supple."[119] He superimposed these Taine-esque divisions on binaries culled from the Chinese critical tradition by associating the cold, unsentimental practicality of the north with the quality of "substance" (Ch. *zhi*, Jp. *shitsu*), and the elegant refinement and "idealism" (*risōteki*) of the south with "polish" or "craft" (Ch. *wen*, Jp. *bun*). In contrast to disciplines like philosophy and history, Sasagawa elevated the latter and presented it as a metonym for the neologism *bungaku* as it was understood in late nineteenth-century Japan:

The elegant literature of the region of Chu [in southern China] was rich in conception and something incomparable to the literature of the north, where the quality of utility was most developed. It's for this reason that the south produced the parables of the *Zhuangzi*, the emotional laments of Qu Yuan and his *Li sao*, and all manner of tales about spirits and immortals. In other words, the sprouts of Chinese fiction first took root in this region.[120]

As with Kojō Teikichi's claim that Chinese literature had been compromised and diluted as early as the Zhou dynasty, Sasagawa's view of Chinese literary development was characterized by a similar process of early derailment. Unsurprisingly, the culprit was the emergence of Confucianism, whose utilitarian focus and alleged hostility to the kind of fanciful imagination Sasagawa identified with literature itself stifled the development of fiction and drama from its inception:

The north was the historical center of China in high antiquity, and for this reason the practical-minded northern race [*hoppō jinshu*] was the historical people of high antiquity. The southern race [*nanpō jinshu*] was never able to penetrate this historical center. Thus, the northern way of thinking was to overturn all of China, and the Confucian ideology it produced—an ideology that links together three millennia—took root in all people's hearts. Regardless of how rich and fecund the thinking underpinning southern literature was, the reason that fiction and drama were unable to develop [in China] was because of the overpowering dominance of northern thought.[121]

The fact that the south literally stands outside history in Sasagawa's framework made it unsurprising that a long-overdue invigorating influence would come from even farther north. At this point, Sasagawa's interest in the Yuan period as a formative moment in the development of Chinese belles lettres becomes clear. It was only during this time that "immature" genres such as fiction and drama could be allowed to fully germinate and flourish free of stifling forces:

The reason [for the sluggish development of fiction described previously] must be traced to the power and authority enjoyed by Confucian ideology. Now, Confucianism venerates the realization of action [kyūkō jissen] and encourages whatever benefits either society or the development of the individual. Fiction and drama, which concern themselves with truths hidden in the midst of falsehood and reality cloaked in the unreal, were naturally despised. Northern thought, which tends toward the practical and utilitarian, overflowed China throughout its long history. And as a result, fiction and drama were eternally trampled and suppressed. But then, in a corner of deepest Heilongjiang, a force rose up that summoned wind and rain and startled the very heavens! This fresh act [katsugeki] strode onto the stage of the Central Plains and introduced a new episode in the setting of a newly unified China. Not only that, Chinese philosophy was turned on its head, and all the old systems and culture were swept aside. The sudden development of fiction and drama were unquestionably a side consequence of this momentum.[122]

In his quite literally histrionic description of the Song–Yuan transition, Sasagawa established a direct causal link between the Mongol invasion and the florescence of fiction and drama in the thirteenth and fourteenth centuries. While viewed as an anomaly from political, economic, and racial standpoints in the hands of Meiji-period literary historians, the Mongol conquest paradoxically contributed to a *purification* of the Chinese literary scene. By sweeping aside the oppressive and sclerotic institutions of traditional Confucian culture, the invasion provided a setting in which the types of more "authentic" expression Sasagawa described earlier could flourish. Far from being a period of cultural or racial dilution and oppression under a putative Mongol "yoke," this period of foreign intervention and political administration allowed Chinese culture to flourish in an atmosphere free of the strictures that had held it back for two millennia.

Like the nomenclature "Shina" itself, which denoted both a contemporary nation-state and a timeless cultural essence, this period of stagnation from antiquity to the Yuan explained how China could be both "an ancient country of literature" and relatively young when it came to sophisticated genres like fiction and drama. Though "uncultured barbarians" from the margins of the empire, the Mongols were consistently presented by Chinese-literature historiographers as unselfconscious avatars of a startling progressivism. By doing away with the institutions associated with Confucianism, the Mongols were credited with nudging China back onto a "normal" path of development that resulted in an apotheosis of the novel and drama as the highest forms of expression—a path of development completed by Japan and the West, it was argued, in far shorter time. Unwitting catalysts in a chain reaction, the Mongols supported Chinese fiction not owing to any moral imperatives or the civilizing properties of *bun* but, rather, because of their willingness to honestly and sincerely embrace less-praiseworthy desires. As Sasagawa's colleague and frequent collaborator Kubo Tenzui explained,

The Yuan valued "light" genres [*keibungaku*] like drama and fiction, and in doing so they opened up a new aspect of Chinese literature. When we inquire into the reasons for this, then we find that it's the same set of circumstances surrounding poetry in the Jin dynasty [1115–1234]. These groups underwent a dramatic leap in terms of progress in China. These barbaric people who had passed their lives in the frosty steppes and wastes of the north suddenly found themselves in China, where the climate is warmer and gentler. Bedazzled by traditional culture, their natures underwent a massive transformation. Their stoicism and austerity were transformed into indulgence, and pleasing their eyes and ears became their highest concern. Now, light genres [like drama and fiction] had always been criticized within strict Confucian ideology, but the Yuan emperors didn't revere Confucian ideals all that much. As a result, ties to traditional ways of thinking were weakened. The authors of these light genres stood outside traditional ideology. In other words, these authors were leftover subjects or savants from the lower echelons of society. *The important thing is this: China's "pure literature" [jun bungaku] availed itself of a once-in-a-millennium opportunity to attach itself to the natural passion of humanity and develop as a result.*[123]

There is a great deal to unpack in this remarkable statement: the sudden equation of "light" or "frivolous" literature with "pure literature" (*junbungaku*); the "natural" (*shizen*) affection humans feel for these light/ pure texts; and the role of foreign invasion in the seemingly preordained ascension of previously marginalized genres. If, as Japanese historians argued, each dynasty has a representative literary genre, then in the Yuan period a great "hole" in the canon had finally been patched.[124] In the words of Miyazaki Shigekichi (1871–1933), whose lecture notes on Chinese fiction and drama were published in the first decade of the twentieth century, "The works of fiction and drama that came to fruition during the eighty-year auspice of the Yuan were not simply the glory of the Yuan; rather, they opened up a new epoch in the four-millennia-plus history of Chinese literature as a whole."[125] Though anomalous in terms of government structure and ethnic composition, the Yuan was thus smoothly fitted into a larger narrative of development and progress in which earlier genres like *shi*, *yuefu*, and *ci* were now contextualized as discrete steps on an evolutionary scale culminating in fiction and drama. The barbarous "reaction" (*handō*) against these repressive institutions had only returned China to a normal path of development.[126] Even the most glorious centers, it was argued, required invigoration from the periphery.

CODA

Since there is no single work of Chinese-literature historiography that might be deemed more representative than the others, I have attempted to center on discursive commonalities between a number of these works—keeping in mind, of course, that authors differed in their educational training, pedagogical goals, and understanding of *bungaku* itself. In dealing with the potentially overwhelming body of information presented by the first wave of Japanese Chinese-literature historiography, it is perhaps most useful to arrange them on a spectrum. On the one hand, most of these works were composed by people who had devoted their lives to the study of China and its institutions. "Scientific" methodologies notwithstanding, the products of their labor evinced a compelling and sincere desire to proselytize the joys of reading a wide range of Chinese texts. In terms of the comparative literary studies demanded with such frequency during the Meiji period, China provided an alternative genealogy and body of literary thought that could act as a counterweight to the potentially overwhelming influx of Western ideas and methodologies. It was not only that Chinese literary texts dwarfed

Western output in terms of volume and venerability, but also that they provided a body of critical thought that could be used to evaluate East Asian texts by East Asian standards.

On the other hand, these early works of historiography nearly all voice a belief that, despite its temporal primacy, the "development" of Chinese literature was marked by disruption, lacuna, and delay. Although they were the clearest example, fiction and drama were not the only genres to be deemed "belated" (*osoi*)[127] by Japanese historiographers. Kojō Teikichi excluded fiction and drama from consideration, but similarly lamented the suppression of true expression by autocratic government and the sycophantic pressures of the imperial examination system. A consistent and uniting theme in these texts is the idea that Confucianism and the system of government it engendered had derailed a promising start. A common response in dealing with this schema was to suggest that the people who had acted as traditional intellectual guardians of Chinese civilization were not as authentically "Chinese" as the overwhelming numbers of people excluded from China's literary patrimony. From this standpoint, Chinese intellectuals themselves, who were products of traditional Confucian educations, were victims: either entirely unable to appreciate the fruits of their civilization, or, as discussed later, forced to adopt a bifurcated and potentially hypocritical stance toward its consumption.

Sasagawa Rinpū was perhaps the first to advance the argument that the institutional state required a shake-up before a more authentic Chinese voice could be recognized, but he was by no means the only voice in this chorus. In the highly charged political atmosphere of the period following the First Sino-Japanese War, the implications of these theories were anything but anodyne. In her study of the global reception of Yuan-period drama, Patricia Sieber noted that "Japanese academic institutions played a significant role in reconstructing the Chinese past for modern ends."[128] As Sieber demonstrates, Aoki Masaru's *Shina kinsei gikyoku shi* (*History of Chinese Drama of the Early Modern Period*, 1930) also argued that the development and refinement of drama as an art form was a direct result of the Mongol invasion of China. Aoki credited his lifelong obsession with Chinese drama to an encounter with Sasagawa Rinpū's *Shina shōsetsu gikyoku shōshi*, and in retrospect, his championing of foreign invasion as a catalyst for civilizational growth seems directly indebted to Sasagawa's pioneering study. Sieber concludes by noting:

Inscribing ethnicity into civilizational hierarchies was of course all the more insidious given that some modern Japanese scholars not only portrayed the Japanese as belonging to the same ethnic group as the Mongols, but also because the Japanese government prepared to "enter and rule" China from the very same geographic region, that is, the northern forest lands of Manchuria, as had the Manchus three hundred years earlier.[129]

Regardless of whether this tendency was rooted directly in imperialist aspirations, a key hallmark of Chinese-literature historiography—one that connects it to parallel excursions in Japanese-literature historiography—was the idea that literary history possessed the potential to reveal a hidden and authentic self occluded in other disciplines. Authors like Fujita Toyohachi, Kubo Tenzui, and Sasagawa claimed to offer a perspective on an "inner China" that could not be discerned in other fields—an inner China variously embodied in an indeterminate "people," subaltern shepherds and mulberry farmers, or a set of disembodied "natural affections." As Kano Naoki put it,

I want to lecture on fiction and drama as one pillar of Chinese literature. Beforehand, I should say what is known by all, which is that this facet of literature is undeveloped when compared with other nations. Popular literature—that is to say, fiction and drama—is nothing more than one branch of Chinese literature, and it doesn't occupy a very exalted place. Not only that, but traditionally scholars of Sino-Japanese topics haven't even considered it literature.[130]

And, later,

But what I want you to pay attention to is this: If you ask Chinese people if they really look down on novels and refuse to read them, you'll find that's not the case at all. The Chinese have an inner self and an outer self. On the outside, they say that novels are not for gentlemen and that they revile them, but on the inside there's no one who doesn't read them with gusto. It's like with *Dream of the Red Chamber*: "No one will admit to reading *Dream of the Red Chamber*, but there's no one who hasn't read it." *Popular literature exists as an inverse reaction to the austere demands of Confucian scholarship.*[131]

Kano credited this disjuncture to the differences between a private "inner" (*ri*) self and the "outer" (*hyō*) selves the Chinese present to one another (and presumably to nosy Japanese literary historians as well). Kano's relationship of "outer" to "inner" paralleled the status of the Confucian classics to works of fiction, and his statement suggested a more direct point of access to something previously unknown. The question became finding a representative work that would allow this interrogation to take place, a work that would lay bare all the alleged contradictions in the Chinese character and complexity inherent in the "fresh act" inaugurated by the Yuan transition. It was, of course, sometime during the Mongol invasions and the restoration of Chinese rule during the Ming that Shi Nai'an was alleged to have composed *Shuihu zhuan*, and it is perhaps small wonder that this novel in particular, as the next chapter demonstrates, was selected as the crowning embodiment of a putative Chinese character.

Chapter Four

CIVILIZATION AND ITS DISCONTENTS

Travel, Translation, and Armchair Ethnography

The Hell's Angels as a group are often willfully stupid, but they are not without savoir-faire, and their predilection for travelling in packs is a long way from being all showbiz. Nor is it entirely due to warps and defects in their collective personality. The streets of every city are thronged with men who would pay all the money they could get their hands on to be transformed—even for a day—into hairy, hardfisted brutes who walk over cops, extort free drinks from terrified bartenders and thunder out of town on big motorcycles.

—HUNTER S. THOMPSON, *HELL'S ANGELS: A STRANGE AND TERRIBLE SAGA*

To treat *Romance of the Three Kingdoms* and *Shuihu zhuan* as simple novels is to make a grave error.

—TOKUTOMI SOHŌ, *RECORD OF A LEISURELY TRIP THROUGH CHINA*

Though often impenetrable to outsiders and jarring in their unexpected eruptions of violence, the rituals and conventions governing outlaw societies are no less defined than those that add comfort and stability to interactions in the social center. When he chronicled his exploits following the Bay Area Hells Angels in the mid-1960s, for instance, Hunter S. Thompson astutely noted how the incongruous "savoir-faire" apparent among the members of the homely outfit of motorcycle outlaws served a centripetal function by consolidating group identity and providing a blueprint for social engagement within the hierarchy.[1] In the context of *Shuihu zhuan*, travelers are often preceded by their reputations, and the bonds of brotherhood celebrated throughout the lengthy novel are established through a two-part pas de deux of misrecognition and apology. When an outlaw realizes that his chance acquaintance or heretofore concealed travel companion is a fellow denizen of the "rivers and lakes" (*jianghu*) where outlaws dwell, he displays his respect with the set phrase, "I have eyes but failed to recognize Mount Tai!" (*youyan bushi Taishan*), an utterance that establishes a bond that is indissoluble until one member of the party's gory demise. One is what he is, the formulation suggests; and although identities might be concealed through disguises and esoteric noms de guerre, it is incumbent upon the first party to discern the reality beyond appearances.

This trope of recognition serves as an ideal point of entry into a discussion of *Shuihu zhuan*'s reception during the Meiji and Taishō periods. Just as the Chinese Yannan Shangsheng—quoted in the opening pages of the preceding chapter—"discovered" *Shuihu zhuan* to be the world's first political novel, so, too, did many modern Japanese writers and scholars revisit the novel in their adulthood, only to realize that a literary giant had been hiding in plain sight all along. Itō Gingetsu, who fulsomely praised the revolutionary potential of *Shuihu zhuan* in the preface to his 1908 retranslation, described the novel as a text he had previously "enjoyed without any understanding of its meaning" (*mu imi-ni aidoku shita mono*) and claimed that it was not until he reencountered it as an adult that he "realized it was in fact a work with profound significance" (*sukoburu imi aru o oboeru*).[2] These epiphanies were often softened by an almost palpable sense of nostalgia, from the young Mori Kainan, who remembered seeking the "samadhi" of *Shuihu zhuan* from his teacher, Yoda Gakkai; to the critic and historian Yamaji Aizan's recollections of hearing the novel read aloud on the knee of his grandfather, who remarked that "the period described in *Shuihu zhuan* was just like the time of our own Restoration."[3]

What is perhaps most remarkable about engagement with *Shuihu zhuan* in the years between 1890 and 1930 is the shared conviction among Japanese literati that the classic Chinese novel had something pressing to offer in the *present* moment, although what that message was and to whom it was addressed were subject to extensive debate. For some rereaders of *Shuihu zhuan*, the novel's muddy morality and painstaking attention to characterization were potential sources of inspiration for contemporary novelists, who objected to earlier "didactic" models of composition but struggled to establish new forms in an increasingly constricted milieu. For rereaders interested in contemporary Chinese politics, the dynamic and complex world of the Liangshan marshes acted as a "snapshot" (*shashin*) or microcosm of China as a whole, promising a mode of understanding and explicating a territory that Japanese travelers encountered firsthand in increasing numbers throughout the period in question. Finally, in an era temporally removed enough from the initial establishment of *bunmei kaika* to allow postmortem analysis, *Shuihu zhuan* offered a referendum on the larger project of Enlightenment itself: a way of positing difference between Japan and its continental neighbor and establishing a network of clear binaries that tallied the respective failures and accomplishments of two linked civilizations.

These new interpretations were engendered by the emergence of a new understanding of literature that emerged during the late nineteenth and early twentieth centuries. As demonstrated by the writing of critics from Mikami Sanji to Haga Yaichi to Sasagawa Rinpū, there is a remarkable structural consistency apparent in Meiji- and Taishō-period literature historiography (*bungakushi*)—even if the architects of both *Nihon bungakushi* and *Shina bungakushi* quibbled over what should be included within the purview of literature itself. Whatever it was, the authors agreed, literature functioned as an index of a nation's development, and it represented the site of unitary and unifying cultural essences that might be placed in a comparative framework. These critics presented the history of literature as a process of continuous development (*hatten*) and progress (*shinpo*), with the novel and drama usually presented as the endpoint. Historiographers of Chinese literature devoted considerable attention to the role of the Mongol conquest in nudging China back onto a "normal" track of development, and in doing so bringing to fruition a lengthy process of incremental literary advancement. Long overdue, the appearance of the novel during the Yuan dynasty was described as nothing less than the completion or fulfillment of a three-thousand-year process of evolution.

Within this basic conceptual framework, *Shuihu zhuan* occupied a special position in the Chinese literary canon as the telos of the telos: a privileged point of insight into a putative Chinese character that acted as both foil and supplement to Japanese modernity. Although other Chinese novels like *Romance of the Three Kingdoms* continued to be avidly read and enjoyed throughout the period discussed in this chapter, engagement with *Shuihu zhuan* operated on a different scale, as demonstrated both by the hyperbolic intensity of critical utterances and by extant material evidence. In his encyclopedic and compulsively readable history of *Shuihu zhuan* in Japan, for instance, Takashima Toshio has tallied well over a dozen republications and retranslations of the novel between 1880 and 1915, a lineage that ranged from cheap serialized pamphlets like the *Hiragana e-iri kan Kara daiko* (Kana compendium of illustrated Chinese texts) to the handsome two-volume edition of the novel published as part of the Hakubunkan publishing house's Teikoku bunko series in 1895—the edition nostalgically recalled by Akutagawa Ryūnosuke in his semiautobiographical "Half-Life of Daidōji Shinsuke" (Daidōji Shinsuke no hansei, 1925).[4] The prefaces and paratextual features of these new editions enlisted *Shuihu zhuan* in a series of both long-standing and contemporary debates concerning the function of literature, the morality of *Shuihu zhuan* in particular, and the novel's relation to the present. The preface to Hiraoka Ryūjō's sprawling *Hyōchū kun'yaku Suikoden* (An annotated and translated *Water Margin*) of 1914, for example, justified the monumental effort needed to translate and annotate *Shuihu zhuan* by situating it within a larger surge of interest in translated literature—lamenting Japanese readers' ignorance of Chinese texts and equation of translation with French, British, and Russian literature alone.[5] Similarly, Takasu Baikei's *Suikoden monogatari*, a simple digest aimed at children, was published as part of the Fuzanbō publishing house's *Tsūzoku sekai bungaku* (Easy reading from around the world), where *Shuihu zhuan* appeared alongside works by Shakespeare, Dante, Homer, and Milton.[6] The academic discipline of *bungakushi* had forged an equivalence between *Shuihu zhuan* and other "novels" (*shōsetsu*) from the Japanese and Western traditions, and the editors of *Tsūzoku sekai bungaku* suggested a similar cross-cultural structural parity by including the word *monogatari* in the title of each volume.[7]

Although readers advanced various justifications for their obsession with *Shuihu zhuan*, it is clear that the novel was seen as more than just a work of fiction by its Japanese explicators. In their many discussions of *Shuihu zhuan*, critics invariably described the text as not simply a novel but also a "product" (*sanbutsu*) or "unique specialty" (*tokusan*) of China as a whole, emphasizing *Shuihu zhuan*'s status as something fundamentally and irreducibly Chinese. Whereas Edo-period critics like Seita Tansō and Kyokutei Bakin had explored the significance of *Shuihu zhuan* with respect to "universal" Confucian norms such as loyalty (*chū*) and duty (*gi*), Meiji-period explication of the novel took a quasi-ethnographic swerve by grounding it in a specific geographical and cultural context: in this case, both late imperial China in general and, far more anachronistically, the fin de siècle Qing dynasty to which Japanese travelers flocked in increasingly large numbers in the first decades of the Meiji period.

In the attempt to utilize *Shuihu zhuan* as a hermeneutic for current events, we see a curious return to much earlier ideas about the writing and function of "fiction." As nearly all Chinese-literature historiographers were quick to point out, the word recently adopted as a translational equivalent for fiction—*shōsetsu* (Ch. *xiaoshuo*)—had quite different connotations in its earliest history. Mori Kainan was but one of the many scholars who traced the term to its locus classicus: the "Treatise on the Arts and Writing" (Yiwen-zhi) included in Ban Gu's (32–92 CE) *History of the Western Han* (*Hanshu*). In the treatise, writers of *xiaoshuo* are listed last among ten lineages or schools (*jia*), including Confucianism, Daoism, Legalism, and Mohism. Ban Gu himself rooted the composition of *xiaoshuo* in the Zhou-dynasty political office of *baiguan*, the "petty historian" charged with collecting rumors, gossip, and other small or insignificant talk (the literal meaning of *xiaoshuo/shōsetsu*) among the alleys and byways (*xiaodao*) of the sovereign's domain. In contrast to late nineteenth-century conceptions of "fiction," the term *xiaoshuo/shōsetsu* in its original context might best be thought of as a branch of history. As Sheldon Hsiao-peng Lu writes, "*Xiaoshuo* is a discourse of limits. It constitutes the furthest point to which official discourse wishes to go, the point from which it must step back. The office of *xiaoshuo* is a legitimate establishment if and only if it contributes to the rule of the sovereign by fulfilling the tasks of social reporting, 'reportage,' and admonition."[8] In emphasizing, as Mori Kainan did in his discussion of *shōsetsu*, this original tradition of "petty historiography" (*baishi*), Meiji-period writers built on a long-standing discourse about the utility of fiction in representing and reporting the living conditions and customs of the lower echelons of society in particular.[9] In Zhou-dynasty China, the *baiguan* served as the emperor's direct conduit into the thoughts and feelings of his people; similarly, during the Meiji period, novels like *Shuihu zhuan* were presented as a way of understanding the lived experiences of a putative "national people" (*kokumin*) effaced in political journalism and more elite academic disciplines like history and philosophy.[10] Thus, at the same time the *shōsetsu* was being elevated as a critically respectable and artistically autonomous genre—most famously, but by no means exclusively, in Tsubouchi Shōyō's *Shōsetsu shinzui* (*The Essence of the Novel*)—we see a concomitant return to the premodern idea of fiction as an "unofficial history" (*yashi*) or "mirror" (*kagami*) of the present.

THE VALUE OF *BUNGAKUSHI* AND THE UNCANNY
MODERNITY OF *SHUIHU ZHUAN*

Revelations about the value of *Shuihu zhuan* were often given academic sanction by the ostensibly objective form of literature historiography, where authoritative critical pronouncements were accompanied by chastisement of Chinese readers for failing to recognize their own literary Mount Tai. An 1897 joint review of Fujita Toyohachi's *Sen-Shin bungaku* and Sasagawa Rinpū's *Shina shōsetsu gikyoku shōshi* began with the statement, "If you climb Mount Lu, then you are unable to see its faces; only when you leave the mountain do they become clear."[11] Similarly, the reviewer explained, the Chinese themselves were too close to their own literary corpus to analyze it in the detached and scientific manner necessary for literature historiography. The reviewer concluded that the Japanese were better equipped to pursue the study of Chinese texts, echoing contemporaneous statements by scholars like Kano Naoki, who pointed out (anachronistically) that the Japanese had always recognized fiction and drama as integral parts of literature, whereas the Chinese had not.[12]

That *Shuihu zhuan* was central to the formation of Meiji- and Taishō-period theories of literary development is easily demonstrated. With the exception of works that explicitly did not address fiction and drama (like the first edition of Kojō Teikichi's *Shina bungakushi*),[13] all the works discussed earlier engaged *Shuihu zhuan* at length and treated it as not only an inflection point in Chinese literary history but also the culmination of an entire tradition. *Shuihu zhuan* was, of course, a work that most Meiji-period Sinophiles had read at some point in their lives—usually in childhood through the translation of Kyokutei Bakin and Takai Ranzan—and Mori Kainan and Kubo Tenzui were not the only scholars to forgo a summary of the novel's contents in their histories, since "certainly by this point, everyone has read the work."[14] Despite the patina of detachment offered by scientific methodologies, many of the scholars in question presented the novel in a distinctly nostalgic light. Mori Kainan's "Chats on Chinese Fiction" (Shina shōsetsu no hanashi), published in *Waseda bungaku* in the early 1890s, might well have been called "Chats on *Shuihu zhuan*," since Mori devoted three out of six installments of the series to the novel, and even sections 2 and 6, ostensibly devoted to other texts, focused largely on *Shuihu zhuan* as well. Mori recounted his first experience with the novel at the age of fourteen or fifteen, and he recalled becoming so engrossed that "he had no mind for either food or sleep."[15] Mori found a fellow enthusiast in Hashimoto Yōtō (1844–1884), a *kanshi* poet in the circle of Mori's father, Shuntō (1819–1889), and the two whiled away many hours debating important issues like the validity of Jin Shengtan's truncation and whether or not Bakin had truly understood the meaning of the novel. When Mori and his friend disagreed over particular passages, he sought out the "august opinion" (*kōken*) of Yoda Gakkai (1834–1909), who the young acolyte had heard "attained the samadhi of *Shuihu zhuan*" (*kono sho no sanmai o e-tamaeru*). Mori's portrait of the young reader culminated in an encounter with the famous translator and educator Nakamura Masanao (1832–1891), who at the time would have been fairly fresh from his translations of Samuel Smiles and John Stuart Mill, and who told Mori that *Shuihu zhuan* was really an extended allegory for the early years of the Song dynasty.[16] The nostalgic and quasireligious undertones of this charming *Bildung* account are no doubt meant to be slightly humorous, but Mori's recollections demonstrate the continued popularity of *Shuihu zhuan* among the educated elite, its attraction among even the most fervent Westernizers and reformers, and the firm entrenchment of premodern literary hermeneutics.

Mori was not alone in giving extravagant praise to the novel. In the ten-page addendum to the 1902 reprinting of his *Shina bungakushi*, Kojō Teikichi grudgingly addressed interest in drama and vernacular novels (*hakuwa shōsetsu*) and singled out for unique praise the play *Xixiang ji* (*Romance of the Western Wing*) and "that most remarkable" *Shuihu zhuan*, using them to demonstrate the florescence of previously marginalized genres under Yuan hegemony.[17] The editor and belletrist Nakane Kōtei (1839–1913) claimed that *Shuihu zhuan* was a sui generis work unsurpassed by anything written later, and Kubo Tenzui similarly celebrated the text as the "pinnacle" of Chinese literature.[18] Kojima Kenkichirō described *Shuihu zhuan* as "the most marvelous of marvelous works," and Sasagawa Rinpū situated the novel in a global context by declaring *Shuihu zhuan* to be "a work that tops even Japanese and Western fiction."[19] Finally, Kano Naoki, who had studied extensively in Europe and referenced Western studies of Chinese fiction in his own research, described *Shuihu zhuan* as the "number-one" novel of China and praised the author as a *Menschenkenner*—a modern Teutonic update on Jin Shengtan's familiar praise of Shi Nai'an's ability to create distinct personalities for his characters.[20]

Why were these critics so infatuated with *Shuihu zhuan* in particular, when novels such as *Romance of the Three Kingdoms* and *Journey to the West* were also widely beloved and easily available in translation? Reading their effusive descriptions of *Shuihu zhuan*, it is difficult to escape the suspicion that the novel was entrancing precisely because it failed to conform to the exacting methodological principles outlined in the prefaces to their histories. Nearly as old as the tradition of Chinese-literature historiography in Japan was a reaction against the nascent discipline, by critics who worried that the scientific rubrics and systems of taxonomy presented in these works were insufficient for measuring the intangible qualities of literary enchantment. Takayama Chogyū, for instance, published a review of Fujita Toyohachi's *Sen-Shin bungaku* in 1897, where he took Fujita to task for his overreliance on Hippolyte Taine's triad of race, surroundings, and epoch. Describing the adoption of this framework as "both the strongest and weakest aspect" of Fujita's history, Takayama cautioned the reader that this kind of geographic and racial determinism could potentially occlude subtle but important distinctions between texts produced in similar environments.[21] An example of this elision was highlighted in a quite literally incendiary review of Sasagawa Rinpū's *Shina shōsetsu gikyoku shōshi*, which recommended burning Sasagawa's work to inspire its author to new heights of critical acumen. Among the many items that aroused the reviewer's ire was Sasagawa's interpretation of both *Shuihu zhuan* and *Journey to the West* as "novels." A desire to use Western terminology and taxonomic categories, the reviewer claimed, had led Sasagawa to overlook fundamental distinctions between true novels (*shōsetsu*) like *Shuihu zhuan*, which focused on the description of humanity, and allegorical "Märchen" (*mēruhen*) like *Journey to the West*, which couched a didactic message in the form of fanciful, easily digested tales.[22] Implicit in these criticisms was the suggestion that Western rubrics of development might not apply to China's textual corpus and that literature itself was less easily classified and quantified than exotic flora and fauna, population growth, and steel production.

The enterprise of literature historiography was predicated on the idea of consistent and quantifiable development across civilizations; in other words, texts from different cultures were expected to demonstrate similar characteristics at comparable stages of development. While Japanese critics easily found Japanese and Western parallels for works like *Romance of the Three Kingdoms* (*Heike monogatari*), *Plum in the Golden Vase* (*Genji monogatari*), and the short fiction of Feng Menglong (Ihara Saikaku and the *sewamono* of Chikamatsu Monzaemon), *Shuihu zhuan* stubbornly resisted these attempts at analogue. The many Japanese adaptations of *Shuihu zhuan* were clear candidates for comparative discussion, but Chinese-literature historiographers were acerbic in their evaluation of works like *Hakkenden*, *Keisei Suikoden*, and *Chūshin Suikoden*, characterizing them as Kubo Tenzui and Aoki Masaru both did as "really, really dumb."[23] What separated the Chinese novel from its Japanese adaptations was the fact that *Shuihu zhuan* presented a clear exception to the general rule in traditional East Asian fiction that virtue is rewarded and iniquity punished, a narrative schema embodied in the concept of "retribution" (*bao*) that undergirds famous works like *Plum in the Golden Vase*, Feng Menglong's short stories, and of course the fiction of Kyokutei Bakin. Although Song Jiang and most of his followers are put to death at the end of *Shuihu zhuan* (at least in symbolic form in Jin Shengtan's version), readers consistently identified and sympathized with the outlaws, making the moral calculus of *Shuihu zhuan* far less clear than in other works of Chinese fiction and drama. Bakin's "tripartite" reading of *Shuihu zhuan* was the culmination of a lifetime spent trying to resolve this tension, but his own ambivalence toward the results was evidenced by the fact that he felt compelled to rewrite the narrative from scratch in the form of works like *Keisei Suikoden* and *Hakkenden*. Despite their denigration of the work itself, Bakin's *Hakkenden*, in particular, became a persistent foil in Meiji-period discussions of the Chinese novel.[24] As I demonstrate in the following, these discussions of *Shuihu zhuan* vis-à-vis Bakin's corpus constituted a clear example of what Brian C. Dowdle terms polemical literary history; namely, writing that "remembers and reframes the past in such a way as to use it in a contemporary literary debate."[25]

An elegant resolution to the moral ambiguity apparent in *Shuihu zhuan* was to claim that this aspect of the text was an early attempt at some form of literary realism. What is more surprising than Meiji-period critics' attempts to apply modern interpretive rubrics to *Shuihu zhuan* is the consistent discovery that the classic Chinese novel held up to these new standards of evaluation. A consistent argument advanced in critical writing on *Shuihu zhuan* is the idea that the novel was, in many ways, eerily protomodern. For instance, Shi Nai'an's attention to characterization and ability to craft 108 distinctive personae were presented as an interest in interiority and "psychology" (*shinri*), the focal point and distinguishing characteristic, in many contemporary disquisitions on the novel, of modern literature itself. Often the statements made by modern Japanese critics were based on the arguments of earlier readers like Bakin and Jin Shengtan. Jin, for example, had consistently highlighted the issue of characterization in his exegesis—highlighting the subtle distinctions in *Shuihu zhuan* that he claimed could not be found in other contemporaneous novels: "When the *Shuihu zhuan* describes the personalities of 108 persons, there are truly 108 different personalities. In other books, the people they describe all look the same, be they as many as a thousand or as few as two."[26] Or,

Just in the description of rough men alone, the *Shuihu zhuan* uses many methods of description. For example, the roughness of Lu Zhishen is that of a man of hasty temperament, that of Shi Jin the impulsiveness of youth, that of Li Kui wildness; the roughness of Wu Song is that of an untrammeled hero; the roughness of Ruan the Seventh comes from his pent-up sorrow and anger; and the roughness of Jiao Ting is simply his bad temper.[27]

When Kano Naoki lectured on *Shuihu zhuan* at Kyoto University in the 1910s, he echoed Jin Shengtan almost word for word by praising the description of individual characters as the best part of the book and ending his discussion by distinguishing between the roughness of characters like Wu Song and Shi Xiu.[28] Not only were the characters themselves rough, Kano claimed, but the very "rough abandon" (*sohō*) with which the entire novel itself had been written allowed the reader to "penetrate the intricacies of emotion" (*ninjō no kibi o ugachi*) in a way unparalleled by works like *Romance of the Three Kingdoms* and *Journey to the West*. Meiji-period critics were equally interested in the author's use of dialogue and dialect.[29] Nakane Kōtei, for instance, situated *Shuihu zhuan* in a network of contemporaneous literary debates by pointing approvingly to the coarse language of the novel as an early attempt at "unifying spoken and written registers" (*genbun itchi*).[30] In a hermeneutic environment obsessed with time and temporal development, *Shuihu zhuan* itself was both of its time and oddly timeless: precocious in its uncanny modernity and simultaneously perceived as alarmingly retrograde and savage from the standpoint of civilization.

In a series of articles titled "*Shuihu zhuan*: An Ancient Model for Naturalism" (Shizen shugi no furuki mohan: *Suikoden*), the historian and literary critic Yamaji Aizan (1865–1917) took the logical next step and argued that contemporary writers in Japan could potentially take inspiration from an ancient source. Published in 1910 in Yamaji's *Dokuritsu hyōron* (Independent criticism), the essay began by arguing that naturalism itself was not a new phenomenon. Yamaji defined naturalism in simple, reverent, and almost mystical terms, focusing on the ways in which individual works of art took form through a tension between limitless nature and the artistic, textual, and human "strictures" (*jōboku*) constraining the author's expressive capacity:

Nature is a limitless pool of water, and literature is the dipper that we use to draw from it. There are large dippers, and there are small dippers; there are long dippers, and there are short dippers. When a dipper is filled to its inevitable limit, then we say that literature has encountered a "stricture." For instance, Bashō's poem "the ancient pond / a frog leaps in / the sound of water" is, without question, a work that vividly brings to life a slice of nature. The poem conveys nature in such a way that it's given concrete form in front of our very eyes. However, nature is not a thing that can always be brought to life through an ancient pond, a frog, and the sound of water. Nature is an unfathomable ocean. It is always new; eternally new and fresh. If a creator views nature in terms of the same literary forms and the same emotions they inspire, then this is not transcribing [*shasu*] nature. This is covering it up! The first creator sees nature, but the next sees nature through the eyes of his predecessor. To see nature through the eyes of others is the beginning of the end. It's fine to love Tolstoy, Ibsen, and the others, but to view nature in the same way as Tolstoy and Ibsen is to fall into secondhand description—in other words, to fall into a stricture![31]

For all his emphasis on novelty and fresh expression, Yamaji's essay began in a distinctly nostalgic vein by recalling his first encounter with *Shuihu zhuan* as a young boy on his grandfather's knee. According to Yamaji, his grandfather would say "almost like a tic" that "the period described in *Shuihu zhuan* was just like the time of our own Restoration," pointing to early Meiji oligarch-outlaws like Ōkubo Toshimichi (1830–1878) and Saigō Takamori (1828–1877) as examples of larger-than-life personages who would have been at home in the Liangshan marshes.[32] Revisiting the novel in adulthood, however, Yamaji was more struck by its interest in quotidian life. In "challenging precedent and authority" and presenting a narrative centered on the vicissitudes of petty clerks, rough-hewn constables, and simple villagers, *Shuihu zhuan* is a bizarre outlier in the Chinese literary tradition, Yamaji claimed. Like many of his contemporaries, Yamaji interpreted *Shuihu zhuan* as a subversive reaction (*handō*) against more conventional aspects of Chinese civilization: in this case, the so-called talented scholar and beautiful lady (*caizi jiaren*) romances that flourished beginning in the middle of the seventeenth century. These works, which Daria Berg characterizes as "celebrat[ing] chastity, chivalry, virtue, and wit," focus on harmonious and companionate marriage between gifted literati and equally talented brides.[33] In contrast to the handsome civil-examination licentiates and chaste beauties that populate *caizi jiaren* fiction, Yamaji highlighted *Shuihu zhuan*'s unusual focus on characters like Song Jiang, a low-level clerk who despises sex and the company of women, possesses only modest skills in the martial arts, and is described unflatteringly by the author as swarthy, short, and unattractive. By centering the narrative on such a physically unprepossessing character, Yamaji argued, the author of *Shuihu zhuan* signaled his resistance to the thematic and descriptive strictures found in *caizi jiaren* fiction.

Yamaji's remarkable analysis of *Shuihu zhuan* centered on the twentieth and twenty-first chapters of the novel, in which Song Jiang takes as his bride the dancing girl Yan Poxi, only to slay her in a fit of anger when she embarks on an affair with Song's assistant and threatens to divulge her husband's outlaw connections to the authorities. To be sure, there is no shortage of drama in these chapters, and Yan's licentious depiction, spousal neglect, and grisly murder are all consonant with the generally androcentric and misogynistic tenor of the novel as a whole. However, it was not these sensationalistic sections that interested Yamaji the most, and in choosing to focus on the marital over the martial, the Meiji-period critic presents *Shuihu zhuan* as a domestic drama rather than a tale of warrior valor. Conditioned as readers are to happy unions between physically and literarily endowed partners, the case of the unhappy Song Jiang and his partner with the roving eye is confusing and startling to the reader. As Yamaji explains,

From the point of view of conventional literature, an ugly man who is detested by his wife and ultimately suffers the humiliation of having her stolen away by a friend is someone to look down on. This is the constraining convention of literature at work. But *Shuihu zhuan* doesn't operate this way at all. This novel breaks free of convention by giving us a central character who doesn't inspire desire in women and suffers the indignity of having her stolen away by a friend. This is truly an instant where the author pulls back the curtain, breaks the rules that people have placed on literature, and reveals the true face of humanity in such a way that it's like the joyful feeling you get when the clouds break to reveal a sunny sky.[34]

A homely character who inspires contempt in women and allows his wife to be stolen away should also inspire contempt in the reader, we are told, but the author of *Shuihu zhuan* uses this unusual and fresh situation to create a more intriguing character. There is perhaps even a modicum of (historically rare) sympathy for Yan Poxi herself, who, the novel tells us, is rarely visited by her husband and might best be described in modern parlance as sexually frustrated.[35] Song Jiang is Yamaji's central focus, however, and in the remainder of the essay, the critic focuses on the author's even more startling attention to the true object of the clerk's desire: the fraternal company of the Liangshan outlaws:

Shuihu zhuan is emphatically not a record of "secondhand" [*sekondo hando*] description; everything is uniquely set down [*utsushita*] as the author's senses encounter his surroundings. For instance, look at chapter 22, when Song Jiang first meets Wu Song. The text says, "As he took Wu Song in, his heart filled with great joy." Jin Shengtan explicated this passage by saying, " 'Viewing a beautiful woman by lamplight' is an immortal line! But in this passage, he substitutes it with 'Viewing a fellow gallant [*haohan*] by lamplight!' This is truly another immortal line." In other words, Jin is pointing out the author's description of the affection and attraction [*koi*] between two men. When tiger-fierce Wu Song meets Song Jiang, then he's suddenly as timid as a mouse. And when Song Jiang sends Wu Song on his way later on, Wu Song can't stop crying. Imagine such a demon shedding tears! Whereas most novels focus only on the attraction between men and women, the author of *Shuihu zhuan* desired to move beyond these weaker emotions. The attractive forces binding together two virile men can also serve as an outstanding topic for literature, and the author of *Shuihu zhuan* was the first to discover this. Truly, the author of *Shuihu zhuan* was not someone who saw nature with the eyes of others; his work is the result of the new discoveries he made for himself by observing the world around him.[36]

To describe the meeting of a talented scholar and his female companion by lamplight is a tired cliché; to describe the homoerotic undertones of a meeting between rough-hewn and grubby outlaws by lamplight is *naturalism*. Like Kano Naoki's interest in characterization, Yamaji's reading of the passage is rooted in earlier modes of interpretation. Although he gives the author of *Shuihu zhuan* credit for the "discovery" (*hakken*) he describes, it might be more fair to give at least partial credit to Jin Shengtan, who had drawn attention to the passage in question on the basis of the defamiliarizing effect of the incongruously romantic description.

SHUIHU ZHUAN AS SYMBOL AND SNAPSHOT

By 1910, Yamaji Aizan was not the first writer to argue that *Shuihu zhuan*, uniquely among all works of East Asian fiction, was a disconcertingly precocious work. Similar sentiments had been developed in detail as early as 1897, during a literary roundtable hosted by Mori Ōgai (1862–1922) in the pages of his journal *Mezamashigusa* (The eye-opener). The roundtable, devoted exclusively to *Shuihu zhuan*, included a prestigious array of influential Meiji-period literati, including Ōgai's younger brother, Miki Takeji (1867–1908), Yoda Gakkai, Mori Kainan, the translator and journalist Morita Shiken (1861–1897), and the novelist Kōda Rohan (1867–1947).[37] The roundtable, carried out through correspondence so that each contributor would have ample time to develop his points, combined detailed bibliographic analysis with impressionistic reminiscence and criticism. The exegetical heavy lifting was left in this case to Mori Kainan, who dutifully walked his peers through a discussion of the novel's many editions and the vexed question of *Shuihu zhuan*'s authorship. Like their Edo-period predecessors, the members of Ōgai's salon were highly partisan in their selection of editions, united, like Suyama Nantō and his peers a century and a half earlier, by their distaste for the truncated edition of Jin Shengtan. Unlike Nantō, however, the *Mezamashigusa* contributors had Western critical theory at their disposal as a way of justifying their selection of editions. Ōgai, for example, employed the German aesthetician Friedrich Theodor Vischer's (1807–1887) distinction between the symbolic (*Symbolik*) and allegorical (*Allegorie*) to explain why Jin's dream sequence was an inferior and unrepresentative ending:

Consider the ending from the standpoint of Vischer's discussion of *Faust*, where he makes a distinction between symbol and allegory. A symbol may be used to fruitfully draw out an image, but allegory always becomes constrained by a larger concept. When you read *Shuihu zhuan* in its entirety, then there isn't a single instant where the images don't vividly well up in your mind. It's only the dream sequence—up until the point where Jin writes, "Suddenly, he saw an inscription, where the phrase 'All under Heaven Is at Peace' was written in large blue characters"—that gets tangled up and constrained by explanation and didacticism [*rikutsu*].[38]

With the entirety of the Chinese literary corpus at their fingertips, one wonders why Ōgai and his peers selected *Shuihu zhuan* for extended discussion. As with the more formal tradition of Chinese-literature historiography discussed previously, there is a clear sense that *Shuihu zhuan* was intriguing precisely because of its own taxonomic outlaw status. In his bibliographic introduction, Mori Kainan dismissed the traditional theory that *Shuihu zhuan* and *Romance of the Three Kingdoms* were both written by Luo Guanzhong and pointed out that the styles of the two works were completely different. Whereas *Romance of the Three Kingdoms* "gives the impression of listening to an instructor's lecture, even when it makes use of more colloquial language," *Shuihu zhuan* was described as a work that "from start to finish was written by someone who intended to write a novel" (*hajime yori shōsetsu o tsukuru to iu hō kara fude o tsuketa*).[39] According to Kainan, the structure and language of an authentic "novel" like *Shuihu zhuan* differed from both the didactic style of *Romance of the Three Kingdoms* and the highly allegorical *Journey to the West*, which centered on the conveyance of religious tenets. *Shuihu zhuan*, Kainan explained, has no real message to impart to the reader, aside from a generalized lament about the unfairness (*fuhei*) of life, illustrated by Song Huizong's ingratitude toward Song Jiang at the end of the longer edition.[40] Rather than search for an overarching message as one might do with *Journey to the West*, Kainan asserted, the reader should focus on the author's vivid attention to the prosaic quotidian details that, like many contemporaneous critics, he equated with literary modernity: the ability, in his memorable phrase, to "render even the chin hairs and eyebrows of the protagonists visible."[41] In its careful attention to description, spoken language (Kainan praised the author's use of different dialects for different characters), and verisimilitude, *Shuihu zhuan*'s closest analogue, is the equally epic *Plum in the Golden Vase*, which provides a similarly panoptic view of late-Ming mercantile and domestic culture. Although *Shuihu zhuan* and *Plum in the Golden Vase* are presented as similar in their attention to the minutiae of daily life, Kainan held the former up as unique:

> The novel *Plum in the Golden Vase* isn't as exciting as *Shuihu zhuan* in terms of plot [*monogatari*], but when it comes to narrating detail without letting a single thing slip by, then *Shuihu zhuan* can't compete. Consider the section where Li Ping'er is dying: everyone gathers at the side of her pillow as she draws her dying breath, and by the time she's put in her coffin, more than a hundred pages have gone by. . . . If you're combing through Chinese texts looking for the same kind of attention to detail that you find in Western novels, then *Plum in the Golden Vase* and *Dream of the Red Chamber* come the closest. *Shuihu zhuan is ideal for getting a sense of the uniqueness of the Chinese people, but it's neither a historical novel [rekishi shōsetsu] nor a novel of sentiment [ninjō shōsetsu]; instead, it straddles the line between the two.*[42]

It is in this final comment, I believe, that Kainan comes closest to articulating the group's interest in *Shuihu zhuan*—namely, its potential as a means of describing and conveying a "unique" (*tokusei*) Chinese character. While novels like *Plum in the Golden Vase* and *Dream of the Red Chamber* are praised for their mimetic and near-Western attention to narrative detail, *Shuihu zhuan* is of value primarily in its accurate reflection not only of a bygone civilization but also, it seems, of its contemporary incarnation. As the salon progresses, it quickly becomes apparent that the participants have collapsed the distinction between the China of antiquity and the contemporaneous Qing dynasty that many of them had traversed firsthand. Ōgai, for instance, who had spent time in Taiwan and Manchuria as a military medic, lamented,

> *Shuihu zhuan*, from start to finish, never loses its sense of being a *uniquely Chinese product*. Why is it that in China pestilences, crop failures, and floods follow one after another, and why is it that Chinese officials are unable to prevent them? Why is it that convicts and rebels run amok without restraint, and why are the Chinese troops unable to subdue them? We see from *Shuihu zhuan* that these were

problems that existed during the Song and haven't been solved to this day. Every time I reread *Shuihu zhuan*, I always find this thought occurring to me.[43]

Morita Shiken similarly utilized his section of the discussion to enumerate specific social tensions threatening the cohesion of the Chinese state, all of which, he argued, could be accurately recognized and diagnosed by reading *Shuihu zhuan*. These problems were not presented as historically contingent or recent but as deeply rooted in a dehistoricized, timeless Chinese character that was apparent in the "uniquely Chinese product" (*tokushu naru Shina san*) of *Shuihu zhuan*. Morita, who had spent time in China as an overseas correspondent for his patron Yano Ryūkei's (1851–1931) *Yūbin hōchi shinbun*, justified his elision of China past and China present by writing, "*Shuihu zhuan* is unquestionably a snapshot of an aspect of the time in which its author lived. And if we allow that the state of Chinese society hasn't changed very much since the time in which *Shuihu zhuan* was written, then we can say that it's a snapshot of an aspect of the present as well."[44]

"The time in which *Shuihu zhuan* was written," was, of course, more than four centuries prior to Ōgai's salon, but Morita's proposal to read *Shuihu* as a transparent "snapshot" (*shashin*) of contemporary China was taken up by the group with notable alacrity. Much of the *Mezamashigusa* salon is devoted to a near-pathological exegesis of Chinese social woes as the contributors move freely between Song-period and contemporary China and turn to the novel in an ahistorical attempt to find explanations for the problems afflicting late-Qing-dynasty China. The Liangshan outlaws are bandits, the reader is told, and the proliferation of bandits has always been encouraged in China by the competitive atmosphere and slim possibilities for success in the Chinese imperial-exam system. Banditry flourishes also because of the inherently superstitious and susceptible mind-set of the Chinese, as well as because of the lack of loyalty the Chinese feel toward their emperor, a figure who, Morita Shiken emphasized, often rises from a common background and might easily be replaced in turn by a future emperor bearing a different surname. The stability of Chinese society is threatened at the level of the family by rampant female lust, a phenomenon encouraged by the strict gender segregation that relegates Chinese women to the rear quarters of the household, where they are "sequestered like convicts" and left to stew in their lascivious thoughts like Yan Poxi and Pan Jinlian.

Having arrived at a Grand Unified Theory of contemporary Chinese social instability, Morita Shiken voiced the group's conclusion:

Just look how many times in the novel Li Kui turns to Song Jiang and asks him whether or not he'd like to be the "new" Song emperor. Look how frequently magic and sorcery appear in the novel. Consider the fact that the Liangshan gang is founded by Wang Lun, a failed-examination candidate, or that the rebel leader Tian Hu was an average person from Qinzhou who turned to banditry only because he couldn't bear the demands of rapacious officials. Or that Fang La was able to deceive the masses after supposedly seeing his changed reflection in the river.[45] All of this succeeds in representing an aspect of Chinese culture in such a way that the reader can only nod his head in agreement that this is precisely the way things are.[46]

Thus, throughout the *Mezamashigusa* discussion, *Shuihu zhuan* is deeply historicized bibliographically but left alone as a floating signifier purporting to describe a timeless, ahistorical Chinese civilization and character. Rather than interpreting the novel's structure and themes with respect to universal notions of duty and loyalty, all commentators take care to emphasize *Shuihu zhuan*'s unique Chineseness (*Shina tokusan*) and inextricable links to the land of its composition. Works such as *Plum in the Golden Vase* might provide more detail about quotidian life in China, but the members of the group unanimously turn to the more subversive and troubling *Shuihu zhuan* as a social index.

The exploration of *Shuihu zhuan* as a symbol of fin de siècle imperial China and, by extension, a foil to Japanese modernity was further developed in other contemporary disquisitions on the text. In a 1900 essay titled "*The Water Margin* and *Eight Dog Chronicle*" (*Suikoden to Hakkenden*), the poet Masaoka Shiki (1867–1902) agreed with many of the statements advanced by Ōgai's coterie but arrived at opposite conclusions as to their significance. Shiki began the essay by drawing attention to the anachronism of his interest in *Shuihu zhuan*. Whereas Ōgai and his collaborators had largely ignored the state of contemporary Japanese letters, Shiki began his discussion with an apology:

If I pick a topic like *Shuihu zhuan* at this time in history in particular, people might suspect that I've gone a bit nuts. And if you wonder why I'm picking these two immature works for a comparative discussion during the Meiji—the era of the progressive novel, after all—I would say the following: Yes, these novels appear immature from the point of view of today, but if we consider the age in which they were produced, then we find that they were giants of their age and several stages beyond their contemporaries. That is to say, from the point of view of the development of the novel, these two works should be singled out as the outstanding representatives of their respective eras. In this respect, they're different from today's lifeless novels [*kyō no herohero shōsetsu*], which are "progressive" for their time but will never serve as the capstone for an entire era, as these works do.[47]

Like many of his contemporaries, Shiki continued in a nostalgic vein by relating how, as a child, he had read both Bakin's *Hakkenden* and works of Chinese fiction, including *Shuihu zhuan*, obsessively. Recently, Shiki wrote, he had an opportunity to reread the two novels during recuperation from an illness.[48] Revisiting these classics from childhood, Shiki was astounded by the degree to which his attitude toward each had changed. According to Shiki, he devoured *Shuihu zhuan*, finding himself engrossed in the same way that translations of Chinese fiction had captivated him in his youth. As for Bakin's *Hakkenden*, Shiki explained that even though, as a child, he had read Bakin so much that he memorized entire passages,

when I read it later, I found myself feeling a powerful antipathy toward it—to the point that I detested even picking it up. Maybe this was just a reaction to my enthusiasm before. Whatever the reason, the *Hakkenden* I once loved had soured on me, and at the same time *Shuihu zhuan*—which I'd formerly underestimated—grew correspondingly more engrossing. Thus, I started to think of writing a comparative discussion of the two.[49]

After providing a brief introduction to the novel's history—culled largely from the recent analysis in *Mezamashigusa*—Shiki explored his reasons for turning away from Bakin and embracing the alluring chaos of *Shuihu zhuan* in its place. Shiki presented his discussion in the form of a binary by contrasting *Hakkenden*'s belabored attention to "principle" (*rikutsuppoi*) to a certain guileless "innocence" (*mujaki*) that he claimed pervaded *Shuihu zhuan*. On its surface, Shiki's discussion of principle in the context of Bakin's oeuvre appears to be a variation on the critical arguments of Tsubouchi Shōyō and others, who had presented didacticism (*kanzen chōaku*) as the inverse of the modern novel's focus on interiority and psychology (*shinri*).[50]

Although he did object to Bakin's continual evocation of morally edifying messages, Shiki did not understand principle as a simple matter of morality and instruction. The term *rikutsuppoi* referred also to the sense of deliberateness and intentional craft characterizing the construction of Bakin's text, ranging from narratological techniques like foreshadowing and the relationship between protagonists' names and personalities to the carefully calibrated sense of proportion observable in the allotment of punishment and reward.[51]

The "innocence" or "guilelessness" (*mujaki*) that Shiki celebrated in *Shuihu zhuan* referred to both the characters depicted in *Shuihu zhuan* and the reader's reaction to the novel itself. This guilelessness was an amoral quality manifested, for instance, in the maniacal enthusiasm and singular focus characters like "the living Buddha" Li Kui brought to their gory livelihoods. It referred also to readers' natural responses to these figures. Shiki described the paramount affective quality of *Shuihu zhuan* as "a feeling of fineness" (*kanji no yoi*) experienced by the reader, a banal-sounding encomium that Shiki struggled to define in his essay.[52] *Kanji no yoi* was not, he stated, interchangeable with terms such as "interesting" or "intriguing" (*omoshiroi*). *Kanji no yoi* denoted a work of art or literature that inspired a sudden, intuitive rush of joy—a response that Shiki directly contrasted with the cerebral, deliberative appreciation encouraged by Bakin's complex narrative.[53] The heady rush engendered by *Shuihu zhuan* was often a reaction to an unexpected juxtaposition of details, a point that situated *Shuihu zhuan* in the discourse of haiku poetics developed by Shiki elsewhere. Like Yamaji Aizan in his discussion of Song Jiang's marriage to Yan Poxi, Shiki turned away from the novel's many iconic scenes and looked elsewhere in the text for seemingly mundane details that would bolster his theory. In the third chapter of the novel, for example, "The Tattooed Monk" Lu Zhishen takes refuge in Wutaishan Monastery after killing a local bully and attracting the attention of the law. In one of the many overtly comic episodes in the novel, the coarse Lu struggles to adapt to monastic life, where the traditional *haohan* diet of bowls of wine and chunks of meat is explicitly proscribed by Buddhist law. Shortly after his initiation, the intemperate Lu escapes his confines in search of a forbidden drink. As luck would have it, he immediately encounters a wine vendor on the road, who sings a song about the exploits of a legendary warlord as he makes his way down the dusty path. In light of the raucous, over-the-top, lowbrow comedy that pervades Lu

Zhishen's time in the monastery, there is little in this that attracts the reader's attention, but Shiki immediately pounced on the scene and held it aloft as an example of *kanji no yoi*. In his essay, he quoted the original passage in full, along with the commentary of Jin Shengtan, who had annotated the passage by writing, "How great that the wine vendor isn't singing about wine but is instead humming a song about going into battle!"[54] Taking a cue from Jin, Shiki elaborated,

This is one of the finest examples of *kanji no yoi*, which as I explained before, deals with an immediate sensation. . . . The specialness of this passage emerges through contrast [*kontorasuto*], which is when two entities are used to illuminate each other. Here, the elements of the equation are Wutaishan Monastery, Lu Zhishen, the wine vendor, and the wine vendor's song. The disjuncture between the monastery and the murderous Lu Zhishen is a contrast. The fact that the same [coarse and violent] Lu Zhishen becomes a Buddhist monk presents another internal contrast. The monastery and the wine vendor flouting the injunction against alcohol present another contrast. And the fact that the wine vendor is singing a song about an ancient battlefield presents another example of a character's internal contrast.[55]

What entrances Shiki so much about this scene is the random and accidental (*gūzen*) way in which elements of the scene collide. Shiki suggests that this quality of randomness might serve as the best antonym for Bakinesque "principle" (*rikutsu*) and demonstrated how the motif of the accidental encounter structures the entire work, from the overarching narrative of the outlaws' assemblage through chance meetings to the glimpses of inner complexity and depth enabled by a humble wine vendor's interest in an old battle tune. Shiki took this emphasis on the random and chance not only as a form of mimetic fidelity but also as a necessary complication of Bakin's rigid distinction between abstract moral polarities. In contrast to Bakin's dog knights, Shiki pointed out that in *Shuihu zhuan* good characters possess flaws and supposedly evil characters are capable of behaving admirably. Similarly, the characters' use of non sequiturs in dialogue and seemingly portentous omens that end up coming to naught are praised as being far more representative of lived experience than similar signs in Bakin's novel—in which every encounter and detail of the landscape is deployed in the conveyance of a moral message.

Like Mori Ōgai and Morita Shiken in the *Mezamashigusa* roundtable, Shiki connected *Shuihu zhuan* to both classical and contemporary China. A substantial section of Shiki's analysis was devoted to the issue of magic and sorcery in *Shuihu zhuan*, an instance in which the novel clearly moved away from the mimetic paradigm Shiki had discussed earlier. In contrast to Morita Shiken, who dismissed the presence of sorcery in *Shuihu zhuan* as evidence of a superstitious Chinese mindset, Shiki defended the theme on almost ethnographic grounds by presenting it as an alternative window into a Chinese quotidian:

In China, sorcery is something that people not only believed in during ancient times but also believe in in the present. Just look at the Society of Righteous Harmony that's stirring things up at the present moment: isn't it true that most Chinese believe that they are capable of sorcery and magic? . . . And if that's the case, then the author of *Shuihu zhuan* didn't put sorcery in his novel just because he was fond of wild stories; rather, it's better to say that it's in there because it's a reflection of what the Chinese at that time believed.[56]

Like Morita before him, Shiki elides the distinction between the China of *Shuihu zhuan* and the contemporary civilization across the sea: the reference to the contemporary Boxer Rebellion occupies the same breath as his discussion of the Ming-period novel. However, rather than simply being a relic of a backward civilization, as Morita had argued, the novel's interest in magic and sorcery was, for Shiki, an issue of verisimilitude: in this case, accurately reflecting the epistemological parameters of *Shuihu zhuan*'s audience. Shiki's larger point becomes clear when he compares Bakin's use of magic and sorcery in *Hakkenden*: "However, when we come to the case of *Hakkenden*, then we just find a lot of nonsense. . . . It's not that no one in Japan believed that sort of stuff, but it is true that the only people who believed it were ignorant, know-nothing children. Thus, *Hakkenden* comes out looking even more barbaric for blindly following these "*Water Margin*–esque" exaggerations."[57] Thus, paradoxically, even the retrograde elements of *Shuihu zhuan* are more honest (and therefore of more value) than Bakin's attempts to create intrigue through servile imitation of the "*Shuihu*-esque" (*Suikoden-teki*). The *Mezamashigusa* coterie's "snapshot" of a static and backward society is inverted as a positive index of

Shuihu zhuan's verisimilitude, although the unmistakably racist discourse of Japanese spiritual sophistication is preserved intact.

EMBRACING THE *"SHUIHU*-ESQUE": TRAVEL, ENCOUNTER, AND ARMCHAIR ETHNOGRAPHY

Although critics like Mori Ōgai, Morita Shiken, and Masaoka Shiki had experience traveling and working in the Chinese empire, their essays were written while comfortably ensconced back in their homeland of Japan. Other discussions of the *"Shuihu*-esque," however, were composed in situ by writers who sought to describe for their countrymen the geographic and cultural landscape of a region that travelers encountered in increasingly large numbers throughout the final years of the nineteenth and beginning of the twentieth centuries. Many of the first Japanese historians of Chinese literature, for example, spent extensive time in China in the capacity of educators, journalists, translators, and diplomats, and this firsthand contact with contemporary Chinese culture was frequently invoked as a credential for their scholarly output. Writers like Kojō Teikichi and Fujita Toyohachi may be understudied in the contemporary academy, but the list of figures these pioneering authors came into firsthand contact with during their time abroad are names that all historians of modern East Asia are intimately familiar with. In between stints as a foreign correspondent in the 1890s, Kojō, for instance, worked as a Japanese-language translator for Liang Qichao's publication *Shiwubao* (Contemporary affairs), and Fujita Toyohachi labored in a similar capacity for Luo Zhenyu's (1866–1940) *Nongxuebao* (Agricultural bulletin). The indefatigable Fujita later became an instructor at Luo's Dongwen Xueshe academy, where he taught Japanese, English, mathematics, and chemistry and played a seminal role as an intermediary between Chinese scholars such as Luo and Wang Guowei (1877–1927) and Japanese scholars like Kano Naoki, Naitō Konan (1866–1934), and Kuwabara Jitsuzō (1871–1931). Fujita's former classmates and fellow contributors to *Shina bungaku taikō* Taoka Reiun and Shirakawa Riyō interacted extensively with Kang Youwei and Zhang Zhidong, respectively, and Miyazaki Shigekichi (quoted in the conclusion of the previous chapter) spent considerable time on the continent as a correspondent during the Russo-Japanese War. Practitioners of a discipline who had been closely linked at Tōdai found themselves similarly clustered in China, as demonstrated anecdotally by the fact that during one of his early trips to China, a young Kano Naoki took shelter from the Boxer Rebellion in the foreign legation, only to find himself side by side with Kojō Teikichi.[58] Although all these authors had unique experiences and interests in China, it is perhaps not too much of a stretch to imagine that they shared the belief, articulated by Taoka Reiun, that, "Having devoted ourselves to the study of the Chinese classics [in Japan], the continent of China was the greatest stage [butai] for action!"[59]

Although Shina bungakushi was a text-based pursuit, in this respect it had more in common with nascent disciplines such as ethnography and folk studies, which similarly centered on firsthand observation of Chinese culture and displayed a marked distrust toward the elite culture enshrined in the study of government, official historiography, and classical thought. The array of new interpretations of Shuihu zhuan that began to emerge during the Meiji period was largely enabled by the advent of Japanese travel to the Qing empire and the changes in attitude toward China that this firsthand contact engendered. Even a cursory glimpse at Japanese travelogues from the Meiji and Taishō periods demonstrates that many travelers journeyed to China with preconceptions derived from their experiences with Chinese texts—a fact demonstrated by Joshua Fogel in his magisterial study of Japanese travelers in China from the bakumatsu period to World War II.[60] While Fogel rightly observes that none of them was so naive as to hope to find Confucius himself alive and well in Qufu, it is no exaggeration to say that many of them expected to find a world similar to that found in China's second most famous text, Shuihu zhuan, a classic work of fiction that was often explicitly held up as both a parallel and subversive alternative to the epistemological terrain described in the Confucian canon.

Needless to say, the tradition of description that emerged from Japanese travel to China was anything but disinterested and apolitical. What united the utterances of traveling experts and dilettantes alike was the way in which they served the function of what James Clifford has termed ethnographic self-fashioning, a process by which the act of description serves to project an image of represented and representor alike.[61] This line of inquiry often took the form of an ambiguous reckoning with the successful realization of Western-style civilization (bunmei kaika) in Japan. E. Taylor Atkins, for instance, has identified a heady mix of self-disgust and "primordial nostalgia" in the process by which Japanese ethnographers—both professional and amateur—turned their attention to what they considered less-developed regions of East Asia.[62] Atkins's research focuses mainly on Japanese interest in Korean folk culture and the ways in which the collection of information about an "uncontaminated" Korean people served both to reinforce feelings of Japanese self-superiority and to assuage the sense of dislocation and identity crisis that accompanied the tumultuous Meiji transition. Although the case of China differed dramatically from that of Korea—unlike Korea, China was never fully colonized, and traditionally China was seen as a producer rather than a receiver of culture (*bun*)—many of Atkins's observations are equally applicable to late-Qing and Republican-era China. Just as Japanese ethnographers in colonial Korea posited a difference between elite Confucian *yangban* culture and the putative folk spirit manifested in traditions as disparate as textile production and shamanism, works of fiction like *Shuihu zhuan* were presented as the product of a popular milieu uncontaminated by elite Confucian culture.

Kano Naoki, for example, who had traveled extensively in China after his graduation from Tōdai and who played a central role in establishing Chinese folk culture as a legitimate field of study in Japan, elevated *Shuihu zhuan* over its sister novel *Romance of the Three Kingdoms* on precisely these grounds.[63] Kano classified *Shuihu zhuan*, *Romance of the Three Kingdoms*, and similar works as "oral-derived novels" (*kōtōtai*) and contrasted them with both classical tales and—like many of his peers—the main body of Chinese literature itself, which he claimed focused overwhelmingly on the conveyance of moral messages. In his lectures at Kyoto University, Kano traced the term *xiaoshuo* back to its earliest appearance in the *Hanshu* and translated the term's original meaning into English as "minor information," referring to the petty gossip and rumors that the imperial officers collected and conveyed to the emperor. Although Kano was careful to emphasize that this was *not* the way to interpret later "mature" works like *Shuihu zhuan* and *Romance of the Three Kingdoms*, his analysis of specific titles approached them in precisely that way:

In the West, sinologists [*Shinagakusha*] have already translated part of [the Ming short-story collection] *Jingu qiguan* into English and French. Several of the plays from the Yuan dynasty have also been translated into these languages. The reason for this is that literary research is an essential means of understanding Chinese society. From issues of morality and customs all the way down to the structure of the family, there's more information in novels than in any other type of literature. This is why Western scholars turned their attention to these works early on.[64]

Far from adopting a defense of the novel along the lines of *l'art pour l'art*, Kano justified the study of fiction in quasi-ethnographic terms. In contrast to many of his peers, who argued that *Shuihu zhuan* had been written during the Yuan, Kano hypothesized (correctly, according to current consensus) that the novel had been written in the Ming, by a "genius" who had synthesized and combined early story cycles and works of drama. According to Kano, the author's intention in writing the text was political—namely, to demonstrate how people who were not originally bandits were forced to turn outlaw by government malfeasance. This reading centered focus securely on the butchers, constables, clerks, and petty vendors depicted in *Shuihu zhuan*, whose lives, Kano argued, were vividly illustrated in great detail. Kano praised the French sinologist Antoine-Pierre-Louis Bazin (1799–1863), who had translated a portion of *Shuihu zhuan* into French as part of a larger "effort at describing the customs of China."[65] This was a project that Kano endorsed wholeheartedly, and he bolstered his support for Bazin with reference to his own firsthand knowledge of customs on the continent:

Bazin is completely right in saying that *Shuihu zhuan* describes the society and customs of a particular epoch of Chinese history in detail. But you could go one step further: since the social customs of China haven't changed much since high antiquity, then this novel is extremely useful in understanding contemporary China as well. The inverse of this, of course, is that if you don't understand Chinese social customs, then you're not going to appreciate the best parts of *Shuihu zhuan*.[66]

To illustrate his point, Kano discussed an episode in the thirty-third chapter of the novel in which Song Jiang's colleagues' attempt to spring him from jail lands Song in deeper trouble. The interesting part of the section, Kano claimed, was in the outlaws' efforts to sway the governor by claiming Song shared his surname: the section had not made sense, Kano stated, until he witnessed firsthand the affection the Chinese feel for people who share the same name. Thus Kano concluded, "Not only is *Shuihu zhuan* interesting as a work of fiction; it's also a valuable resource in terms of researching Chinese customs."[67]

By this point, Kano's dubious equation of ancient and contemporary China is old hat, running like a leitmotif throughout Meiji- and Taishō-period writing on Chinese literature. At the same time the study of China was grounded in the temporally centered theories of progress and evolution that permeated period scholarship, China itself was dehistoricized as a timeless and unchanging entity in both academic and popular discourse. Indeed, many of the sentiments expressed in Kano's highly specialized lectures on Chinese bibliography and textual exegesis were voiced in far more popular and widely read form by the journalist and newspaper impresario Tokutomi Sohō (1863–1957), whose travels in China were recorded in his 1918 *Shina man'yūki* (Account of a leisurely trip through China). Tokutomi's account of the sights and sounds he encountered during his time abroad is interspersed with polemics dealing with Sino-Japanese political relations and the pressing need to acquire information about China. As a sharp retort to paternalistic reformers who emphasized the need for China to learn from Japan's modern political and technological institutions, Tokutomi argued that Japanese ignorance of Chinese culture was a far greater problem than its inverse. In a chapter succinctly titled "The Japanese Know Nothing About the Chinese" (Nihonjin Shinajin o shirazu), for instance, Tokutomi criticized the misleading rhetoric of *dōbun dōshu* (same culture, same race) and stated instead that "the roots on which the nations of China and Japan are established are entirely different, and the paths by which their respective subjects emerged are not the same at all."[68] Despite the misleading claims of a shared "universal" Confucian culture, both China and Japan had their own mutually foreign sets of rituals and practices. To expect the Chinese to transform themselves into Japanese through the superficial adoption of select customs and institutions was, for Tokutomi, "like asking us Japanese to become European by donning a top hat and a frock coat." China was a great "puzzle" (*nazo*), Tokutomi concluded, referring in this case less to Oriental inscrutability than to the reluctance of his own countrymen to make an effort to understand the Chinese nation.

Tokutomi's prognosis rested on an elision of historical nuance. Whereas Western history could be divided into discrete "historical segments" (*shiteki kaidan*) like classical antiquity, the Middle Ages, and the Renaissance, he claimed, China's history had been experienced as one continuous and cohesive chain (*renzokuteki ni keika se-ri*).[69] In a section called "The Present

Is Just Like the Past" (Ima nao inishie no gotoshi), Tokutomi argued that to investigate Chinese history was to experience historical déjà vu, in which perceived differences between epochs were little more than issues of "leaves and branches." Tokutomi compared the present divide between the republican south and the warlord-torn north of China with other junctures in Chinese history: the Zhou decline during the Warring States period, the fractured geography following the collapse of the Han, the divide between the Northern and Southern dynasties in the medieval period, and the epic face-off between the Qin and Chu states in antiquity. In abruptly histrionic style, Tokutomi asked the reader, "Should the north and south of China be united, or should they stay divided? And if now divided, then how can the rupture be transformed into unity? Conversely, what could occasion a fracture in unity and result in division?"[70] The parallel style and melodramatic phrasing clash with Tokutomi's otherwise workmanlike prose, until the reader remembers that a certain Chinese novel opens with an almost identical meditation. From *Romance of the Three Kingdoms*: "Long has it been said that the empire has a great tendency: what is long divided must be united, and what is long united must be divided. At the end of the Zhou, the seven kingdoms struggled for supremacy before being swallowed up by Qin; and when the state of Qin fell, the houses of Chu and Han fought until the latter triumphed."[71]

Lest the connection seem a stretch, Tokutomi explicitly cited *Romance of the Three Kingdoms* and *Shuihu zhuan* in the same section of his travelogue, arguing that although travel is the ideal means of acquiring knowledge about China, texts provide an analogous function:

For those who wish to observe China while representing the Empire of Japan, I would say that at the very least you have to have knowledge of texts from the *Zuo Commentary* [*Zuozhuan*] and the *Records of the Grand Historian* [*Shiji*] to *Romance of the Three Kingdoms* and *Shuihu zhuan*. I'm not telling you to do this just because "China is a nation of literature" or anything like that. I'm saying this because the China of antiquity is precisely like the China of the present. And if the China of antiquity is like the China of the present, then it's short-sighted to think of the *Zuo Commentary* and *Records of the Grand Historian* as simple records of the past. And to treat *Romance of the Three Kingdoms* and *Shuihu zhuan* as simple novels is to make a grave error. It's no exaggeration to say that these works contain everything— from historical rises and falls on down to daily relationships among the people.

Today's Chinese didn't appear suddenly from outer space: they are a race that bears the weight of four thousand years of history on their backs![72]

From the momentous historical cataclysms related in the *Zuo Commentary* and Sima Qian's *Records of the Grand Historian* to the intricacies of human interactions depicted in fiction, China is best apprehended through its texts—not, as Chinese-literature historiographers argued, because China is a "nation of literature" but because China is literature itself. For Tokutomi, the collapse of distinctions between past and present is paralleled by an elision of the boundaries between China's textual corpus and the lives and experiences, we are told, it transparently encodes.

In his travelogue, Tokutomi famously described China as "a nation poisoned by civilization" (*bunmei chūdoku koku*), a characterization that arraigned the stultifying effects of traditional Confucian culture but—like so many other utterances made by Japanese travelers in China—contained the seeds of a self-criticism as well. The fiction writer and poet Akutagawa Ryūnosuke, who traveled to China in 1921 at the invitation of the *Ōsaka mainichi shinbun*, discovered that Japanese *bunka* was even more stagnant than Chinese *bun*, and as with Tokutomi and Kano Naoki before him, the discovery was predicated on both the textual and experiential. Half a decade after Tokutomi's trip, it seems that Japanese intellectuals were no closer to solving the "riddle" of China, and Akutagawa's employers described their dispatch of the young author as another attempt at bringing the emerging face of "New China" (*atarashiki Shina*) into relief.[73] Editorial dramatics aside, the China of 1921 probably was a more puzzling environment for a Japanese traveler, since Sino-Japanese relations had deteriorated noticeably in the aftermath of the Japanese annexation of Shandong, a series of Chinese boycotts against Japanese economic interests, and the rapidly growing Japanese presence in continental Asia. Akutagawa encountered a number of symbols of anti-Japanese sentiment in the course of his travels, and, pairing such encounters with his antiquarian interest, it is perhaps unsurprising that he spent much of his time abroad looking for various spots of relief from political concerns. Akutagawa interviewed cultural luminaries and government officials such as Zhang Binglin, Zheng Xiaoxu, and Gu Hongming, but his treatment of these discussions in his travelogue was fairly superficial.[74] Although he had been dispatched to chronicle the political and cultural contours of New China, Akutagawa appeared most intrigued by the sights familiar to him from his reading: the tutelary shrine he recognized from the supernatural tales of Pu Songling (1640–1715), the grave of the Six Dynasties courtesan Su Xiaoxiao, and a bustling Shanghai alleyway, where he experienced a literary epiphany:

We went to see a number of open-air shops. There were socks, toys, sprouts of sugarcane, buttons made of mother-of-pearl, handkerchiefs, peanuts, and a number of other, slightly dirty, comestibles. Of course, there was really no difference between the Chinese out and about and Japanese enjoying themselves on festival days. Across the way, there was a modern dandy strolling about in a gaudy striped suit and purple quartz necktie. But just as I was taking this sight in, I saw an old-style granny with silver bracelets around her wrists and bound feet that couldn't have been more than two or three inches in length. In the midst of all these people, it seems that we had both Chen Jingji from *Plum in the Golden Vase* and Xi Shiyi from *A Precious Mirror for Judging Flowers*. However, Du Fu, Yue Fei, Wang Yangming, and Zhuge Liang were nowhere to be found.[75] *To put it another way, contemporary China is not the China of classical poetry. It is the lascivious, cruel, rapacious China of the novel.* Those cheap "mock Orientalists" who delight in Chinese porcelain, water lilies, embroidered birds, and the like have gradually died out in the West. It's time for you same dilettantes, who know nothing about China beyond the [literary anthologies] *Models for Literary Composition* [*Wenzhang guifan*] and *Anthology of Tang Poetry* [*Tangshi xuan*], to disappear from Japan as well![76]

Despite his continual search for the literary geography represented in classical poetry, prose fiction once again serves as the closest hermeneutic for deciphering his experience.

Whereas the mercantile-centered *Plum in the Golden Vase* had encapsulated the bustling urban chaos of Shanghai for Akutagawa, his subsequent journey to the famous West Lake in Hangzhou put him in mind of a different work. By the time he reached West Lake, Akutagawa had already been hospitalized with pleurisy, and his energy and temper were at a nadir. Made increasingly peevish by the "prosaic" (*sanbunteki*) details of modernity he encountered in China—the red paint slopped onto the monuments and steles celebrated in classical verse, ubiquitous and ill-mannered American tourists, and so forth—Akutagawa escaped his escorts and stumbled upon a secluded café, where, he tells us, he was finally able to penetrate the disappointing facade of the modern and successfully merge with the timeless literary ideal he had been seeking:

In that moment, I forgot about the red brick and ubiquitous American tourists. No, I was able to summon a "novel" feeling [*shōsetsu meita kimochi*] as I watched the peaceful scenery. There, in the light of late spring beneath the willow trees in Stone Tablet Village, [the outlaw] Ruan Xiaoer was sitting on the stump with his fishing pole and not a care in the world. His brother Ruan Xiaowu had washed off a chicken and gone inside to get a butcher knife. And how I loved Ruan Xiaoqi with "the pomegranate flower tucked in his hair and panther tattoos," who was washing some old clothes. Wait, someone was coming! Ah, no. It wasn't the outlaw military strategist Wu Yong, after all. No, it was just a prosaic candy seller with a basket slung over his arm. He sidled over and asked if I would like to buy a caramel or something like that. And that was the end of that. Like a flea, I was yanked right out of my *Shuihu zhuan* reverie.

With the rueful observation that "there is not a single candy-selling hero among the 108 gallants of *Shuihu zhuan*," Akutagawa shrugged off his trance and reluctantly reentered the distasteful landscape of modernity.

Shuihu zhuan was a novel Akutagawa returned to repeatedly in his account of China. And in keeping with the trends discussed in this chapter, he connected the well-known novel to the national ethos he claimed to have uncovered during his time abroad—in Akutagawa's memorable phrase, a certain "*Shuihu*-esque" (*Suikoden rashii*) quality to human interaction:

The reader probably doesn't understand what I mean by "*Shuihu*-esque." Of course, the novel *Shuihu zhuan* is well known in Japan through Kyokutei Bakin's *Hakkenden* and [the *yomihon*] *Shintō Suikoden* and *Nihon Suikoden*. But I don't think that any of those works really give a sense of what I mean by "*Shuihu*-esque." "*Shuihu*-esque" is a kind of Chinese philosophical insight. It says that the 108 *haohan* weren't the loyal men of valor that Bakin, for example, made them out to be. No, they were just a bunch of hoodlums from start to finish. But they didn't come together just because they delighted in evil. . . . It's that an outlaw-gallant isn't constrained by trifling things like arson and murder. Among the Liangshan group there was a mind-set that said mere questions of good and evil were there to be trampled underfoot. Even a career military man like Lin Chong or a compulsive gambler like Bai Sheng could be a brother as long as they adopted that mind-set.

It's a kind of "supramoral" philosophy that's not limited just to the characters in the novel. It has always had a strong root in the Chinese mindset—at least when compared with us Japanese. . . . If you think I'm making this up, you'd better take a look at Nietzsche's *Thus Spake Zarathustra*.

Akutagawa's ambiguous praise is noteworthy for the division he draws between Chinese and Japanese fiction and the putative ethos each imparts to its readers. While Japanese adaptations of *Shuihu zhuan*, exemplified by the sternly moralizing *Hakkenden* of Bakin, explore a classical Confucian understanding of duty and loyalty (*chūshin*), the original *Shuihu zhuan* embodies a supramoral (*chōdōtoku*), almost "Nietzschean," disregard for social order. Though Akutagawa professed an ambiguous admiration for this alleged quality of Chinese thought, he simultaneously presented it as a fault line threatening the stability of contemporary Chinese society.

CODA

While the reification of *Shuihu zhuan* as a privileged point of entry into a unique national psyche was paralleled by the Meiji-period elevation of Edo *gesaku* writers like Saikaku, Chikamatsu, and especially Bakin, the case of *Shuihu zhuan* was complicated by the conflicted and often contradictory feelings many Japanese intellectuals harbored toward contemporary China.[77] If *Shuihu zhuan* were to be consecrated as the pinnacle of Chinese literary achievement—and a number of Meiji-period historians asserted that it should—then it was presented as the endpoint of a particularly troubled history, one characterized by aporia, instability, and the "barbarism" that Japanese intellectuals had hoped to overcome or suppress in their own rapidly modernizing nation.

One of the goals of this chapter has been to demonstrate the rhetorical and conceptual similarity in the ways in which China was approached as an object of knowledge by credentialed expert and amateur aficionado alike. These similarities include a collapsing of the distance between archaic and contemporary China, the agreement that works of literature provide a window into the circumstances of their composition, and the idea that research on Chinese textual culture could potentially shed light on the contours of Japanese cultural uniqueness as well. Like their peers in parallel disciplines, Japanese literary scholars often presented their work as a way of cultivating self-knowledge in an imperial context. As Robert Thomas Tierney has argued,

In the late nineteenth century, Japanese scholars imported new academic disciplines from the West, but they quickly established autonomous branches of these disciplines within Japan. These disciplines offered paradigms of knowledge that were sometimes applied to solving the practical problems of ruling an empire. In return, the realities of ruling an empire informed the conceptual framework of these disciplines and shaped representations that the Japanese made of themselves and their nation.[78]

Tierney's research focuses chiefly on the emergence of ethnography, colonial policy studies, folklore, and eugenics as academic disciplines, but one could add "literary historiography" to the list without substantially modifying the statement here. In a manner comparable to the "triangular structure" of imperialism described in Tierney's discussion, the development of Chinese literary historiography in Japan was an undertaking in which Western benchmarks of culture and progress were never far from the historians' minds, and one characterized by rapid oscillation between identification and self-imposed distancing from the subject under scrutiny.[79]

As a universally known and perennially republished and retranslated text, *Shuihu zhuan* played a profoundly important role in the Meiji period in terms of constructing a public imaginary of the political and cultural state of China during the final years of the Qing. On the one hand, this imagined China was retrograde and static, violent and backward, hopelessly beset on all sides by warfare, government corruption, and famine, and—most important—desperately in need of Japanese intervention and support. At the same time, a number of Japanese literati shocked themselves (and probably their readers, as well) by finding something attractive in this chaos: a pure, unsullied, and unpretentious dynamism and vigor that were nostalgically reimagined as the vital elements that Japan had jettisoned in its single-minded quest for Western-style modernity.

A FINAL VIEW FROM THE MARGINS

Anthropologist or historian, we are now so cognizant of the manifold subtleties of cultural artifacts, their genealogies, and our interpretations of them that we hardly know where literally or figuratively to begin tracing their trajectory.

—JOHN WHITTIER TREAT, *THE RISE AND FALL OF MODERN JAPANESE LITERATURE*

It is true that there are many works written in the colloquial, but if you truly become conversant with *Shuihu zhuan*, then approaching the others is as easy as crushing bamboo. The reason for this is that, in the case of *Shuihu zhuan*, there is a "real water margin" beyond the surface of the text.

—SEITA TANSŌ, *EXPLICATION OF "THE WATER MARGIN" AND ITS COMMENTARY*

In this study, I have attempted to walk a fine line by employing *Shuihu zhuan* as both case study and hermeneutic prism, using the novel as an entry point into a network of larger questions about cultural encounter and textual circulation while simultaneously drawing attention to the irreducibly unique features of Japanese interest in a particular work of Chinese fiction. On a thematic macroscale, Japanese engagement with *Shuihu zhuan* is inextricably intertwined with a range of discussions pertaining to the composition, interpretation, and social functions of literary fiction, a network of discussions that I have charted from a period before the term "literary fiction" itself would have had any meaning whatsoever to Japanese readers to the ascension of *Shuihu zhuan* to a preeminent position in the recently constituted field of literature (*bungaku*) in the late nineteenth and early twentieth centuries. The selection of a focal point provides concrete form and direction to the forbiddingly vast array of texts and abstract topoi that might be selected to construct an argument about these processes. Thus, although in chapters 1 and 3 of my monograph *Shuihu zhuan* has played the role of focal point, discussion of the narrative and structure of the novel itself has ceded center stage to larger issues of language, canonization, and literary historiography.

At the same time, I have desired to demonstrate *Shuihu zhuan*'s status as a unique monolith in the early modern Japanese experience of late imperial Chinese fiction, and the remaining two chapters in my study have centered on the ways in which the novel's complex structure and ethically ambiguous message engendered a variety of singular interpretations and moral reactions—from Kyokutei Bakin's tortured endorsement of the language, if not the content, of the novel to Akutagawa Ryūnosuke's uneasy embrace of its "Nietzschean" elements. My motivation for fixing central focus on *Shuihu zhuan* among the innumerable works of late imperial Chinese fiction and drama imported into Japan during the early modern period is rooted in my contention that much of the novel's appeal to Japanese readers had to do with its own taxonomic outlaw status—in particular, its subversive rejection of the neo-Confucian and Buddhist discourses of duty, loyalty, and self-cultivation that could be used to analyze works such as *Romance of the Three Kingdoms*, *Journey to the West*, and even *Plum in the Golden Vase*.[1] By virtue of its resistance to these hermeneutic paradigms, *Shuihu zhuan* provides a singular point of entry into an alternative history of Japanese literary culture, one that emphasizes previously marginalized perspectives, the transnational circulation of texts, and cross-cultural interrogations of genre and narratology.

In the introduction to this monograph, I suggested that there is a connection to be made between the present academic moment and the second half of the Meiji period, when the academic discipline of literature historiography began to take institutional shape and in many ways determined, for better or for worse, what would be accepted as the Japanese literary canon in subsequent decades. Recent years have witnessed a vibrant debate among Japanologists over the content and contours of "Japanese literature"; in particular, the ways in which the canon as it has been traditionally constituted might be historicized and expanded to include previously occluded genres, genders, scripts, and individual voices. This discussion has been paralleled on the "China side" of East Asian studies, which is marked by growing interest in the dissemination and reception of Chinese texts in transplanted contexts, primarily, if not altogether exclusively, in the so-called Sinographic cultural sphere of influence (*kanji bunkaken*). It may not require an extensive study of early modern literary historiography to see how these vectors of inquiry are rooted in contemporary geopolitical concerns, but it is my hope that such a study might help us approach the tasks of selection, anthologization, and canonization with more nuance and sensitivity. The central contention of this monograph has been that Japanese engagement with Chinese fiction provides a new avenue by which to interrogate the binaries that have traditionally served as ideological anchors for Japanese and East Asian literary historiography. These binaries—which include tensions between barbarism and civilization, newly reified distinctions between Western and Eastern culture, arbitrary divisions in periodization, and the relationship of a universalized world civilization to the particularities of the nation-state—emerged during the first decades of the Meiji period but continue to have a profound effect on the way in which the literatures of both Japan and China are approached in the contemporary academy. Research by scholars such as Wiebke Denecke, Matthew Fraleigh, Miura Kanō, Saitō Mareshi, and Brian Steininger among others has done much to confirm and reestablish the status of Sinitic *écriture* as an indissoluble part of Japanese literature. By examining the Japanese afterlife of a late imperial Chinese novel and attempting to read that novel as a part of Japanese literature itself, I hope to further critically interrogate the teleological narratives of literary and linguistic nationalism that have traditionally divided academic scholarship on China and Japan.

To devote a monograph to the trajectory of a particular work of Chinese fiction in its transplanted Japanese context is an undertaking that seems at once claustrophobically specific and woefully insufficient. The sense of insufficiency stems from the undeniable presence of a potentially overwhelming volume and diversity of primary material. In the case of *Shuihu zhuan*, the simple act of selecting and treating a particular source text in depth (as I have done with works as disparate as Suyama Nantō's *Chūgi Suikodenkai*, Santō Kyōden's *Chūshin Suikoden*, and the literary criticism of Masaoka Shiki) necessarily requires the neglect of scores of alternative instances of engagement. Indeed, the composition of an encyclopedic and full account of *Shuihu zhuan*'s impact on early modern Japanese literary culture starts to resemble the perfect map described by Borges in his "On Exactitude in Science," in which cartographers create a "Map of the Empire that was of the same Scale as the Empire and that coincided with it point for point."[2]

On the other hand, devotion of one's attention to a single text risks running afoul of the charge the eighteenth-century historian Seita Tansō leveled at his Chinese predecessor, Jin Shengtan: the danger of overlooking the most important issues in the myopic pursuit of minor details. In his extended explication of Jin's criticism, Tansō argued that the more a reader delved into the text of *Shuihu zhuan*, the more he or she would realize that the novel was about far more than the title's eponymous water margin. Although I am skeptical of Tansō's claim that the novel should be read instead as an allegorical roman à clef dealing with the foundation of the Song dynasty, I am in basic agreement with his larger point—namely, that any inquiry into the dissemination, translation, and canonization of a particular work of Chinese fiction in early modern Japan necessarily merges into a far vaster field of inquiry. As Tansō and his peers were quick to note, it is only by standing in the peripheries that we are better able to interrogate and reconsider the center.

TITLES, NAMES, AND SELECTED KEY TERMS

Since this list includes terms from three languages (and makes use of three Romanization systems), I have itemized entries purely by alphabetical order, ignoring macrons and spaces between Romanized words. Thus, Mōri Yoshinari follows Moriyama Sukehiro, Xie Zhaozhe precedes *Xixiang ji*, and the Chinese names Shi Nai'an and Shi Qian are bisected by *Shin'yaku Suikoden* and Shionoya On, among other terms.

Akutagawa Ryūnosuke 芥川龍之介
Akutagawa Tankyū 芥川丹丘
Amakawaya Gihei 天河屋義平
Amenomori Hōshū 雨森芳洲
An Daoquan 安道全
Andō Tameakira 安藤為章
Aoki Masaru 青木正児
Arai Hakuseki 新井白石
Ashikaga Takauji 足利尊氏

Bai Sheng 白勝
Ban Gu 班固
Bendō 弁道
Bowuzhi 博物志
Bungei shunjū 文藝春秋

Cai Jing 蔡京
Chai Jin 柴進
Chanzhen yishi 禪真逸史
Chao Gai 晁蓋

Chen Jingji 陳敬濟
Chikamatsu Monzaemon 近松門左衛門
Ch'oe Pu 崔溥
Chūgi Suikoden 忠義水滸傳
Chūgi Suikodenkai 忠義水滸傳解
Chūka 中華
Chūshin Suikoden 忠臣水滸傳

"Daidōji Shinsuke no hansei" 大導寺信輔の半生
Dai Zong 戴宗
Da Ming lü 大明律
Danfu 亶父
Da Song zhongxing tongsu yanyi 大宋中興通俗演義
Dazai Shundai 太宰春臺
Di Baoxian 狄葆賢
Diwu caizishu Shi Nai'an Shuihu zhuan 第五才子書施耐庵水滸傳
Dokuritsu hyōron 独立評論
Doku zokubun sanjō 讀俗文三條
Dong Xi liang Jin yanyi 東西兩晉演義
Du Fu 杜甫

Emura Hokkai 江村北海
Enya Hangan 塩冶判官
Etsū 慧通

Fang La 方腊
Fang Ruhao 方汝浩
Feng Menglong 馮夢龍
Fujita Toyohachi 藤田豊八
Fūryū Shidōkenden 風流志道軒傳

Gao Qiu 高俅
Gazoku kango yakkai 雅俗漢語譯解
Genji monogatari 源氏物語
Gensei 元政
Goroku jigi 語録字義
Goroku yakugi 語録譯義
Guben xiaoshuo jicheng 古本小說集成
Gu Hongming 辜鴻銘
Guo Xun 郭勛
Guoyu 國語

Haga Yaichi 芳賀矢一
Hagino Yoshiyuki 萩野由之
Hagiwara Hiromichi 萩原廣道
Hakusai shomoku 舶載書目
Hanshu 漢書

Han Wudi (Emperor Wu of Han) 漢武帝
Han Yu 韓愈
Hara Nensai 原念斎
Hashimoto Yōtō 橋本蓉塘
Hattori Nankaku 服部南郭
Hayano Kanpei 早野勘平
Hayashi Gitan 林義端
Hayashi Hōkō 林鳳岡
Hiraga Gennai 平賀源内
Hiragana e-iri kan Kara daiko 平仮名絵入咸唐題庫
Hiraoka Ryūjō 平岡龍城
Hitorine ひとりね
Honchō Suikoden 本朝水滸傳
Hongloumeng 紅樓夢
Hong Xin 洪信
"Honsho o aratani yaku shitaru riyū" 本書を新たに譯したる理由
Hou Meng 侯蒙
Huang Ming yinglie zhuan 皇明英烈傳
Hu Shi 胡適
Huyan Zhuo 呼延灼
Hu Yinglin 胡應麟
Hyōchū kun'yaku Suikoden 標註訓譯水滸傳

Ichikawa Seiryū 市川清流
Ichimura Sanjirō 市村瓚次郎
Ihara Saikaku 井原西鶴
Ikebe Yoshikata 池辺義象
"Ima nao inishie no gotoshi" 今なお古の如し
Inoue Tetsujirō 井上哲次郎
Itō Gingetsu 伊藤銀月
Itō Jinsai 伊藤仁斎
Itō Ryūshū 伊藤龍洲
Itō Tōgai 伊藤東涯

Jingben zengbu xiaozheng quanxiang Zhongyi shuihu zhizhuan pinglin 京本増補校正全
  像忠義水滸志傳評林
Jingu qiguan 今古奇觀
Jin Shengtan 金聖歎

Kakogawa Honzō 加古川本蔵
Kana dehon Chūshingura 仮名手本忠臣蔵
Kanbun taikei 漢文大系
"Kangaku yoroshiku seisoku ikka o mōke shōnen shūsai o erami Shin-koku ni
  ryūgaku seshimu-beki ronsetsu" 漢學宜しく正則一科を設け少年秀才を選み清國に留學せ
  しむべき論説
Kang Youwei 康有為
Kano Naoki 狩野直樹

Kanseki kokujikai 漢籍國字解
Katsushika Hokusai 葛飾北斎
Kawahigashi Hekigotō 河東碧梧桐
Keisei Suikoden 傾城水滸傳
Kibi no Makibi 吉備真備
Kinoshita Jun'an 木下順庵
"Kin Seitan o najiru" 詰金聖歎
Kitamura Kigin 北村季吟
Kitamura Saburō 北村三郎
Kōda Rohan 幸田露伴
Kogetsushō 湖月抄
Kojima Kenkichirō 児島献吉郎
Kojō Teikichi 古城貞吉
Kokubungaku 國文學
Kokubungaku taikō 國文學大綱
Kokubungaku tokuhon 國文學讀本
Kokuyaku Chūgi Suikoden zensho 國譯忠義水滸傳全書
Kōmyō 光明
Kō no Moronao 高師直
Kosugi Misei 小杉未醒
Koten Kōshūka 古典講習科
Kōtoku Shūsui 幸徳秋水
Kubo Tenzui 久保天隨
Kujakurō hikki 孔雀楼筆記
Kŭmnam p'yohae rok 錦南漂海錄
Kusunoki Masashige 楠木正成
Kuwabara Jitsuzō 桑原隲蔵
Kyokutei Bakin 曲亭馬琴

Liang Qichao 梁啓超
Liezi 列子
Li Kui 李逵
Lin Chong 林沖
"Li sao" 離騷
Liu Xie 劉勰
Li Yu 李漁
Li Zhuowu 李卓吾
Li Zhuowu xiansheng piping Zhongyi shuihu zhuan 李卓吾先生批評忠義水滸傳
Luguibu xubian 錄鬼簿續編
Lu Junyi 盧俊義
"Lun xiaoshuo yu qunzhi zhi guanxi" 論小說與群治之關係
Luo Guanzhong 羅貫中
Luo Ye 羅燁
Luo Zhenyu 羅振玉
Lu Xun 魯迅
Lu Zhishen 魯智深

Man'yōshū 萬葉集
Mao Zonggang 毛宗崗
Masaoka Shiki 正岡子規
Mezamashigusa めさまし草
Mikami Sanji 三上参次
Miki Takeji 三木竹二
Minagawa Kien 皆川淇園
Mishima Chūshū 三島中洲
Miyajima Daihachi 宮島大八
Miyazaki Shigekichi 宮崎繁吉
Miyoshi Shōraku 三好松洛
Mori Kainan 森槐南
Mori Ōgai 森鴎外
Morishima Chūryō 森島中良
Mori Shuntō 森春濤
Morita Shiken 森田思軒
Moriyama Sukehiro 守山祐弘
Mōri Yoshinari 毛利吉就
Motoori Norinaga 本居宣長
Muro Kyūsō 室鳩巣

Naitō Konan 内藤湖南
Nakamura Masanao 中村正直
Nakane Kōtei 中根香亭
Namiki Senryū 並木千柳
Nansō Satomi hakkenden 南総里見八犬傳
Narushima Ryūhoku 成島柳北
Nihon bungaku 日本文學
"Nihon bungaku no hitsuyō" 日本文學の必要
Nihon bungakushi 日本文學史
Nihon bungaku zensho 日本文學全書
"Nihonjin Shinajin o shirazu" 日本人支那人を知らず
Nihon kaika shōshi 日本開化小史
Nihon risshihen 日本立志編
Nihon shishi 日本詩史
Nihon Suikoden 日本水滸傳
Nise Murasaki inaka Genji 偐紫田舎源氏
Nitta Yoshisada 新田義貞
Nongxuebao 農學報

Ochiai Naobumi 落合直文
Ogyū Sorai 荻生徂徠
Oka Hakku 岡白駒
Okajima Kanzan 岡島冠山
Ōkubo Toshimichi 大久保利通
Ōkuma Shigenobu 大隈重信

Ōmachi Keigetsu 大町桂月
Ono Sadakurō 斧定九郎

Pan Jinlian 潘金蓮
Pinhua baojian 品花寶鑑
Pu Songling 蒲松齡

Qu Yuan 屈原

Rouputuan 肉蒲團
Ruan Xiaoer 阮小二
Ruan Xiaoqi 阮小七
Ruan Xiaowu 阮小五
Rusu Kisai 留守希斎
Ryōzan ippodan 梁山一歩談
Ryūtei Tanehiko 柳亭種彦

Saigō Takamori 西郷隆盛
Sakushihō 作詩法
Sanguo yanyi 三國演義
Santō Kyōden 山東京傳
Sasagawa Rinpū 笹川臨風
Seita Tansō 清田儋叟
Sekai hyakketsuden 世界百傑傳
Sen-Shin bungaku 先秦文學
"*Sen-Shin bungaku o yomu*" 先秦文學を讀む
"*Sen-Shin bungaku to Shina shōsetsu gikyoku shōshi o hyō-su*" 先秦文學と支那小説戯曲
　小史を評す
Sentetsu sōdan kōhen 先哲叢談後編
Shaoshi shanfang bicong 少室山房筆叢
Shen Deqian 沈德潛
Shennong 神農
Shigeno Yasutsugu 重野安繹
Shiji 史記
Shi Jin 史進
Shijing 詩經
Shimada Kōson 島田篁村
Shina 支那
Shina bungaku gairon kōwa 支那文學概論講話
"*Shina bungaku no kachi*" 支那文學の価値
Shina bungakushi 支那文學史
Shina bungaku shikō 支那文學史綱
Shina bungaku shiyō 支那文學史要
Shina bungaku taikō 支那文學大綱
Shina bungaku zensho 支那文學全書
Shi Nai'an 施耐庵
Shina kaika shōshi 支那開化小史

Takayama Chogyū 高山樗牛
Takebe Ayatari 建部綾足
Takeda Izumo 竹田出雲
Takeda Shun'an 竹田春庵
Taketori monogatari 竹取物語
Takezoe Shin'ichirō 竹添進一郎
Tanaka Taikan 田中大観
Tangshi xuan 唐詩選
Taoka Reiun 田岡嶺雲
Teikoku bungaku 帝國文學
Teikoku hyakka zensho 帝國百科全書
Tengō suiyōryū 天剛垂楊柳
Tenkai 天海
Teraoka Heiemon 寺岡平右衛門
Tō 唐
Tōjō Kindai 東條琴臺
Tokugawa Tsunayoshi 德川綱吉
Tokutomi Sohō 德富蘇峰
Tonomura Yasumori 殿村安守
Tō'on gazoku gorui 唐音雅俗語類
Tōwa 唐話
Tōwagaku 唐話學
Tōwa san'yō 唐話纂要
Tōyō 東洋
Tōyō tetsugaku 東洋哲學
Tsubouchi Shōyō 坪内逍遥
Tsuga Teishō 都賀庭鐘
tsūzokubon 通俗本
Tsūzoku Kō Min eiretsuden 通俗皇明英列傳
Tsūzoku sekai bungaku 通俗世界文學

Ueda Akinari 上田秋成
Ueda Kazutoshi 上田萬年
Utagawa Kuniyoshi 歌川國芳

wakan 和漢
wakokubon 和刻本
Wang Guowei 王國維
Wang Jin 王進
Wang Wangru 王望如
Wang Yangming 王陽明
Waseda bungaku 早稲田文學
Wenxin diaolong 文心雕龍
Wenzhang guifan 文章規範
Wu Song 武松
Wu Yong 吳用
Wu za zu 五雜俎

Xie Zhaozhe 謝肇淛
Ximen Qing 西門慶
Xin xiaoshuo 新小說
Xiong Damu 熊大木
Xi Shiyi 奚十一
Xixiang ji 西廂記
Xiyou ji 西遊記
Xuanhe yishi 宣和遺事

Yakubun sentei 譯文筌蹄
"Yaku *Suiko* ben" 譯水滸辨
Yamaji Aizan 山路愛山
Yanada Zeigan 梁田蛻巖
Yanagisawa Kien 柳沢淇園
Yang Erzeng 楊爾曾
Yang Lin 楊林
Yang Zhi 楊志
Yannan Shangsheng 燕南尚生
Yano Ryūkei 矢野龍溪
Yan Poxi 閻婆惜
Yan Qing 燕青
Ye Zhou 葉晝
Yiwenzhi 藝文志
"Yiyin zhengzhi xiaoshuo xu" 譯印政治小說序
Yōda Gakkai 依田學海
Yōjikaku 用字格
Yuan Hongdao 袁宏道
Yūbin hōchi shinbun 郵便報知新聞
Yu Chu 虞初
Yue Fei 岳飛
Yu Xiangdou 余象斗

Zhang Binglin 章炳麟
Zhang Heng 張橫
Zhang Hua 張華
Zhang Qing 張清
Zhang Shun 張順
Zhang Shuye 張叔夜
Zhang Zhidong 張之洞
Zhang Zhupo 張竹坡
Zhaoshi bei 照世杯
Zhao Yi 趙翼
Zheng Xiaoxu 鄭孝胥
Zhiyanzhai 脂硯齋
Zhongguo xiaoshuo shilüe 中國小說史略
"Zhongyi shuihu zhuan xu" 忠義水滸傳序
Zhongyong 中庸

Zhou Dunyi 周敦頤
Zhuangzi 莊子
Zhuge Liang 諸葛亮
Zhu Gui 朱貴
Zhu Tong 朱仝
Zhu Xi 朱熹
Zhu Youdun 朱有燉
zokugo 俗語
Zokugokai 俗語解
Zuiweng tanlu 醉翁談錄
Zuozhuan 左傳

NOTES

INTRODUCTION: ENTERING THE MARGINS

1. This essay is included in Li Zhi [Zhuowu], *Fenshu* (Beijing: Zhonghua shuju, 1974), 303–7. It has also been translated by Huiying Chen and Drew Dixon in *A Book to Burn and a Book to Keep (Hidden): Selected Writings*, ed. and trans. Rivi Handler-Spitz, Pauline C. Lee, and Haun Saussy (New York: Columbia University Press, 2016), 125–28.

2. Adapted from James Legge's translation, included in *Classical Chinese Literature: An Anthology of Translations*, ed. John Minford and Joseph S. M. Lau (New York: Columbia University Press, 2000), 144–45.

3. David Rolston, *Traditional Chinese Fiction and Fiction Commentary: Reading and Writing Between the Lines* (Stanford, Calif.: Stanford University Press, 1997), 1–11.

4. To be sure, as chapter 2 makes clear, Jin Shengtan wrote many things with varying degrees of commitment to the arguments he advanced. In other sections of his commentary he praised the outlaws for their preservation of these cardinal virtues.

5. For a discussion of the principle of retribution and its imprint on late imperial Chinese fiction, see Patrick Hanan, *The Chinese Vernacular Story* (Cambridge, Mass.: Harvard University Press, 1981), 26–27.

6. No relation to the Song dynasty itself, although the characters in the novel remark on the coincidence of Song Jiang's surname.

7. Glynne Walley, *Good Dogs: Edification, Entertainment, and Kyokutei Bakin's* Nansō Satomi hakkenden (Ithaca, N.Y.: Cornell University East Asia Program, 2017), chapter 4.

8. Tomiko Yoda, *Gender and National Literature: Heian Texts in the Constructions of Japanese Modernity* (Durham, N.C.: Duke University Press, 2004); Haruo

Shirane and Tomi Suzuki, eds., *Inventing the Classics: Modernity, National Identity, and Japanese Literature* (Stanford, Calif.: Stanford University Press, 2000).

9. Joshua A. Fogel, "Introduction: My Route into Asian Studies," in *Between China and Japan: The Writings of Joshua Fogel* (Leiden: Brill, 2015), 2.

10. David Damrosch, "What Is World Literature?" *World Literature Today* 77, no. 1 (2003): 14.

11. Needless to say, this is not a situation unique to scholars of Sino-Japanese: the nomenclature "Japanese literature" and "Chinese history" (or "Uzbek literature and history," etc.) require the same critical caution, a point made, in the field of Japanese literature historiography, by scholars such as Karatani Kōjin, Haruo Shirane, Tomi Suzuki, and, most recently, Matthew Fraleigh.

12. David Lurie, *Realms of Literacy: Early Japan and the History of Writing* (Cambridge, Mass.: Harvard University Asia Center, 2011), introduction, chapter 1, and 323–34; Matthew Fraleigh, *Plucking Chrysanthemums: Narushima Ryūhoku and Sinitic Literary Traditions in Modern Japan* (Cambridge, Mass.: Harvard University Asia Center, 2016), introduction.

13. Atsuko Sakaki, *Obsessions with the Sino-Japanese Polarity in Japanese Literature* (Honolulu: University of Hawai'i Press, 2006), introduction and chapter 1.

14. As my formulation suggests, I am thinking for instance of Prasenjit Duara, *Rescuing History from the Nation: Questioning Narratives of Modern China* (Chicago: University of Chicago Press, 1995).

15. Asō Isoji, *Edo bungaku to Chūgoku bungaku* (Tokyo: Sanseidō, 1950). By way of briefly introducing Asō's conception of "Japanification," see his discussion on p. 66 of the eighteenth-century *yomihon* author Tsuga Teishō vis-à-vis the far better-known Ueda Akinari.

16. Nakamura Yukihiko, "*Suikoden* to kinsei bungaku," in *Nakamura Yukihiko chojutsushū*, vol. 7 (Tokyo: Chūō kōronsha, 1984), 214–68; Takashima Toshio, *Suikoden to Nihonjin: Edo kara Shōwa made* (Tokyo: Taishūkan shoten, 1991). Here grateful mention should also be made of the 2010 edition of *Ajia yūgaku*, edited by Inada Atsunobu, whose provocative title—"*Suikoden* no shōgeki"—might be taken as an exploration of either the "impact" of the novel on Japanese literary culture (the actual focus of most of the articles in the collection) or the sense of "shock" the subversive novel imparted to its readers.

17. Saitō Mareshi, *Kanbunmyaku no kindai: Shin-matsu = Meiji no bungakuken* (Nagoya: Nagoya daigaku shuppankai, 2005).

18. Fraleigh, *Plucking Chrysanthemums*, introduction. Fraleigh's argument builds on Victor Mair, "Buddhism and the Rise of the Written Vernacular in East Asia: The Making of National Languages," *Journal of Asian Studies* 53, no. 3 (1994): 707–51.

19. Gideon Toury, *Descriptive Translation Studies and Beyond* (Amsterdam: John Benjamins, 2012), 17–23.

20. *Shina bungaku taikō* and the discursive environment in which it emerged are the subject of chapter 3.

21. Emanuel Pastreich, *The Observable Mundane: Vernacular Chinese and the Emergence of a Literary Discourse on Popular Narrative in Edo Japan* (Seoul: Seoul National University Press, 2011).

22. Patrick Caddeau's excellent study of Hagiwara Hiromichi's engagement with the *Genji* is similarly structured as a narrative of increasingly literary readings of Heian

literature that are contrasted with the ethical and philological concerns of writers like Andō Tameakira, Motoori Norinaga, and others; *Appraising Genji: Literary Criticism and Cultural Anxiety in the Age of the Last Samurai* (Albany: State University of New York Press, 2006).

23. Michael C. Brownstein, "From *Kokugaku* to *Kokubungaku*: Canon-Formation in the Meiji Period," *Harvard Journal of Asiatic Studies* 47, no. 2 (1987): 435–60; Haruo Shirane, "Curriculum and Competing Canons," in *Inventing the Classics: Modernity, National Identity, and Japanese Literature*, ed. Haruo Shirane and Tomi Suzuki (Stanford, Calif.: Stanford University Press, 2000), 220–49.

24. Karen Laura Thornber, *Empire of Texts in Motion: Chinese, Korean, and Taiwanese Transculturations of Japanese Literature* (Cambridge, Mass.: Harvard University Asia Center, 2009).

25. See Satoru Hashimoto, "1900, February 10: Liang Qichao's Suspended Translation and the Future of Chinese New Fiction," in *A New Literary History of Modern China*, ed. David Der-wei Wang (Cambridge, Mass.: Belknap Press, 2017), 161–66.

26. Kōno Kimiko, Wiebke Denecke, and Jinnō Hidenori, eds., *Nihon "bun"gakushi*, 2 vols. (Tokyo: Bensei shuppan, 2015).

27. P. F. Kornicki, "The Survival of Tokugawa Fiction in the Meiji Period," *Harvard Journal of Asiatic Studies* 41, no. 2 (1981): 461–82; Atsuko Ueda, *Concealment of Politics, Politics of Concealment: The Production of "Literature" in Meiji Japan* (Stanford, Calif.: Stanford University Press, 2007); Jonathan E. Zwicker, *Practices of the Sentimental Imagination: Melodrama, the Novel, and the Social Imaginary in Nineteenth-Century Japan* (Cambridge, Mass.: Harvard East Asia Center, 2006).

28. And from Tansō we could undoubtedly go back even further, until finally arriving back at the *Book of Odes*, which were often interpreted allegorically as glimpses into the affairs of the states in which they were composed.

29. Saitō Mareshi has highlighted, for instance, the epistemological incongruity between the modern formulation "Sino-Japanese" and earlier dyads like *wakan*. Whereas "Sino-Japanese" highlights China and Japan as geographically and culturally bounded *entities*, for Saitō, *wakan* focuses on a *process*: in particular, a productive dialectic characterized by the absorption and contrast of particular texts and motifs; see *Kanbunmyaku no kindai*, chapter 1. At the risk of making a difficult concept even more esoteric, I think of it this way: if China and Japan are conceived of as the two halves of the yin-yang diagram, "Sino-Japanese" focuses on the border separating black from white, while *wakan* highlights their reconcilability as well as the presence of yang in yin and yin in yang.

30. Atsuko Ueda, *Concealment of Politics*, chapters 2 and 3.

31. References to and quotations from the original novel cite the particular edition of the novel in question (i.e., Jin Shengtan's Guanhuatang edition, the Rongyutang edition, etc.), which are briefly described in the following section and analyzed in greater detail throughout the study. For simple issues of plot summary, readers are also directed to the two English-language translations I've consulted: Sidney Shapiro, *Outlaws of the Marsh*, 3 vols. (Beijing: Foreign Languages Press, 1980) (100 chapters), and John and Alex Dent-Young, *The Marshes of Mount Liang*, 4 vols. (Hong Kong: Chinese University Press, 1994) (120 chapters).

32. The Song empire would be invaded by Jurchen forces from the north in 1125, and Huizong himself was captured and taken prisoner the following year. Incidentally,

the fall of the Northern Song and Huizong's humiliating capture by the Jurchens are both portrayed in Chen Chen's early-Qing *Sequel to "The Water Margin"* (*Shuihu houzhuan*).

33. Richard Gregg Irwin, *The Evolution of a Chinese Novel: Shui-hu chuan* (Cambridge, Mass.: Harvard University Press, 1953), 9–13.

34. Reprinted in *Shuihu zhuan ziliao huibian*, ed. Zhu Yixuan and Liu Yuchen (Tianjin: Nankai daxue chubanshe, 2002), 20.

35. For a summary and discussion of these plays, see Irwin, *Evolution of a Chinese Novel*, chapter 3. As scholars such as W. L. Idema, Stephen West, and Patricia Sieber have demonstrated, however, many of these "Yuan-period" works are available only in the form of Ming editions and are thus potentially more representative of Ming-period aesthetics and literary ideologies. See, for example, Patricia Sieber, *Theaters of Desire: Authors, Readers, and the Reproduction of Early Chinese Song-Drama, 1300–2000* (New York: Palgrave Macmillan, 2003).

36. A final source worth mentioning is the "simple story" (*pinghua*) *Xuanhe yishi* (Anecdotes of the Xuanhe period, thirteenth century?), a collection of tales surrounding the collapse of the Northern Song that includes rudimentary versions of well-known episodes from the later novel. As late as the fifteenth century, when the playwright and scion of the Ming imperial family Zhu Youdun (1379–1439) authored a series of plays about the outlaws, he described *Xuanhe yishi* as the most detailed account in existence. See W. L. Idema, *The Dramatic Oeuvre of Chu Yu-Tun (1379–1439)* (Leiden: Brill, 1985), 176–81.

37. The source that mentions Luo Guanzhong is *A Record of Ghosts, Continued* (*Luguibu xubian*) and identifies Luo as the author of several works of drama.

38. For example, once the novel was transplanted to Japan, the historian Seita Tansō accepted Jin's attribution to Shi Nai'an, whereas Kyokutei Bakin gravitated toward the Luo Guanzhong hypothesis (discussed in chapter 2).

39. For a summary of sixteenth-century literary library inventories that mention *Shuihu zhuan*, see Andrew Plaks, *The Four Masterworks of the Ming Novel* (Princeton, N.J.: Princeton University Press, 1987), 279–86.

40. The fact that one of the earliest editions of *Shuihu zhuan* was produced by the Ming Censorate is highly ironic in light of the fact that the novel was banned by the same government organ in the final years of the dynasty.

41. W. L. Idema, *Chinese Vernacular Fiction: The Formative Period* (Leiden: Brill, 1974), discusses this issue from the standpoint of publishing and material culture, while Plaks focuses on the sophisticated use of irony and symbolism in what he terms the sixteenth-century literary novel. Most recently, Scott Wentworth Gregory has analyzed the circumstances of production and possible social functions of the Wuding and Censorate editions of *Shuihu zhuan* in "'The Wuding Editions': Printing, Power, and Vernacular Fiction in the Ming Dynasty," *East Asian Publishing and Society* 7 (2017): 1–29.

42. Gregory, "'The Wuding Editions,'" 3.

43. David Rolston provides a descriptive bibliography for *Shuihu zhuan* and other works of late imperial Chinese fiction in *How to Read the Chinese Novel* (Princeton, N.J.: Princeton University Press, 1990). This has been my main source of information for the preceding summary.

44. David Damrosch, *What Is World Literature?* (Princeton, N.J.: Princeton University Press, 2003), 12.

45. Contemporary scholars of late imperial Chinese fiction distinguish between two major genealogical lines in the diffusion of *Shuihu zhuan*: simplified recensions (*jianben*) and full recensions (*fanben*). The *jianben* are broadly characterized by lower-quality printing, simpler language, and the inclusion of more discrete episodes: a result, perhaps, of popular demand for more adventures. The *fanben*, by contrast, contain fewer episodes but make use of more elaborate language. At present, most scholars believe that the full recensions of *Shuihu zhuan* came first and the simplified recensions were abridgements and extrapolations of these preexisting narratives.

46. As evidenced by Edo-period descriptions of Jin Shengtan as the true creator (*sakusha*) of *Shuihu zhuan*, or Kōda Rohan's confident declaration as late as 1923 that "all readers" were familiar with the commentator's work, margins between text and paratext were permeable until fairly recently.

47. Michael Emmerich, *The Tale of Genji: Translation, Canonization, and World Literature* (New York: Columbia University Press, 2013), 10.

48. Emmerich, *The Tale of Genji*, 11; emphasis added.

49. Other scholars have been hesitant to accept Emmerich's presentation of these items as constitutive, rather than reflective, of canonical status. See Rebekah Clements and Peter Kornicki, "The Latter Days of the *Genji*," *Monumenta Nipponica* 64, no. 2 (2009): 363–72, and Emmerich's response to their criticism, *The Tale of Genji*, 52.

50. See Linda Hutcheon's rebuttal of fidelity criticism and defense of "adaptations as adaptations" in *A Theory of Adaptation*, 2nd ed. (London: Routledge, 2013), chapter 1.

1. SINOPHILIA, SINOPHOBIA, AND VERNACULAR PHILOLOGY IN EARLY MODERN JAPAN

1. Nakamura Yukihiko, "*Suikoden* to kinsei bungaku," in *Nakamura Yukihiko chojutsushū*, vol. 7 (Tokyo: Chūō kōronsha, 1984), 214–68.

2. Preface to Suyama Nantō, *Chūgi Suikodenkai*, in *Tōwa jisho ruishū*, ed. Nagasawa Kikuya, vol. 3 (Tokyo: Kyūko shoin, 1970).

3. Keiko Suzuki, "The Making of Tōjin Construction of the Other in Early Modern Japan," *Asian Folklore Studies* 66 (2007): 83–105; Ronald Toby, "Carnival of the Aliens: Korean Embassies in Edo-Period Art and Popular Culture," *Monumenta Nipponica* 41, no. 4 (1986): 415–56.

4. Yanagisawa Kien, *Hitorine*, in *Nihon koten bungaku taikei*, vol. 96 (Tokyo: Iwanami shoten, 1965), 81–82.

5. Yoshikawa Kōjirō, *Jinsai, Sorai, Norinaga: Three Classical Philosophers of Mid-Tokugawa Japan*, trans. Yūji Kikuchi (Tokyo: Tōhō gakkai, 1983), 203–5.

6. *Ga* and *zoku* had never occupied fully mutually exclusive terrain in either China or Japan, and they were often invoked in order to delineate fluid hierarchies in both genre and style. Though often deployed pejoratively, the aesthetic category of *zoku* had acquired an artistically authoritative presence of its own by the beginning of

the eighteenth century in fields such as haikai, painting, and prose fiction. See Nakano Mitsutoshi, *Jūhasseiki no Edo bungei: Ga to zoku no seijuku* (Tokyo: Iwanami shoten, 1999).

7. I use the term "philology" cautiously. In his study of Chinese evidentiary scholarship (*kaozhengxue*) during the Qing period (1644–1911), Benjamin Elman provides a useful warning against conflating different conceptions of textual exegesis under the rubric "philology." The term's suggestions of a "purely" scholastic, politically disinterested agenda are particularly misleading in the early modern East Asian context, and Elman's caution is helpful in assessing the significance of Kanzan and Nantō with respect to their predecessors. See *From Philosophy to Philology: Intellectual and Social Aspects of Change in Late Imperial China* (Los Angeles: University of California Press, 2001), 30.

8. Maruyama Masao, *Studies in the Intellectual History of Tokugawa Japan*, trans. Mikiso Hane (Princeton, N.J.: Princeton University Press, 1974), 69–92.

9. Ōba Osamu, ed., *Hakusai shomoku*, 2 vols. (Fukita: Kansai daigaku tōzai gakujutsu kenkyūjo, 1972).

10. Tokuda Takeshi, *Nihon kinsei shōsetsu to Chūgoku shōsetsu* (Musashimurayamashi: Seishōdō, 1987), 9–22.

11. For an introduction to the content and structure of these works, see Komatsu Ken, *Chūgoku rekishi shōsetsu kenkyū* (Tokyo: Kyūko shoin, 2001).

12. From Yang Erzeng's late-Ming preface to *Dong Xi liang Jin yanyi* (Explication of the history of the Eastern and Western Jin), in *Guben xiaoshuo jicheng*, series 3, vols. 61–63 (Shanghai: Shanghai guji chubanshe, 1990).

13. Preface to *Tsūzoku Kō Min eiretsuden*, trans. Okajima Kanzan. The microfilm of the 1705 print is in the collection of the National Institute of Japanese Literature, Tokyo.

14. Included in volume 8 of Nagasawa, *Tōwa jisho ruishū*.

15. Yoshikawa Kōjirō, *Jinsai, Sorai, Norinaga*, 77–200; Emanuel Pastreich, "Grappling with Chinese Writing as a Material Language: Ogyū Sorai's *Yakubun sentei*," *Harvard Journal of Asiatic Studies* 61, no. 1 (2001): 119–70.

16. *Yakubun sentei* has been translated and annotated in Pastreich, "Grappling with Chinese Writing."

17. Kiri Paramore, *Japanese Confucianism: A Cultural History* (Cambridge: Cambridge University Press, 2016), 43–44.

18. A copy of *Yōjikaku* is preserved in the Special Collections, Waseda University Library, Waseda University, Tokyo. The "trap and snare" are a *Zhuangzi* reference to language's status as an intermediary that can be discarded once its object has been attained. For further discussion of this metaphor in the context of Sorai's more famous work, see Emanuel Pastreich, *The Observable Mundane: Vernacular Chinese and the Emergence of a Literary Discourse on Popular Narrative in Edo Japan* (Seoul: Seoul National University Press, 2011), 143–46.

19. Dazai Shundai, *Sekihi*, in *Sorai gakuha*, ed. Rai Tsutomu, vol. 37 of *Nihon shisō taikei* (Tokyo: Iwanami shoten, 1972), 146.

20. Amenomori Hōshū, *Kissō chawa*, in *Amenomori Hōshū zensho*, ed. Kansai Daigaku Tōzai Gakujutsu Kenkyūjo Nitchū Bunka Kōryū no Kenkyū Rekishihan (Suita: Kansai daigaku shuppan kōhōbu, 1980), 138.

21. Presumably the classical scholar Kinoshita Jun'an (1621–1699), under whom Hōshū, Muro Kyūsō (1658–1734), and Arai Hakuseki (1657–1725) studied.

22. Amenomori, *Kissō chawa*, 189–90.

23. This quotation is taken from a letter to Hori Keizan (1688–1757). The letter is reproduced in *Ogyū Sorai*, in *Nihon shisō taikei*, vol. 36, ed. Yoshikawa Kōjirō (Tokyo: Iwanami shoten, 1973), 527–33; emphasis added.

24. *Ogyū Sorai*, 526.

25. *Bendō* in *Ogyū Sorai*, 200.

26. The letter, "Addressed to Master Kōkoku," is reproduced in *Ogyū Sorai*, 545–46.

27. Pastreich, *The Observable Mundane*, 121–50. Nakamura Yukihiko, "Kogidō no shōsetsuka tachi," in *Nakamura Yukihiko chojutsushū*, vol. 8 (Tokyo: Chūō kōronsha, 1984).

28. Yoshikawa Kōjirō, *Jinsai, Sorai, Norinaga*, 203.

29. Yanagisawa, *Hitorine*, 192.

30. *Tōwa san'yō* is included in Nagasawa, *Tōwa jisho ruishū*, vol. 3.

31. For a discussion of the language of *Tōwa san'yō* and its relationship to various Chinese dialects, see Richard VanNess Simmons, "A Second Look at the *Tōwa san'yō*: Clues to the Nature of the *Guanhuah* Studied by Japanese in the Early Eighteenth Century," *Journal of the American Oriental Society* 117, no. 3 (1997): 419–26.

32. Okajima, *Tōwa san'yō*, 117–20.

33. Okajima, *Tōwa san'yō*, 291.

34. Okajima Kanzan, *Tō'on gazoku gorui*, in Nagasawa, *Tōwa jisho ruishū*, vol. 6, 301.

35. Okajima, *Tōwa san'yō*, 1–5. In deciphering the script, I was greatly assisted by Okada Kesao's transcription in *Edo igengo sesshoku: Rango, Tōwa to kindai Nihongo* (Tokyo: Kasama shoin, 2006), 228.

36. Literally, as a *benbō* (Ch. *bianmao*)—the cap and forelocks that are discarded when a child comes of age. This is a set phrase for something of no use.

37. Okajima, *Tōwa san'yō*, 7–9.

38. In the preface to the translation, Gitan wrote, "Last autumn, I requested explicated translations of *Tales of Valor* and *Shuihu zhuan* that could be made available to all. This spring, *Tales of Valor* was finished and taken to press first."

39. Preface to the 1719 *Taiheiki engi*, in the collection of the National Archives of Japan, Tokyo.

40. See volume 13 of Nagasawa, *Tōwa jisho ruishū*, 276–78. Emanuel Pastreich discusses Hakku's interest in *Shuihu zhuan* and describes the contents of the lectures in *The Observable Mundane*, 189–94.

41. Nakamura Yukihiko, "Kogidō no shōsetsuka tachi," 200–201.

42. Suyama, *Chūgi Suikodenkai*, 1.

43. Romanization is based on the kana glosses Nantō provides and not on modern (Mandarin) pronunciation.

44. Suyama, *Chūgi Suikodenkai*, 8.

45. Suyama, *Chūgi Suikodenkai*, 8.

46. Suyama, *Chūgi Suikodenkai*, 6; emphasis in original. Strictly speaking, Jin Shengtan's edition consists of seventy chapters with five fascicles of prefatorial material.

47. Nantō's stern dismissal of Jin Shengtan is even more remarkable in light of its apparent hypocrisy. As Nakamura Aya, building on earlier work by Takashima

Toshio, has shown, several of the individual entries in *Suikodenkai* do not appear in the one-hundred-twenty-chapter edition of the novel and are found instead in Jin Shengtan's seventy-chapter edition! See Nakamura Aya, "*Suikoden* wakokubon to tsūzokubon—*Chūgi Suikodenkai* hanrei to Kin Seitan hon o megutte," in Suikoden *no shōgeki*, in *Ajia yūgaku*, no. 131, ed. Inada Atsunobu (Tokyo: Bensei shuppan, 2010), 113–24.

48. Suyama, *Chūgi Suikodenkai*, 3.

49. Writing of the *kundoku* text attributed to Kanzan, Nantō states, "The first ten chapters of *Shuihu zhuan* have been glossed and annotated by Okajima Kanzan. There are, however, mistakes in his work, which I have corrected in my explication. Please do not construe this as my being eager to point out faults in my predecessors. I only wish to benefit the readers of the text" (Suyama, *Chūgi Suikodenkai*, 7).

50. Suyama, *Chūgi Suikodenkai*, 7.

51. Again, romanization is based on the kana provided by Nantō and does not reflect modern pronunciation.

52. Kunjo is the monk Etsū—a native of Nagasaki and contact of Ogyū Sorai; see Takashima Toshio, *Suikoden to Nihonjin: Edo kara Shōwa made* (Tokyo: Taishūkan shoten, 1991), 77.

53. Suyama, *Chūgi Suikodenkai*, 11.

54. Watanabe Kazuyasu, *Meiji shisōshi: Jukyōteki dentō to kindai ninshikiron* (Tokyo: Perikansha, 1985), 343–56.

55. Murakami Masataka, "Zokugokai shōkō," in *Nihongo no rekishi chiri kōzō*, ed. Katō Masanobu (Tokyo: Meiji shoin, 1997); William David Fleming, "The World Beyond the Walls: Morishima Chūryō (1756–1810) and the Development of Late Edo Fiction" (Ph.D. diss., Harvard University, 2011), 424–30.

56. Shigeno Yasutsugu, "Kangaku yoroshiku seisoku ikka o mōke shōnen shūsai o erami Shin-koku ni ryūgaku seshimu-beki ronsetsu," *Tōkyō gakushi kaiin zasshi* 1 (1879): 76–93.

57. 1829 edition of *Sentetsu sōdan kōhen* in the National Diet Library, Tokyo.

58. In Nakamura's translation, *Saikoku risshihen* (Tales of ambition from Western countries).

59. Higashi Kan'ichi, *Nihon risshihen*, fascicle 7 (1882).

2. HISTORIES OF READING AND NONREADING

1. Both the *wakokubon* and the *tsūzokubon* have been attributed to Okajima Kanzan, although there is little substantial evidence for either attribution, and modern scholars are unanimous in arguing that Kanzan could not have been involved in both projects. For this vexed question of attribution, see Nakamura Aya, "*Suikoden* wakokubon to tsūzokubon—*Chūgi Suikodenkai* hanrei to Kin Seitan hon o megutte," in Suikoden *no shōgeki*, in *Ajia yūgaku*, no. 131, ed. Inada Atsunobu (Tokyo: Bensei shuppan, 2010), 113–24.

2. Takashima Toshio, *Suikoden to Nihonjin: Edo kara Shōwa made* (Tokyo: Taishūkan shoten, 1991), 85–103. It is with considerable trepidation that I use the term "translation" to refer to the *tsūzokubon* and other rewritings of *Shuihu zhuan*. As Rebekah Clements has demonstrated, early modern writers employed a wide range of

overlapping terms to denote the act of translation. The deployment of these terms was by no means standardized or universally agreed upon, and the difficulty of determining an adequate equivalent for "translation" is only compounded by the instability of the term in English. *Yaku*—the most common equivalent for translation in general—has a broader range than is implied by the English term and, in the case of *Shuihu zhuan*, could be applied to *kundoku* editions of the original Chinese text like the aforementioned *wakokubon*, popularizations (*tsūzoku*) written in a combination of kana and Sinographs, and even simplified digests like the two *Shuihu zhuan*–themed *kibyōshi* published by Santō Kyōden in 1793. See Rebekah Clements, *A Cultural History of Translation in Early Modern Japan* (Cambridge: Cambridge University Press, 2015), 10–13, and Judy Wakabayashi, "The Reconceptualization of Translation from Chinese in 18th-Century Japan," in *Translation and Cultural Change*, ed. Eva Hung (Amsterdam: John Benjamins, 2005), 119–45.

3. Three well-known examples being Takebe Ayatari's early *yomihon*, *Honchō Suikoden* (*The Water Margin* of our land, 1773); Santō Kyōden's later *yomihon*, *Chūshin Suikoden* (A treasury of loyal retainers from *The Water Margin*, 1799–1801); and the *Suikoden gōketsu hyaku-hachi nin no hitori* (One hundred eight heroes of *The Water Margin*) series of *musha-e* prints by Kuniyoshi.

4. A copy of the board, in the possession of the National Diet Library, Tokyo, can be viewed at http://dl.ndl.go.jp/info:ndljp/pid/1310623.

5. The anecdote comes from a letter included in the third fascicle of Gensei's *Sōzanshū* and is discussed in Nakamura Yukihiko, "*Suikoden* to kinsei bungaku," in *Nakamura Yukihiko chojutsushū*, vol. 7 (Tokyo: Chūō kōronsha, 1984), 214–68.

6. Unless, of course, the *wakokubon* that appeared twenty-three years later was indeed Kanzan's work.

7. Kien is discussed later in this chapter. For Bakin's bibliographic quest, see Kanda Masayuki, "*Suikoden* no shohon to Bakin," in *Fukkō suru Hakkenden*, ed. Suwa Haruo and Takada Mamoru (Tokyo: Bensei shuppan, 2008), 249–86.

8. Kyokutei Bakin, *Gendō hōgen* (Tokyo: Yoshikawa kōbunkan, 1993), 260.

9. For a discussion of *Shinpen Suiko gaden*, see Takashima, *Suikoden to Nihonjin*, 172–82.

10. Michael Emmerich, *The Tale of Genji: Translation, Canonization, and World Literature* (New York: Columbia University Press, 2013), 14.

11. Emmerich, *The Tale of Genji*, 11; emphasis added.

12. Emmerich, *The Tale of Genji*, 23.

13. Linda Hutcheon, *A Theory of Adaptation*, 2nd ed. (London: Routledge, 2013), chapter 1.

14. See, for example, Terry Eagleton, *Literary Theory: An Introduction* (Oxford: Blackwell Publishing, 1983), 10–16.

15. How many nonspecialists, for example, have read Fang Ruhao's *Anecdotal History of Buddhist Monks* (*Chanzhen yishi*)? A summary of Tenkai's holdings is provided in Nagasawa Kikuya, ed., *Nikkōsan Tenkaizō shuyō kosho kaidai* (Nikkō: Nikkōsan Rinnōji, 1966).

16. Jonathan E. Zwicker, *Practices of the Sentimental Imagination: Melodrama, the Novel, and the Social Imaginary in Nineteenth-Century Japan* (Cambridge, Mass.: Harvard East Asia Center, 2006), 135.

17. William D. Fleming, "Strange Tales from Edo: *Liaozhai zhiyi* in Early Modern Japan," *Sino-Japanese Studies* 20 (2013): 77.

18. Amenomori Hōshū, *Kissō chawa*, in *Amenomori Hōshū zensho*, ed. Kansai Daigaku Tōzai Gakujutsu Kenkyūjo Nitchū Bunka Kōryū no Kenkyū Rekishihan (Suita: Kansai daigaku shuppan kōhōbu), 157–58.

19. *Shuihu zhizhuan pinglin*, 3 vols., in *Guben xiaoshuo jicheng* (Shanghai: Shanghai guji chubanshe, 1990), 94.

20. *Shuihu zhizhuan pinglin*, 220–21.

21. The former category would include *Shuihu zhuan*'s traveling companion, *Romance of the Three Kingdoms* (*Sanguo yanyi*), which also contains a self-descriptor as a *yanyi*, or "explication," of official historiography.

22. Yu's rough contemporary Xiong Damu (1506–1578) presented this goal most bluntly when he described his *Da Song zhongxing tongsu yanyi* (Explication of the restoration of the great Song dynasty) as a work that will "make it so that even the most ignorant men and women will be able to understand the meaning [of the histories]"; reprinted in *Ming Qing shanben xiaoshuo congkan* (Taipei: Tianyi chubanshe, 1985).

23. My formulation is inspired by Atsuko Ueda's statement *shōsetsu* ≠ "fiction" in *Concealment of Politics, Politics of Concealment: The Production of "Literature" in Meiji Japan* (Stanford, Calif.: Stanford University Press, 2007).

24. David Rolston, *Traditional Chinese Fiction and Fiction Commentary: Reading and Writing Between the Lines* (Stanford, Calif.: Stanford University Press, 1997), introduction and chapter 1.

25. Rolston, *Traditional Chinese Fiction*, 12. Much of the information in the following section has been taken from Rolston.

26. Kōda Rohan, "Kin Seitan" [Jin Shengtan], *Bungei shunjū* 5, no. 6 (1923): 2.

27. Rolston, *Traditional Chinese Fiction*, 4.

28. And in truth the situation is even more complicated, since several publishing houses—including the Hangzhou-based Rongyutang publishing house—published a version of the novel bearing Li Zhuowu's name.

29. For other descriptions of editions of *Shuihu zhuan*, see Ōba Osamu, ed., *Hakusai shomoku*, 2 vols. (Fukita: Kansai daigaku tōzai gakujutsu kenkyūjo, 1972).

30. Yanada Zeigan, *Zeigan shū*, ed. Tokuda Takeshi (Tokyo: Perikansha, 1985), 90. Wang Wangru (active mid-seventeenth century) published another critical edition of *Shuihu zhuan* in 1657, which added his own postchapter discussions to the Jin Shengtan–edited text.

31. Minagawa Kien, *Kien bunshū*, ed. Takahashi Hiromi (Tokyo: Perikansha, 1986), fascicle 7.

32. John C.Y. Wang, *Chin Sheng-t'an* (New York: Twayne, 1972), provides a thorough description of Jin's literary activities.

33. Li Zhi [Zhuowu], *Fenshu* (Beijing: Zhonghua shuju, 1974), 303–7.

34. Lu Lin, ed., *Jin Shengtan quanji* (Nanjing: Fenghuang chubanshe, 2008), 17.

35. For Jin's full description of Shi Nai'an, see John C.Y. Wang's translation in David Rolston, ed., *How to Read the Chinese Novel* (Princeton, N.J.: Princeton University Press, 1990), 131.

36. Lu Lin, *Jin Shengtan quanji*, 926.

37. Lu Lin, *Jin Shengtan quanji*, 643.

38. My primary sources of information about Tansō's life have been Tokuda Takeshi, ed., *Shōseihai* (Tokyo: Yumani shobō, 1976), and Nakamura Yukihiko, "Kaku-retaru hihyōka: Seita Tansō no hihyōteki gyōseki," in *Nakamura Yukihiko chojutsushū*, vol. 1 (Tokyo: Chūō kōronsha, 1982).

39. Tokuda, *Shōseihai*, 13–15. In the passage I elided, Tansō continues his list of figures at the Song court and their fictional avatars in *Shuihu zhuan*.

40. Seita Tansō, *Kujakurō hikki*, ed. Nakamura Yukihiko et al., in *Nihon koten bungaku taikei*, vol. 96 (Tokyo: Iwanami shoten, 1965), 299.

41. Lu Lin, *Jin Shengtan quanji*, 22.

42. Seita Tansō, *Suikoden hihyōkai*, in *Tōwa jisho ruishū*, ed. Nagasawa Kikuya, vol. 3 (Tokyo: Kyūko shoin, 1970), 345–46; emphasis in original.

43. Seita Tansō, *Suikoden hihyōkai*, 354.

44. Marginal comment in Seita Tansō, owner, *Diwu caizishu Shi Nai'an Shuihu zhuan*, fascicle 3.

45. The first ruler of the Song, Zhao Kuangyin, was succeeded by his younger brother, Guangyi, instead of by one of his two surviving sons. Taizong's legitimacy was brought into question by both his unusual succession and by rumors that he had schemed to murder his older brother. In their readings of *Shuihu zhuan*, both Jin Shengtan and Tansō claimed that Song Jiang was responsible for the death of Chao Gai. They disagreed, however, about the significance of this interpretation. For Jin, Song Jiang's alleged culpability served as evidence of his ruthless ambition; for Tansō, Chao Gai's death and Song Jiang's ascension were hints toward the allegorical nature of the novel. For information surrounding Taizong's succession, see F. W. Mote, *Imperial China: 900–1800* (Cambridge, Mass.: Harvard University Press, 1999).

46. Seita Tansō, *Suikoden hihyōkai*, 347.

47. See John C.Y. Wang's translation in Rolston, *How to Read the Chinese Novel*, 134.

48. Lu Lin, *Jin Shengtan quanji*, 749.

49. As Nakamura Yukihiko noted, Tansō's contemporary Tsuga Teishō (1718–1794) also drew connections between characters from *Shuihu zhuan* and figures at the Song court; Nakamura Yukihiko, "*Suikoden* to kinsei bungaku," in *Nakamura Yukihiko chojutsushū*, vol. 7 (Tokyo: Chūō kōronsha, 1984), 235–37.

50. Seita Tansō, *Suikoden hihyōkai*, 352.

51. Allan H. Barr, "The Later Classical Tale," in *The Columbia History of Chinese Literature*, ed. Victor H. Mair (New York: Columbia University Press, 2001), 689.

52. Hu Yinglin, *Shaoshi shanfang bicong* (Shanghai: Shanghai guji chubanshe, 2009), 437.

53. Xie Zhaozhe, *Wu za zu* (Beijing: Zhonghua shuju, 1959), 447.

54. See, for example, William Fleming's discussion of Tansō's rough contemporary Morishima Chūryō (1756–1810), "The World Beyond the Walls: Morishima Chūryō (1756–1810) and the Development of Late Edo Fiction" (Ph.D. diss., Harvard University, 2011), 444. Chūryō quoted Xie Zhaozhe in the preface to his *yomihon The Tale of Izumi Chikahira*, claiming that he took Xie's prescription as his mantra in fiction writing.

55. Seita Tansō, *Suikoden hihyōkai*, 479.

56. Marginal comment to Seita Tansō, *Diwu caizishu Shi Nai'an Shuihu zhuan*, fascicle 3.

57. Lu Lin, *Jin Shengtan quanji*, 30–31.

58. A claim developed nearly a century later by Hagiwara Hiromichi in his exegesis of the *Genji*. See Patrick W. Caddeau, *Appraising Genji: Literary Criticism and Cultural Anxiety in the Age of the Last Samurai* (Albany: State University of New York Press, 2006).

59. Seita Tansō, *Suikoden hihyōkai*, 439.

60. Seita Tansō, *Suikoden hihyōkai*, 502.

61. Seita Tansō, *Suikoden hihyōkai*, 434.

62. Glynne Walley, *Good Dogs: Edification, Entertainment, and Kyokutei Bakin's* Nansō Satomi hakkenden (Ithaca, N.Y.: Cornell University East Asia Program, 2017), chapter 4.

63. Walley, *Good Dogs*, 156–58.

64. *Shinpen Suiko gaden*, fascicle 1 (1805), in Special Collections, Waseda University Library, Waseda University, Tokyo.

65. These are all claims made in Jin's *dufa* essay in the prefatorial material to the Guanhuatang edition.

66. Ro Shungi is the Japanese pronunciation of Lu Junyi. Like its homophone, the pronunciation of 鶏鶲 is *junyi* in Chinese and *shungi* in Japanese.

67. Making 俊義.

68. Kyokutei Bakin, *Gendō hōgen*, 252.

69. For additional support, Bakin pointed to an earlier collection of anecdotes called *Xuanhe yishi* (Anecdotal history of the Xuanhe period, thirteenth century?), which provides the story of the Liangshan outlaws in capsule form and served as a source for the later novel. In *Xuanhe yishi*, Lu Junyi's name is given as Lu Jinyi 盧進義, suggesting, Bakin claimed, that the author of the novel had deliberately changed the character's name to provide a clue toward his later demise. See *Da Song xuanhe yishi*, ed. Zhou Jialu (Changsha: Yuelu shushe, 1993), 252.

70. Kyokutei Bakin, *Gendō hōgen*, 253. The reference to lifting one corner is, of course, from Confucius's description of the ideal student in *Analects* 7.8.

71. Kyokutei Bakin, *Gendō hōgen*, 251.

72. Kyokutei Bakin, *Nansō Satomi hakkenden*, ed. Hamada Keisuke, vol. 11 (Tokyo: Shinchōsha, 2004), 11.

73. Walley, *Good Dogs*, 123–26.

74. Kyokutei Bakin, *Gendō hōgen*, 13.

75. Kyokutei Bakin, *Keisei Suikoden*, fascicle 8; woodblock edition in Special Collections, Waseda University Library, Waseda University, Tokyo.

76. Kanda, "*Suikoden* no shohon to Bakin," 274–77.

77. Referring to the characters Hong Xin 洪信 and Wang Jin 王進, respectively.

78. Bakin refers to the key roles in traditional Chinese theater: the female lead 旦 (*dan*), the male lead 末 (*mo*), and the clown 淨 (*jing*).

79. Kyokutei Bakin, letter to Tonomura Yasumori, in Kyokutei Bakin, *Bakin shokan shūsei*, ed. Shibata Mitsuhiko and Kanda Masayuki, vol. 6 (Tokyo: Yagi shoten, 2003), 192–93.

80. *Chūshin Suikoden* is included in volume 15 of Santō Kyōden, *Santō Kyōden zenshū*, ed. Mizuno Minoru et al. (Tokyo: Perikansha, 1992).

81. *Chūshin Suikoden* was not, however, the first time Kyōden had engaged *Shuihu zhuan*. In 1793, he published two short *kibyōshi* providing a summary (which Kyōden termed a translation [*yaku*]) of the first twelve chapters of the novel. The

two *kibyōshi*, *Ryōzan ippodan* and *Tengō suiyōryū*, are included in volume 3 of *Santō Kyōden zenshū*.

82. *Chūshin Suikoden* is preserved in *Santō Kyōden zenshū*, vol. 15.

83. For information about Kyōden's sources in the composition of *Chūshin Suikoden*, see Inoue Keiji, "Kyōden *Chūshin Suikoden* to *Suikoden* sanshu," in Suikoden *no shōgeki*, ed. Inada Atsunobu, 150–59 (Tokyo: Bensei shuppan, 2010).

84. For instance, when the villainous Ono Sadakurō coerces a corrupt doctor into giving him a sleeping elixir that he will use to steal a convoy of gifts intended for the shogun, he reminds him that the elixir is "the same one used by the gallants of Mount Liang during the Song dynasty"; see *Santō Kyōden zenshū*, 145.

85. *Santō Kyōden zenshū*, 93.

86. See Keith McMahon, *Causality and Containment in Seventeenth-Century Chinese Fiction* (Leiden: Brill, 1988), 51–56.

87. Lu Lin, *Jin Shengtan quanji*, 292.

88. *Santō Kyōden zenshū*, vol. 15, 87.

89. Inge Klompmakers, *Of Brigands and Bravery: Kuniyoshi's Heroes of the* Suikoden (Leiden: Hotei, 2016), 22–25.

90. Klompmakers, *Of Brigands and Bravery*, 114–15.

91. Sarah E. Thompson, *Tattoos in Japanese Prints* (Boston: MFA Publications, 2017).

92. Klompmakers helpfully includes a list of the thirty-three characters who were not painted. The only other even minutely memorable characters left out of the series are "Small Whirlwind" Chai Jin, who acts as a patron for the outlaws, and the warrior chief Huyan Zhuo.

93. There is evidence that Kuniyoshi created a draft for a print of at least ten other heroes, including Song Jiang, but these were not included in the original series; see Klompmakers, *Of Brigands and Bravery*, 30.

94. David Damrosch, *What Is World Literature?* (Princeton, N.J.: Princeton University Press, 2003), introduction and chapter 1.

3. JUSTIFYING THE MARGINS

1. Reprinted in A Ying, *Wan Qing wenxue congchao: Xiaoshuo xiqu yanjiu juan* (Beijing: Zhonghua shuju, 1960), 125.

2. The two essays have been translated by Gek Nai Cheng in Kirk Denton, ed., *Modern Chinese Literary Thought: Writings on Literature, 1893–1945* (Stanford, Calif.: Stanford University Press, 1996), 71–81.

3. For a discussion of these stylistic and thematic changes, see Chen Pingyuan, *Zhongguo xiaoshuo xushi moshi de zhuanbian* (Shanghai: Shanghai renmin chubanshe, 1988).

4. A Ying, *Wan Qing wenxue congchao*, 125–26.

5. Incidentally, "wedge" (Jp. *kesshi*, Ch. *xiezi*) is the same word that Jin Shengtan used to describe the introductory chapter of the Guanhuatang edition of *Shuihu zhuan*.

6. Itō Gingetsu, preface to *Shin'yaku Suikoden* (Tokyo: Hidaka Yūrindō, 1908), 1–2.

7. Itō, *Shin'yaku Suikoden*, 3; emphasis added.

8. To clarify terminology at the outset, I am employing the admittedly cumbersome "Chinese-literature historiography" as a translation of the term *Shina bungakushi*

to distinguish it from both Japanese-literature historiography (*kokubungakushi*, *Nihon bungakushi*) and Chinese-literature historiography written by Chinese historians (Ch. *wenxueshi*). I translate *bungakushi* as "literary historiography" rather than "literary history" because most of the authors discussed in this chapter included lengthy introductions to the concept of "literary history" before turning attention to the texts themselves. As Mikami Sanji and Takatsu Kuwasaburō noted in their seminal *Nihon bungakushi* of 1890, European historians could assume that their audiences were familiar with the concept of literary history, while Japanese historians could not.

9. Presumably Kitamura Saburō's *Sekai hyakketsuden*, discussed earlier.

10. Di's argument is reprinted in Zhu Yixuan and Liu Yuchen, eds., *Shuihu zhuan ziliao huibian* (Tianjin: Nankai daxue chubanshe, 2002), 339. The Buddhist-inflected *shangcheng* (highest conveyance) was also used by Liang Qichao to describe the potentially uplifting effects of the novel; see Denton, *Modern Chinese Literary Thought*, 74–81.

11. Lydia H. Liu, *Translingual Practice: Literature, National Culture, and Translated Modernity—China, 1900–1937* (Stanford, Calif.: Stanford University Press, 1995), 8.

12. Watanabe Kazuyasu, *Meiji shisōshi: Jukyōteki dentō to kindai ninshikiron* (Tokyo: Perikansha, 1985), 343–56.

13. As my description suggests, I have little interest in determining who composed the "first" history of Chinese literature. There was little consensus on what precisely constituted Chinese literature or even literature (*bungaku*) in general, and the contents of works with the title *Shina bungakushi* differ dramatically, making any claim to primacy difficult and, in my opinion, unnecessary.

14. Fujita Toyohachi, "Shina bungaku no tokushitsu," *Kōko bungaku* 1 (1896): 46–54.

15. Quoted in Miura Kanō, *Meiji no kangaku* (Tokyo: Kyūko shoin, 1998), 293.

16. Joshua A. Fogel, "The Sino-Japanese Controversy over *Shina* as a Toponym for China," in *The Cultural Dimensions of Sino-Japanese Relations: Essays on the Nineteenth and Twentieth Centuries*, 66–79 (Armonk, N.Y.: M.E. Sharpe, 1995); Stefan Tanaka, *Japan's Orient: Rendering Pasts into History* (Berkeley: University of California Press, 1993), 1–54.

17. Takayama Chogyū, "Shina bungaku no kachi," in *Chogyū zenshū*, ed. Saitō Shinsaku and Anezaki Masaharu, vol. 2 (Tokyo: Hakubunkan, 1912), 486. The article was originally published in 1897.

18. Saitō Mareshi, *Kanbunmyaku no kindai: Shin-matsu = Meiji no bungakuken* (Nagoya: Nagoya daigaku shuppankai, 2005), chapter 1.

19. In his study of nineteenth-century Chinese perceptions of Japan, Douglas Howland contrasts a "Chinese worldview based on hierarchy and unification to a Euro-American world view based on [ontological] equality and differentiation" (*Borders of Chinese Civilization: Geography and History at Empire's End* [Durham, N.C.: Duke University Press, 1996], 4).

20. Prasenjit Duara, *Rescuing History from the Nation: Questioning Narratives of Modern China* (Chicago: University of Chicago Press, 1995), 29.

21. Taguchi Ukichi, preface to *Shina bungakushi*, by Kojō Teikichi (Tokyo: Keizai zasshisha, 1897), 3.

22. Takayama, "Shina bungaku no kachi," 486–87.

23. For an excellent discussion of the history of the Koten Kōshūka, see Michael C. Brownstein, "From *Kokugaku* to *Kokubungaku*: Canon-Formation in the Meiji Period," *Harvard Journal of Asiatic Studies* 47, no. 2 (1987): 435–60.

24. Tomi Suzuki, "Gender and Genre: Modern Literary Histories and Women's Diary Literature," in *Inventing the Classics: Modernity, National Identity, and Japanese Literature*, ed. Haruo Shirane and Tomi Suzuki (Stanford, Calif.: Stanford University Press, 2000), 77.

25. Brownstein, "From *Kokugaku* to *Kokubungaku*," 455.

26. Mikami Sanji and Takatsu Kuwasaburō, preface to *Nihon bungakushi*, Meiji Taishō bungakushi shūsei, nos. 1–2 (Tokyo: Nihon tosho sentā, 1982), 10.

27. Ochiai Naobumi et al., eds., *Nihon bungaku zensho*, vol. 1, (Tokyo: Hakubunkan, 1890), "*Taketori monogatari* kaidai," 1. It is interesting to note that contrary to the claim that the novel was the last genre to be folded into the respectable frame of literature, early histories of Japanese literature describe an undeserved dominance of the novel in considerations of literary development. The preface of Mikami and Takatsu's *Nihon bungakushi*, for example, argued that "while the flourishing of the novel is certainly something to be happy about, it is, after all, only *one* type of *belles lettres* [*bibungaku*]."

28. Mikami and Takatsu, *Nihon bungakushi*, 3–4.

29. Mikami and Takatsu, *Nihon bungakushi*, 1.

30. Haga Yaichi and Tachibana Sensaburō, *Kokubungaku tokuhon* (Tokyo: Fuzanbō, 1890), よ-や.

31. Haga and Tachibana, *Kokubungaku tokuhon*, を-わ; Ochiai et al., "*Taketori monogatari* kaidai," 1.

32. Haga and Tachibana, *Kokubungaku tokuhon*, へ.

33. Quoted in Tomi Suzuki, "Gender and Genre," 76.

34. Haga and Tachibana, *Kokubungaku tokuhon*, わ-か.

35. Ochiai Naobumi, "Nihon bungaku no hitsuyō," in *Meiji bungaku zenshū*, vol. 44 (Tokyo: Chikuma shobō, 1984), 3.

36. Ochiai, "Nihon bungaku no hitsuyō," 3.

37. The cosmopolitan Ochiai could, of course, have quoted Socrates's dictum to "know thyself" but undoubtedly preferred to utilize an East Asian source.

38. For this reason, I am extremely reluctant to read Mikami and Takatsu's *Nihon bungakushi* as derivative and imitative of "Western models" of literature historiography. Despite their clear indebtedness to Western sources, even a brief survey of these early histories reveals the degree to which Japanese-literature historiographers questioned the suitability of applying Western theory to Japanese texts. Mikami and Takatsu, for instance, described their own work as a "compromise" (*sesshoku*) with Western historiographies, and throughout the work they argued that Japanese-literature historiography would, by definition, be different from its Western counterpart (7–8).

39. Brownstein, "From *Kokugaku* to *Kokubungaku*," 439–40.

40. Hippolyte Taine, *History of English Literature*, trans. H. Van Laun (New York: Holt, 1883), 10.

41. Memorably described by Taine as an area in which "rain, wind, and surge leave room for naught but [the] gloomy and melancholy thoughts" reflected in the literature of England; Taine, *History of English Literature*, 34.

42. Taine, *History of English Literature*, 1.

43. Mikami and Takatsu, *Nihon bungakushi*, 1–2; emphasis added.

44. Mikami and Takatsu, *Nihon bungakushi*, 8.

45. Hutcheson Macaulay Posnett, *Comparative Literature* (New York: Appleton, 1886), 4–5.

46. Posnett, *Comparative Literature*, 5–6; emphasis in original.

47. By way of example, Posnett argues that in Chinese drama, "the *dénoûment* is the triumph of virtue. Any play without a moral purpose is in Chinese eyes only a ridiculous work in which one can find no meaning." After telling the reader that the writers of frivolous Chinese plays are condemned to "hell (*ming-fou*)," Posnett points out that if these standards were to be applied universally, "Aristophanes, it is to be feared, stands condemned by Chinese judgment to a very lengthy experience of *ming-fou*" (*Comparative Literature*, 16).

48. Mikami and Takatsu, *Nihon bungakushi*, 2–3.

49. Mikami and Takatsu, *Nihon bungakushi*, 2.

50. Mikami and Takatsu, *Nihon bungakushi*, 11.

51. Mikami and Takatsu, *Nihon bungakushi*, 11.

52. Written 純文学.

53. Mikami and Takatsu, *Nihon bungakushi*, 13.

54. Posnett, *Comparative Literature*, 18–19.

55. Mikami and Takatsu, *Nihon bungakushi*, 19–20.

56. An observation identical down to the very details to Liang Qichao's argument for the reform of fiction in *Xin xiaoshuo*.

57. Mikami and Takatsu, *Nihon bungakushi*, 22.

58. Mikami and Takatsu, *Nihon bungakushi*, 26–27.

59. Haga and Tachibana, *Kokubungaku tokuhon*, を–わ.

60. Mikami and Takatsu, *Nihon bungakushi*, 26. At the precise moment "didacticism" (*kanzen chōaku*) was coming under fire for being inimical to the progress of "pure literature," historians conveniently discovered that these principles were rooted in continental influence.

61. Ochiai, "Nihon bungaku no hitsuyō," 4.

62. Matthew Fraleigh, *Plucking Chrysanthemums: Narushima Ryūhoku and Sinitic Literary Traditions in Modern Japan* (Cambridge, Mass.: Harvard University Asia Center, 2016), 4.

63. This taxonomic uncertainty is evidenced even in the modern American academic context. Matthew Fraleigh provides a highly instructive analysis of the posthumous vicissitudes of the Meiji *kanshi* poet Narushima Ryūhoku and his contemporaries through the Library of Congress classification system—a system in which they were regrouped as part of "Japanese literature" only in 2000; *Plucking Chrysanthemums*, 8–9.

64. Mikami and Takatsu, *Nihon bungakushi*, 11–12.

65. Mikami and Takatsu, *Nihon bungakushi*, 29.

66. Both quotations, for instance, come from the multivolume *Shina bungaku taikō* of 1897 edited by Ōmachi Keigetsu, Fujita Toyohachi, Taoka Reiun, Kubo Tenzui, Shirakawa Riyō, and Sasagawa Rinpū.

67. Tanaka, *Japan's Orient*, 108.

68. Takayama, "Shina bungaku no kachi," 485.

69. Kojō Teikichi, for instance, studied the Confucian canon as a young man with fellow Kyushu native Takezoe Shin'ichirō, and Kojima Kenkichirō spent time at Mishima Chūshū's Nishōgakusha academy before matriculating at Tōdai. In fact, in the field of literature historiography, the division between "classical" and "university" studies is misleading, since the Chinese literature track at Tōdai was helmed by educators like Chūshū, Nakamura Masanao, and Shimada Kōson.

70. Not only did the twin traditions of Japanese- and Chinese-literature historiography emerge from the same academic context but also many of the authors collaborated on parallel ventures. For instance, Ōmachi Keigetsu helmed the editorship of both the *Kokubungaku taikō* (three volumes, published 1896–1897) and the *Shina bungaku taikō*, which consisted of fifteen volumes and was published between 1897 and 1904. On the latter project, Ōmachi collaborated with Fujita Toyohachi, Taoka Reiun, Kubo Tenzui, Shirakawa Riyō, and Sasagawa Rinpū, who all wrote extensively on *Shina bungaku*.

71. Andō Hikotarō, *Nihonjin no Chūgokukan* (Tokyo: Keisō shobō, 1971), 155.

72. The institutionalization of Chinese-literature historiography as an academic discipline was mirrored (and likely enabled) by a boom in the publication of a wide range of Chinese literary texts in popular and accessible editions. Contra familiar narratives about the decline of Chinese learning in the Meiji period, Machida Saburō has written extensively about the role of major publishing houses in making Chinese texts of all varieties easily available. These included classic-centric series like the *Kanbun taikei* and *Kanseki kokujikai*, as well as endeavors such as the Hakubunkan publishing house–sponsored *Shina bungaku zensho* and *Teikoku hyakka zensho*, which included works of fiction and drama alongside more canonical works. See Machida Saburō, *Meiji no kangakusha-tachi* (Tokyo: Kenbun shuppan, 1998), 185–230.

73. See Rebekah Clements, "Suematsu Kenchō and the First English Translation of *Genji monogatari*: Translation, Tactics, and the 'Women's Question,' " *Japan Forum* 23, no. 1 (2011): 25–47.

74. Suematsu Kenchō, *Shina kobungaku ryakushi*, 2 vols. (Tokyo, 1882), 1.

75. Kubo Tenzui, *Shina bungakushi* (Tokyo: Jinbunsha, 1903), 1.

76. Kōtoku Shūsui, "*Sen-Shin bungaku to Shina bungakushi*," *Tōyō tetsugaku* 4, no. 6 (1897): 313–14.

77. Kojō Teikichi, "Yoron," in *Shina bungakushi*, 576–85 (Tokyo: Fuzanbō, 1902).

78. Kubo, *Shina bungakushi*, 3. Needless to say, Kubo did not agree with this assessment.

79. Kano Naoki, *Shina shōsetsu gikyoku shi* (Tokyo: Misuzu shobō, 1992), 3.

80. In an 1897 essay, for instance, Takayama Chogyū claimed that "recently, there have been numerous discussions of Chinese literature by young scholars of *kangaku*." The essay was published in the same year as Kojō Teikichi's *Shina bungakushi*, whose preface (by Inoue Tetsujirō) claims that "there have been a few histories of Japanese literature in recent years, but never have I heard of someone writing one for China." It should be noted that neither Takayama nor Inoue penned their own comprehensive history of Chinese literature; the authors themselves were relatively immodest in proclaiming the newness of their endeavor.

81. Kojima Kenkichirō, *Shina bungaku shikō* (Tokyo: Fuzanbō, 1912), 1–2.

82. Fujita Toyohachi, *Shina bungakushi* (Tokyo: Tōkyō senmon gakkō, 1895–1897), 1.

83. Kubo, *Shina bungakushi*, 2.
84. And its sister volume *Shina kaika shōshi* (A brief history of Chinese civilization) (Tokyo: Keizai zasshisha, 1887).
85. Taguchi, preface to *Shina bungakushi*, 2.
86. Shionoya On, preface to *Shina bungaku gairon kōwa* (Tokyo: Dai Nihon yūbenkai, 1919), 1.
87. Saitō Mareshi and Michael Weiner have discussed the prominence of the terms "comparison" and "competition" in the rhetoric of Meiji-period intellectuals interested in explaining the development of Japanese culture and the reasons for Japan's emergence as a beacon of civilization and enlightenment in the early modern era. See Saitō, *Kanbunmyaku no kindai*, chapter 1, and Michael Weiner, "The Invention of Identity: Race and Nation in Pre-War Japan," in *The Construction of Racial Identities in China and Japan*, ed. Frank Dikötter, 96–117 (Honolulu: University of Hawai'i Press, 1997).
88. From the preface to the multivolume *Shina bungaku taikō* (Compendium of Chinese literature) edited by Ōmachi Keigetsu, Fujita Toyohachi, Taoka Reiun, Kubo Tenzui, Shirakawa Riyō, and Sasagawa Rinpū. Each volume centered on a different author, but the same preface was reprinted in all volumes.
89. Kojō, *Shina bungakushi*, 9.
90. Taguchi, preface to *Shina bungakushi*, 3–4.
91. Ōmachi Keigetsu et al., preface to *Shina bungaku taikō* (Tokyo: Dai Nihon tosho kabushiki gaisha, 1897–1900), 4.
92. Inoue Tetsujirō, preface to *Shina bungakushi*, by Kojō Teikichi (Tokyo: Keizai zasshisha, 1897), 1.
93. Presumably Giles's *A History of Chinese Literature*, which was published in 1901.
94. Ichimura Sanjirō, preface to Kojima, *Shina bungaku shikō*, 2–3.
95. Inoue, preface to *Shina bungakushi*, 4. Knowledge of Inoue's histrionic tendencies encourages healthy skepticism about the preface's veracity, and Kojō's own preface provides a far less-titillating narrative. For the surprisingly vexed question of when and in what capacity Kojō spent time in China, see Du Yiwen, "Kojō Teikichi to *Shina bungakushi* ni tsuite," *Nishōgakusha daigakuin kiyō* 17 (2003): 387–409.
96. Kubo, *Shina bungakushi*, 1.
97. Kubo, *Shina bungakushi*, 3.
98. Stephen Owen, *Readings in Chinese Literary Thought* (Cambridge, Mass.: Harvard University Press, 1992), 183.
99. Literally, "weft texts," anonymous works offering esoteric interpretations of the canonical Confucian "warp" texts (*jing*).
100. Liu Xie, *Zengding Wenxin diaolong*, ed. Huang Shulin et al. (Beijing: Zhonghua shuju, 2012), 41. The passage has been translated by Vincent Yu-chung Shih in *The Literary Mind and the Carving of Dragons* (New York: Columbia University Press, 1959).
101. Mori Kainan, "Shina shōsetsu no hanashi," *Waseda bungaku* (1891): 41–46. To his credit, Mori acknowledges that the term *shōsetsu* as used in antiquity referred to different types of texts than more recent works like *Shuihu zhuan* and *Journey to the West*. However, he credited statements like the quotation by Liu Xie with imprinting a defense of potentially marginalized genres on subsequent generations of Chinese writers.

102. Brownstein, "From *Kokugaku* to *Kokubungaku*," 454.

103. For instance, Sasagawa Rinpū, who praised Jin Shengtan and devoted much of his research to the critic's commentarial activities, noted that "although Jin's criticism is not 'philosophical' [*tetsugakuteki*], there are still many places where he opened our minds to hidden secrets." In his insightful contribution to Kawai Kōzō's *Chūgoku bungaku shikan* (Tokyo: Sōbunsha, 2002), Nishigami Masaru convincingly argues that the Meiji-period elevation of the novel and drama vis-à-vis classical poetry and prose might have been inspired by the literary criticism of Jin, Li Yu (1610–1680), and other late imperial critics; see esp. 226–27.

104. Mori Kainan, "Shina shōsetsu no hanashi," 21.

105. Kano, *Shina shōsetsu gikyoku shi*, 10.

106. This connection was enshrined in Lu Xun's seminal *Zhongguo xiaoshuo shilüe* (An outline of Chinese literature) of 1930 and became a dominant narrative pertaining to the development of fiction. Recent scholarship on Six Dynasties *zhiguai* and Tang *chuanqi* has challenged this connection and understanding of these texts as "early fiction." See, for example, Robert Campany, *Strange Writing: Anomaly Accounts in Early Medieval China* (Albany: State University of New York Press, 1996).

107. Kojō, *Shina bungakushi*, 12; emphasis added. The elided section details some of these myths, such as the stone used by Nüwa to bolster Heaven.

108. Kubo, *Shina bungakushi*, 2.

109. Sasagawa Taneo [Rinpū], *Shina shōsetsu gikyoku shōshi* (Tokyo: Tōkadō, 1897), 1.

110. I.e., Mori Kainan, Kubo Tenzui, et al.

111. Kojō, *Shina bungakushi*, 3.

112. Kojō, *Shina bungakushi*, 5–7.

113. Kojō, *Shina bungakushi*, 18.

114. Fujita, *Shina bungakushi*, 1–3. He also noted the similarity between this process and invasions happening in other parts of the world—namely, the Aryan conquest of India, which resulted in the creation of the Vedic classics.

115. For instance, the mythical sage-king Shennong, who conferred knowledge of agriculture.

116. For example, Fujita, *Shina bungakushi*, 9.

117. Sasagawa, *Shina shōsetsu gikyoku shōshi*, 1.

118. Written with the characters 神仙譚 and glossed ふぇやりー・テールス; Sasagawa, *Shina shōsetsu gikyoku shōshi*, 5.

119. Sasagawa, *Shina shōsetsu gikyoku shōshi*, 2–3. Sasagawa treats the region of Shu in modern-day Sichuan province as a separate area but does not pursue this topic in any detail.

120. Sasagawa, *Shina shōsetsu gikyoku shōshi*, 3.

121. Sasagawa, *Shina shōsetsu gikyoku shōshi*, 3–4.

122. Sasagawa, *Shina shōsetsu gikyoku shōshi*, 11.

123. Kubo, *Shina bungakushi*, 319–20; emphasis added.

124. Miyazaki Shigekichi, *Shina kinsei bungakushi* (Tokyo: Waseda shuppanbu, 1905), 60.

125. Miyazaki, *Shina kinsei bungakushi*, 60.

126. Miyazaki, *Shina kinsei bungakushi*, 60–67.

127. Kano, *Shina shōsetsu gikyoku shi*, 4.

128. Patricia Sieber, *Theaters of Desire: Authors, Readers, and the Reproduction of Early Chinese Song-Drama, 1300–2000* (New York: Palgrave Macmillan, 2003), 32.
129. Sieber, *Theaters of Desire*, 35.
130. Kano, *Shina shōsetsu gikyoku shi*, 1.
131. Kano, *Shina shōsetsu gikyoku shi*, 4; emphasis added.

4. CIVILIZATION AND ITS DISCONTENTS

1. Hunter S. Thompson, *Hell's Angels: A Strange and Terrible Saga* (New York: Ballantine Books, 1995).
2. Itō Gingetsu, preface to *Shin'yaku Suikoden* (Tokyo: Hidaka Yūrindō, 1908).
3. Yamaji Aizan, *Dokuritsu hyōron* (1910; repr., Tokyo: Misuzu shobō, 1987–1988), 2.
4. Takashima Toshio, *Suikoden to Nihonjin: Edo kara Shōwa made* (Tokyo: Taishūkan shoten, 1991).
5. Hiraoka Ryūjō, *Hyōchū kun'yaku Suikoden* (Tokyo: Kinsei kanbun gakkai, 1914).
6. Takasu Baikei, *Suikoden monogatari* (Tokyo: Fuzanbō, 1903).
7. In addition to *Suikoden monogatari*, the series included Homer's *Iliad* (*Iriaddo monogatari*), stories from the Old Testament (*Kyūyaku Baiburu monogatari*), plays by "Old Man Shakespeare" (*Saō monogatari*), and Milton's *Paradise Lost* (*Miruton shitsurakuen monogatari*).
8. Sheldon Hsiao-peng Lu, *From Historicity to Fictionality: The Chinese Poetics of Narrative* (Stanford, Calif.: Stanford University Press, 1994), 43.
9. Mori Kainan, *Sakushihō* (Tokyo: Bunkaidō, 1911), 312.
10. Seen in this light, Hippolyte Taine's assertion that literature reflects the geographic and racial circumstances of its composition is not such a new idea after all; in fact, the superficial similarities between the two epistemes likely contributed to their rapid acceptance and assimilation in Japan.
11. "*Sen-Shin bungaku to Shina shōsetsu gikyoku shōshi* o hyō-su," *Teikoku bungaku* 3, no. 7 (1897): 89.
12. Kano Naoki, *Shina shōsetsu gikyoku shi* (Tokyo: Misuzu shobō, 1992), 4.
13. Although, as mentioned in the previous chapter, Kōjō did include a discussion of fiction in a set of "additional considerations" (*yoron*) published in the 1902 reprint of his text.
14. Kubo Tenzui, *Shina bungakushi* (Tokyo: Jinbunsha, 1903), 348. As Takashima Toshio notes, prior to the turn of the century new editions of *Shuihu zhuan* were often republications of the Bakin–Ranzan collaboration *Suiko gaden*, which was utilized, for instance, as the basis for the high-quality Teikoku bunko edition.
15. Mori Kainan, "Shina shōsetsu no hanashi," *Waseda bungaku* (1892): 133.
16. An interpretation that Nakamura no doubt encountered in Seita Tansō's writing on the novel—most likely in the preface to the *kundoku* edition of *Zhaoshibei*.
17. Kōjō Teikichi, "Yoron," in *Shina bungakushi* (Tokyo: Fuzanbō, 1902), 583–85.
18. Nakane Kiyoshi [Kōtei], *Shina bungaku shiyō* (Tokyo: Kinkadō, 1900), 116–17. Kubo, *Shina bungakushi*, 346.
19. Kojima Kenkichirō, *Shina bungaku shikō* (Tokyo: Fuzanbō, 1912), 291. Sasagawa Taneo [Rinpū], *Shina shōsetsu gikyoku shōshi* (Tokyo: Tōkadō, 1897), 33.
20. Kano, *Shina shōsetsu gikyoku shi*, 87.

21. Takayama Chogyū, "*Sen-Shin bungaku o yomu*," in *Chogyū zenshū*, ed. Saitō Shinsaku and Anezaki Masaharu, vol. 2 (Tokyo: Hakubunkan, 1912), 649–51.

22. "*Sen-Shin bungaku to Shina shōsetsu gikyoku shōshi o hyō-su*," 89–91.

23. Kubo, *Shina bungakushi*, 349.

24. Most of the authors discussed in this chapter excoriated Bakin's single-minded insistence upon "didacticism" (*kanzen chōaku*) as the linchpin of fictional narrative, but it is important to note that these were by no means universally shared sentiments. Peter Kornicki, Maeda Ai, Atsuko Ueda, and most recently Brian C. Dowdle have all convincingly demonstrated that, far from evidencing a turn away from Bakin, Meiji-period criticism of Bakin's didacticism was rather proof of the author's universal popularity and enduring appeal among the general reading public.

25. Brian C. Dowdle, "Why Saikaku was Memorable but Bakin was Unforgettable," *Journal of Japanese Studies* 42, no. 1 (2016): 118.

26. Translated by John C. Y. Wang in *How to Read the Chinese Novel*, ed. David Rolston (Princeton, N.J.: Princeton University Press, 1990), 135. The original passage is taken from the edition of *Shuihu zhuan* in Lu Lin, ed., *Jin Shengtan quanji* (Nanjing: Fenghuang chubanshe, 2008), 30.

27. Rolston, *How to Read the Chinese Novel*, 136.

28. Kano, *Shina shōsetsu gikyoku shi*, 88–89.

29. Something Jin Shengtan had also pointed out.

30. Nakane, *Shina bungaku shiyō*, 117.

31. Yamaji, *Dokuritsu hyōron*, 4.

32. Yamaji, *Dokuritsu hyōron*, 2.

33. Daria Berg, "Traditional Vernacular Novels: Some Lesser-Known Works," in *The Columbia History of Chinese Literature*, ed. Victor Mair (New York: Columbia University Press, 2001), 666.

34. Yamaji, *Dokuritsu hyōron*, 4.

35. Compare Yamaji's discussion, for instance, with Kosugi Misei's (1881–1964) *Shin'yaku ehon Suikoden* of 1911, which interspersed a simplified translation of the text with Kosugi's sketches. The image of Yan Poxi lying bare breasted next to a toppled vase and the murder weapon combines a titillating eroticism with an almost *Guernica*-esque twisted agony.

36. Yamaji, *Dokuritsu hyōron*, 5.

37. Certainly the group had impeccable *Shuihu* credentials. Mori Kainan's engagement with the novel has been discussed. Yoda Gakkai was the author of an introductory preface in the popular 1895 Teikoku bunko edition of the novel, and Kōda Rohan would later translate *Shuihu zhuan* in his 1923–1924 *Kokuyaku Chūgi Suikoden zensho*.

38. Mori Ōgai, ed., *Mezamashigusa*, 1897, 22. Getting "tangled up in concepts" (*gainen ni kō-shi*) was, of course, the charge frequently leveled at Kyokutei Bakin's *Hakkenden* in the wake of such works as Tsubouchi Shōyō's *Shōsetsu shinzui*.

39. *Mezamashigusa*, 4–5.

40. Kainan employs the traditional saying, "Once the rabbit is caught, the hunting dogs are cooked and eaten as well."

41. Ōgai, *Mezamashigusa*, 8.

42. Ōgai, *Mezamashigusa*, 8–9; emphasis added.

43. Ōgai, *Mezamashigusa*, 26; emphasis in original.

44. Ōgai, *Mezamashigusa*, 33.

45. A reference to a vision by the rebel Fang La that convinces him he is destined to be the new emperor.

46. Ōgai, *Mezamashigusa*, 41.

47. Masaoka Shiki, "*Suikoden to Hakkenden*," in *Shiki zenshū*, vol. 14 (Tokyo: Kōdansha, 1976), 253. In a preface, Shiki mentions that he wrote the essay with the help of his disciples Takahama Kyoshi and Kawahigashi Hekigotō. For the sake of concision, I refer to Shiki as the author of the work.

48. In the case of *Shuihu zhuan*, Shiki read the original Chinese edition of the text with commentary by Jin Shengtan.

49. Masaoka Shiki, "*Suikoden to Hakkenden*," 254.

50. Although Shōyō did not, contra popular understanding, refute Bakin or didacticism categorically. See Atsuko Ueda, *Concealment of Politics, Politics of Concealment: The Production of "Literature" in Meiji Japan* (Stanford, Calif.: Stanford University Press, 2007), chapter 3.

51. Bakin had, of course, exerted himself to the utmost to attain this type of narrative resonance, and what Shiki denounced as belabored effort he would have undoubtedly called a tightly constructed plot!

52. Masaoka Shiki, "*Suikoden to Hakkenden*," 275.

53. Shiki also irritably criticized Bakin for abusing his authorial privilege by pointing out his own contributions and considerations in the form of the autocriticism found in *Hakkenden*.

54. Lu Lin, *Jin Shengtan quanji*, 112–13.

55. Masaoka Shiki, "*Suikoden to Hakkenden*," 277.

56. Masaoka Shiki, "*Suikoden to Hakkenden*," 269.

57. Masaoka Shiki, "*Suikoden to Hakkenden*," 269.

58. Kawai Kōzō's *Shina bungaku shikan* (Tokyo: Sōbunsha, 2002) provides capsule biographies of the figures associated with *Shina bungakushi*, and much of the preceding information has been taken from there.

59. Quoted in Miura Kanō's study of Taoka Reiun in *Meiji no kangaku* (Tokyo: Kyūko shoin, 1998), 167.

60. Joshua A. Fogel, *The Literature of Travel in the Japanese Rediscovery of China, 1862–1945* (Stanford, Calif.: Stanford University Press, 1996).

61. James Clifford, *The Predicament of Culture: Twentieth-Century Ethnography, Literature, and Art* (Cambridge, Mass.: Harvard University Press, 1988).

62. E. Taylor Atkins, *Primitive Selves: Koreana in the Japanese Colonial Gaze, 1910–1945* (Berkeley: University of California Press, 2010), chapter 2.

63. And to be clear, Kano was absolutely essential in drawing attention to and conducting seminal research on Chinese popular culture. My critical reading is not to downplay the accomplishments described in Joshua A. Fogel, "Kano Naoki's Relationship to *Kangaku*," in *New Directions in the Study of Meiji Japan*, ed. Helen Hardacre and Adam Lewis Kern (Leiden: Brill, 1997).

64. Kano, *Shina shōsetsu gikyoku shi*, 9.

65. Kano, *Shina shōsetsu gikyoku shi*, 82.

66. Kano, *Shina shōsetsu gikyoku shi*, 82–83.

67. Kano, *Shina shōsetsu gikyoku shi*, 82–83.

68. Tokutomi Sohō, *Shina man'yūki* (Tokyo: Tokyo: Min'yūsha, 1918), 423–24.

69. Tokutomi, *Shina man'yūki*, 424.

70. Tokutomi, *Shina man'yūki*, 428.

71. *Sanguo yanyi xiaozhu* (Taipei: Liren shuju, 1994), 1.

72. Tokutomi, *Shina man'yūki*, 426.

73. See William C. Hedberg, "Akutagawa Ryūnosuke's Uncanny Travels in Republican-Era China," *Japan Forum* 29, no. 2 (2017): 236–56, for a discussion of the circumstances surrounding Akutagawa's trip.

74. He spent much of his time with Zhang Binglin, for example, distracted by a stuffed crocodile on Zhang's wall—even though in other places of his fictional corpus he explored the issues he and Zhang discussed (e.g., "Momotarō").

75. Chen Jingji is Ximen Qing's nephew in *Plum in the Golden Vase*, who carries out an incestuous affair with Ximen's wife. Xi Shiyi is a character in the mid-nineteenth-century novel *A Precious Mirror for Judging Flowers* (*Pinhua baojian*), which centers on relationships between opera patrons and young male performers. The type of relationships described in these vernacular novels is contrasted with the classical-language output of the Tang poet Du Fu (712–770), the southern Song general Yue Fei (1103–1142), the Ming philosopher Wang Yangming (1472–1529), and the Three Kingdoms–era military strategist Zhuge Liang (181–234).

76. Akutagawa Ryūnosuke, *Akutagawa Ryūnosuke zenshū*, vol. 6 (Tokyo: Chikuma shobō, 1971), 13; emphasis added.

77. See William Lee's and Haruo Shirane's contributions to Haruo Shirane and Tomi Suzuki, eds., *Inventing the Classics: Modernity, National Identity, and Japanese Literature* (Stanford, Calif.: Stanford University Press, 2000).

78. Robert Thomas Tierney, *Tropics of Savagery: The Culture of Japanese Empire in Comparative Frame* (Berkeley: University of California Press, 2010), 2.

79. David Askew makes a similar point by comparing the development of Western and Japanese ethnography in the context of the scholar's proximity to the object of study. Whereas Western anthropology emerged from analysis of the exotic Others of Africa, Asia, and Oceania, Japanese anthropology focused on discussion of what Askew terms an internal Other or closely related Other; see "Debating the 'Japanese' Race in Meiji Japan: Towards a History of Early Japanese Anthropology" in *The Making of Anthropology in East and Southeast Asia*, ed. Shinji Yamashita, J. S. Eades, and Joseph Bosco (New York: Berghahn Books, 2004), 74–78.

EPILOGUE: A FINAL VIEW FROM THE MARGINS

1. After all, Ximen Qing, the wastrel protagonist of *Plum in the Golden Vase*, is punished in spectacularly gruesome fashion at the end of the novel, and, more important, there is absolutely no doubt in the reader's mind why he is being punished. In contrast, the appropriateness of the deaths of the outlaws (either actual or oneiric) in *Shuihu zhuan* is much more ambivalent, owing partly to the aura of illegitimacy that surrounds the punishing institution (the Song court) and to the charismatic attractiveness of the outlaws themselves.

2. Jorge Luis Borges, "On Exactitude in Science," in *A Universal History of Infamy*, trans. Norman Thomas di Giovanni (New York: Dutton, 1972), 141.

BIBLIOGRAPHY

EDITIONS OF *SHUIHU ZHUAN* CONSULTED

Following is a list of all Chinese-, Japanese-, and English-language editions of *Shuihu zhuan* mentioned in this study. Since similar titles are easily confused, I have provided the basic bibliographic information for particularly important editions (indicated by an asterisk). It must be emphasized that this is *not* a comprehensive list of all editions of the novel, nor is it a catalogue of variations within each edition. For more detailed information, readers are directed to David Rolston's annotated bibliography in *How to Read the Chinese Novel* (Princeton, N.J.: Princeton University Press, 1990) and Takashima Toshio's *Suikoden to Nihonjin: Edo kara Shōwa made* (Tokyo: Taishūkan shoten, 1991), which have been my primary sources of information.

*1. *Chūgi Suikoden* 忠義水滸傳 (aka the *wakokubon* edition). 1728 *kundoku* edition of *Shuihu zhuan* (first 10 chapters only).

    The first systematic attempt at making *Shuihu zhuan* accessible to a wider readership in Japan was published in Kyoto by the Bunkaidō publishing house in 1728. The text is a *kundoku* edition of the first ten chapters of the original Chinese novel, with glosses affixed to the side of the text. These glosses provide the inflections and syntax markers that would allow a Japanese reader to read the text in accordance with Japanese grammar. In his *Chūgi Suikodenkai* of 1757 (discussed in chapter 1), the Tosa scholar Suyama Nantō credited Okajima Kanzan with the preparation of the text, although Kanzan's name does not appear on the work itself. The *wakokubon* is similar in structure and layout to a one-hundred-chapter edition in the possession of the Mukyūkai Library, suggesting a shared parent text. A second installment containing the next ten chapters was published in 1759. The Harvard-Yenching Library possesses the copy examined for this study.

2. Dent-Young, John and Alex. *The Marshes of Mount Liang*. 4 vols. Hong Kong: Chinese University Press, 1994.

*3. *Diwu caizishu Shi Nai'an Shuihu zhuan* 第五才子書施耐庵水滸傳 (aka Jin Shengtan edition or Guanhuatang edition). In *Guben xiaoshuo jicheng*. Shanghai: Shanghai guji chubanshe, 1990.

> The seventy-chapter truncated edition of *Shuihu zhuan* that enjoyed tremendous popularity in both China and Japan. As discussed in chapter 2, Jin Shengtan excised the second half of the longer editions, in which the outlaws are pardoned, and replaced it with a scene in which they are put to death in a dream. The edition is renowned for its extensive paratextual apparatuses, including prefaces and reading guides by Jin; a (clearly spurious) preface by the alleged author, Shi Nai'an; and copious interlineal, marginal, and prechapter comments.

4. Hiraoka Ryūjō 平岡龍城. *Hyōchū kun'yaku Suikoden* 標註訓譯水滸傳. Tokyo: Kinsei kanbun gakkai, 1914.

5. Itō Gingetsu 伊藤銀月. *Shin'yaku Suikoden* 新譯水滸傳. Tokyo: Hidaka yūrindō, 1908.

6. Jackson, J. H. *The Water Margin*. Shanghai: Commercial Press, 1937.

*7. *Jingben zengbu xiaozheng quanxiang Zhongyi shuihu zhizhuan pinglin* 京本增補 校正全像忠義水滸志傳評林 (aka Tenkai edition). In *Guben xiaoshuo jicheng*. Shanghai: Shanghai guji chubanshe, 1990.

> A one-hundred-four-chapter "simplified recension" (*jianben*) of the novel, apparently based on an earlier, full recension (although no such recensions have survived). As the title suggests, the edition is illustrated, with the text appearing below the illustrations on each page. The edition was prepared by the late-Ming Fujian printer Yu Xiangdou and published in 1594. This particular edition is important in the history of the Japanese reception of the novel since a copy found its way into the library of the Tendai abbot Tenkai, whose death in 1643 provides us with a rough estimate for determining the text's importation date.

8. Kōda Rohan 幸田露伴. *Kokuyaku Chūgi Suikoden zensho* 國譯忠義水滸傳全書. Originally published 1923–1924. In Kōda Rohan, *Rohan zenshū*, vols. 33–37. Tokyo: Iwanami shoten, 1978–1980.

9. Kosugi Misei 小杉未醒. *Shin'yaku ehon Suikoden* 新譯絵本水滸傳. Tokyo: Sakura shobō, 1911.

10. Kubo Tenzui 久保天随. *Shin'yaku Suiko zenden* 新譯水滸全傳. Tokyo: Chiseidō, 1911–1912.

11. *Okajima Kanzan yakuhen Chūgi Suikoden* 岡島冠山譯編忠義水滸傳. Tokyo: Kyōdō shuppan, 1907.

*12. Kyokutei Bakin 曲亭馬琴, Takai Ranzan 高井蘭山, and Katsushika Hokusai 葛飾北斎. *Shinpen Suiko gaden* 新編水滸畫傳.

> A collaboration between two of early modern Japan's most famous cultural luminaries, *Shinpen Suiko gaden* was subject to the same type of vicissitudes and false starts that characterized so many other *Shuihu zhuan*–related projects in Edo Japan. In the "Disquisition on Translating *Shuihu zhuan*" (Yaku *Suiko* ben) that caps the first installment of the translation, Bakin described his undertaking as a result of dissatisfaction with the preexisting *Tsūzoku Chūgi Suikoden* (entry no. 15 in this bibliography). In the same essay, Bakin announced his intention to provide

a translation based on the hundred-chapter edition of the novel while incorporating the commentary of Jin Shengtan. Two volumes of *Shinpen Suiko gaden*, corresponding to the first ten chapters of the Chinese novel, were published in 1805 and 1807. At that point, production of the translation halted, apparently as a result of a falling-out between Bakin and his collaborators. The project was only resumed and finished two decades later, with the writer Takai Ranzan translating in place of Bakin. Bakin's earlier complaints about *Tsūzoku Chūgi Suikoden* notwithstanding, both he and Ranzan appear to have relied extensively on both the *tsūzokubon* translation and the *kundoku* text published in 1728 (entry no. 1 in this bibliography). The Bakin–Ranzan translation remained extremely popular well into the Meiji period, when it was republished in a variety of typeset editions (for instance, entry no. 19 in this bibliography).

*13. *Li Zhuowu xiansheng piping Zhongyi shuihu zhuan* 李卓吾先生批評忠義水滸傳 (aka Rongyutang edition). In *Guben xiaoshuo jicheng*. Shanghai: Shanghai guji chubanshe, 1990.

A one-hundred-chapter edition of the novel named for the Rongyutang printing house in Hangzhou. The edition is available in two main versions, one prepared in 1610 and the second as early as 1602. The edition is associated with the late-Ming philosopher Li Zhuowu (Li Zhi), whose essay "Preface to *The Loyal and Righteous Water Margin*" (*Zhongyi shuihu zhuan* xu) appears at the front of the 1610 edition. Li has also been traditionally attributed with the interlineal, marginal, and post-chapter comments, but currently scholarly consensus credits them to a certain Ye Zhou (fl. 1595–1624).

14. *Daigo saishisho Shi Taian Suikoden* 第五才子書 施耐庵水滸傳. 1894 typeset edition of Jin Shengtan text published by the Matsugyokudō publishing house.

*15. Okajima Kanzan 岡島冠山, trans. (attributed). *Tsūzoku Chūgi Suikoden* 通俗忠義水滸傳 (aka the *tsūzokubon* edition). In *Kinsei hakuwa shōsetsu hon'yakushū*, ed. Nakamura Yukihiko, vols. 6–11. Tokyo: Kyūko shoin, 1987.

A translation written in a mixture of kana and Sinographs, published in four installments in 1757, 1772, 1784, and 1790. Okajima Kanzan is listed as the translator of the first three installments, even though the earliest appeared thirty years after his death. The attribution is highly suspect and is more likely an attempt at cashing in on Kanzan's posthumous reputation. The translation project began with a hundred-chapter edition of the novel as a base text, but the publishers appear to have had a change of heart near the end of the project. The fourth installment consists of "miscellanea" (*shūi*) including material that appears only in the one-hundred-twenty-chapter recensions of the novel.

16. Seita Tansō 清田儋叟, owner. *Diwu caizishu Shi Nai'an Shuihu zhuan* 第五才子書 施耐庵水滸傳. Personal copy of Jin Shengtan edition in possession of the University of Tokyo's Institute for Advanced Studies on Asia.

17. Shapiro, Sidney. *Outlaws of the Marsh*. 3 vols. Beijing: Foreign Languages Press, 1980.

18. Takasu Baikei 高須梅渓. *Suikoden monogatari* 水滸傳物語. Tokyo: Fuzanbō, 1903.

*19. *Kōtei Suikoden* 校訂水滸傳. Tokyo: Hakubunkan, 1895.

The popular edition published in two volumes as part of Hakubunkan's Teikoku bunko series. Like many Meiji editions of the novel, the Teikoku bunko edition was a republication of the earlier translation by Kyokutei Bakin and Takai Ranzan. The edition retained Bakin's prefatorial material but balanced it with a new "Discussion of *Shuihu zhuan*" (*Suikoden* kō) by the scholar Yoda Gakkai.

PRIMARY AND SECONDARY SOURCES IN ENGLISH, JAPANESE, AND CHINESE

Akutagawa Ryūnosuke. *Akutagawa Ryūnosuke zenshū*. 9 vols. Tokyo: Chikuma shobō, 1971.

Amenomori Hōshū. *Kissō chawa*. In *Amenomori Hōshū zensho*, ed. Kansai Daigaku Tōzai Gakujutsu Kenkyūjo Nitchū Bunka Kōryū no Kenkyū Rekishihan. Suita: Kansai daigaku shuppan kōhōbu, 1980.

Anderson, Benedict. *Imagined Communities: Reflections on the Origin and Spread of Nationalism*. London: Verso, 2006.

Andō Hikotarō. *Nihonjin no Chūgokukan*. Tokyo: Keisō shobō, 1971.

Aoki Masaru. *Aoki Masaru zenshū*. 10 vols. Tokyo: Shunjūsha, 1969–1975.

Arai Hakuseki. *Arai Hakuseki zenshū*. Ed. Kokusho Kankōkai. 6 vols. Tokyo: Kokusho kankōkai, 1905–1907.

Askew, David. "Debating the 'Japanese' Race in Meiji Japan: Towards a History of Early Japanese Anthropology." In *The Making of Anthropology in East and Southeast Asia*, ed. Shinji Yamashita, J. S. Eades, and Joseph Bosco, 57–89. New York: Berghahn Books, 2004.

Asō Isoji. *Edo bungaku to Chūgoku bungaku*. Tokyo: Sanseidō, 1950.

Atkins, E. Taylor. *Primitive Selves: Koreana in the Japanese Colonial Gaze, 1910–1945*. Berkeley: University of California Press, 2010.

A Ying. *Wan Qing wenxue congchao: Xiaoshuo xiqu yanjiu bian*. Beijing: Zhonghua shuju, 1960.

Bakhtin, M. M. *The Dialogic Imagination: Four Essays*. Trans. Caryl Emerson and Michael Holquist. Austin: University of Texas Press, 1981.

Baroni, Helen. *Obaku Zen: The Emergence of the Third Sect of Buddhism in Tokugawa Japan*. Honolulu: University of Hawai'i Press, 2000.

Berger, Louis Jacques William, IV. "The Overseas Chinese in Seventeenth-Century Nagasaki." Ph.D. diss., Harvard University, 2003.

Bermann, Sandra, and Michael Wood. *Nation, Language, and the Ethics of Translation*. Princeton, N.J.: Princeton University Press, 2005.

Berry, Mary Elizabeth. "Defining 'Early Modern.'" In *Japan Emerging: Premodern History to 1850*, ed. Karl F. Friday, 42–52. Boulder, Colo.: Westview Press, 2012.

Bonner, Joey. *Wang Kuo-wei: An Intellectual Biography*. Cambridge, Mass.: Harvard University Press, 1986.

Borges, Jorge Luis. "On Exactitude in Science." In *A Universal History of Infamy*, trans. Norman Thomas di Giovanni. New York: Dutton, 1972.

Brownstein, Michael C. "From *Kokugaku* to *Kokubungaku*: Canon-Formation in the Meiji Period." *Harvard Journal of Asiatic Studies* 47, no. 2 (1987): 435–60.

Burke, Peter, and R. Po-Chia Hsia, eds. *Cultural Translation in Early Modern Europe*. Cambridge: Cambridge University Press, 2007.

Burns, Susan. *Before the Nation: Kokugaku and the Imagining of Community in Early Modern Japan.* Durham, N.C.: Duke University Press, 2003.

Caddeau, Patrick W. *Appraising Genji: Literary Criticism and Cultural Anxiety in the Age of the Last Samurai.* Albany: State University of New York Press, 2006.

Campany, Robert. *Strange Writing: Anomaly Accounts in Early Medieval China.* Albany: State University of New York Press, 1996.

Chen Pingyuan. *Zhongguo xiaoshuo xushi moshi de zhuanbian.* Shanghai: Shanghai renmin chubanshe, 1988.

Chen Pingyuan and Xia Xiaohong, eds. *Ershi shiji Zhongguo xiaoshuo lilun ziliao.* 5 vols. Beijing: Beijing daxue chubanshe, 1997.

Chesneaux, Jean. "The Modern Relevance of Shui-hu Chuan: Its Influence on Rebel Movements in Nineteenth- and Twentieth-Century China." *Papers on Far Eastern History* 3 (1971): 1–25.

Clements, Rebekah. *A Cultural History of Translation in Early Modern Japan.* Cambridge: Cambridge University Press, 2015.

——. "Speaking in Tongues? Daimyo, Zen Monks, and Spoken Chinese in Japan, 1661–1711." *Journal of Asian Studies* 76, no. 3 (2017): 603–26.

——. "Suematsu Kenchō and the First English Translation of *Genji monogatari*: Translation, Tactics, and the 'Women's Question.'" *Japan Forum* 23, no. 1 (2011): 25–47.

Clements, Rebekah, and Peter Kornicki. "The Latter Days of the *Genji*." *Monumenta Nipponica* 64, no. 2 (2009): 363–72.

Clifford, James. *The Predicament of Culture: Twentieth-Century Ethnography, Literature, and Art.* Cambridge, Mass.: Harvard University Press, 1988.

Cranston, Edwin. *A Waka Anthology, Volume 1: The Gem-Glistening Cup.* Stanford, Calif.: Stanford University Press, 1993.

Damrosch, David. *What Is World Literature?* Princeton, N.J.: Princeton University Press, 2003.

——. "What Is World Literature?" *World Literature Today* 77, no. 1 (2003): 9–14.

Da Song Xuanhe yishi. Ed. Zhou Jialu. Changsha: Yuelu shushe, 1993.

Davis, Winston. "The Civil Theology of Inoue Tetsujirō." *Japanese Journal of Religious Studies* 3, no. 1 (1976): 5–40.

Dazai Shundai. *Sekihi.* In *Sorai gakuha*, ed. Rai Tsutomu. Vol. 37 of *Nihon shisō taikei.* Tokyo: Iwanami shoten, 1972.

Denton, Kirk, ed. *Modern Chinese Literary Thought: Writings on Literature, 1893–1945.* Stanford, Calif.: Stanford University Press, 1996.

D'haen, Theo, David Damrosch, and Djelal Kadir, eds. *The Routledge Companion to World Literature.* London: Routledge, 2011.

Dikötter, Frank. *The Discourse of Race in Modern China.* London: Hurst, 1992.

Doleželová-Velingerová, Milena. "Traditional Chinese Theories of Drama and the Novel." *Archiv Orientální* 59, no. 2 (1991): 132–39.

Dowdle, Brian C. "Why Saikaku Was Memorable but Bakin Was Unforgettable." *Journal of Japanese Studies* 42, no. 1 (2016): 91–121.

Duara, Prasenjit. *Rescuing History from the Nation: Questioning Narratives of Modern China.* Chicago: University of Chicago Press, 1995.

——. *Sovereignty and Authenticity: Manchukuo and the East Asian Modern.* Lanham, Md.: Rowman and Littlefield, 2003.

Du Yiwen. "Kojō Teikichi to *Shina bungakushi* ni tsuite." *Nishōgakusha daigakuin kiyō* 17 (2003): 387–409.

——. "Sasagawa Rinpū (Taneo) no Chūgoku bungaku kenkyū." *Nishōgakusha daigaku jinbun ronsō* 80 (2008): 125–44.

Eagleton, Terry. *Literary Theory: An Introduction.* Oxford: Blackwell Publishing, 1983.

Elman, Benjamin A. *From Philosophy to Philology: Intellectual and Social Aspects of Change in Late Imperial China.* Los Angeles: University of California Press, 2001.

——, ed. *Rethinking East Asian Languages, Vernaculars, and Literacies, 1000–1919.* Leiden: Brill, 2014.

Emmerich, Michael. "Beyond Between: Translation, Ghosts, Metaphors." *Words Without Borders: The Online Magazine for International Literature,* May 2009. https://www.wordswithoutborders.org/article/beyond-between-translation-ghosts-metaphors.

——. *The Tale of Genji: Translation, Canonization, and World Literature.* New York: Columbia University Press, 2013.

Fleming, William D. "Strange Tales from Edo: *Liaozhai zhiyi* in Early Modern Japan." *Sino-Japanese Studies* 20 (2013): 75–115.

——. "The World Beyond the Walls: Morishima Chūryō (1756–1810) and the Development of Late Edo Fiction." Ph.D. diss., Harvard University, 2011.

Flueckiger, Peter. *Imagining Harmony: Poetry, Empathy, and Community in Mid-Tokugawa Confucianism and Nativism.* Stanford, Calif.: Stanford University Press, 2001.

——. Review of *The Observable Mundane: Vernacular Chinese and the Emergence of a Literary Discourse on Popular Narrative in Edo Japan,* by Emanuel Pastreich. *Monumenta Nipponica* 67, no. 2 (2012): 338–41.

Fogel, Joshua A. *Articulating the Sinosphere: Sino-Japanese Relations in Space and Time.* Cambridge, Mass.: Harvard University Press, 2009.

——. *Between China and Japan: The Writings of Joshua Fogel.* Leiden: Brill, 2015.

——, ed. *Crossing the Yellow Sea: Sino-Japanese Cultural Contacts, 1600–1950.* Norwalk, Conn.: EastBridge, 2007.

——. "Kano Naoki's Relationship to *Kangaku*." In *New Directions in the Study of Meiji Japan,* ed. Helen Hardacre and Adam Lewis Kern, 358–72. Leiden: Brill, 1997.

——, ed. *Late Qing China and Meiji Japan: Political and Cultural Aspects.* Norwalk, Conn.: EastBridge, 2004.

——. *The Literature of Travel in the Japanese Rediscovery of China, 1862–1945.* Stanford, Calif.: Stanford University Press, 1996.

——. *Politics and Sinology: The Case of Naitō Konan (1866–1934).* Cambridge, Mass.: Harvard University Press, 1984.

——, ed. *Sagacious Monks and Bloodthirsty Warriors: Chinese Views of Japan in the Ming-Qing Period.* Norwalk, Conn.: EastBridge, 2002.

——. "The Sino-Japanese Controversy over *Shina* as a Toponym for China." In *The Cultural Dimensions of Sino-Japanese Relations: Essays on the Nineteenth and Twentieth Centuries,* 66–79. Armonk, N.Y.: M.E. Sharpe, 1995.

Fraleigh, Matthew. *Plucking Chrysanthemums: Narushima Ryūhoku and Sinitic Literary Traditions in Modern Japan.* Cambridge, Mass.: Harvard University Asia Center, 2016.

——. Review of *A Cultural History of Translation in Early Modern Japan,* by Rebekah Clements. *Harvard Journal of Asiatic Studies* 77, no. 1 (2017): 184–90.

Fujita Toyohachi. *Sen-Shin bungaku: Shina bungaku shikō*. Tokyo: Tōkadō, 1897.
——. "Shina bungaku no tokushitsu." *Kōko bungaku* 1 (1896): 46–54.
——. *Shina bungkakushi*. Tokyo: Tōkyō senmon gakkō, 1895–1897.
Ge, Liangyan. "Authoring Authorial Intention: Jin Shengtan as Creative Critic." *CLEAR* 25 (2003): 1–24.
——. *Out of the Marshes: The Rise of Chinese Vernacular Fiction*. Honolulu: University of Hawai`i Press, 2001.
Genette, Gérard. *Paratexts: Thresholds of Interpretation*. Trans. Jane E. Lewin. Cambridge: Cambridge University Press, 1997.
Gluck, Carol. *Japan's Modern Myths: Ideology in the Late Meiji Period*. Princeton, N.J.: Princeton University Press, 1985.
Gordon, Andrew. *A Modern History of Japan: From Tokugawa Times to the Present*. 2nd ed. New York: Oxford University Press, 2009.
Gotō Tanji, Kamada Kisaburō, and Okami Masao, eds. *Taiheiki*. In *Nihon koten bungaku taikei*, vols. 34–36. Tokyo: Iwanami shoten, 1960–1962.
Gregory, Scott Wentworth. "'The Wuding Editions': Printing, Power, and Vernacular Fiction in the Ming Dynasty." *East Asian Publishing and Society* 7 (2017): 1–29.
Guben xiaoshuo congkan. Beijing: Zhonghua shuju, 1987–1991.
Guben xiaoshuo jicheng. Shanghai: Shanghai guji chubanshe, 1990–1992.
Gu Ming Dong. *Chinese Theories of Fiction: A Non-Western Narrative System*. Albany: State University of New York Press, 2006.
Haga Yaichi and Tachibana Sensaburō. *Kokubungaku tokuhon*. Tokyo: Fuzanbō, 1890.
Hamada Keisuke. "Bakin no iwayuru haishi shichi hōsoku ni tsuite." In *Bakin*, ed. Nihon Bungaku Kenkyū Shiryō Kankōkai, 136–45. Tokyo: Yūseidō, 1974.
——. "*Kanzen chōaku* hoshi." In *Bakin*, ed. Itasaka Noriko, 214–52. Tokyo: Wakakusa shobō, 2000.
Han, Suk-jung. "The Problem of Sovereignty: Manchukuo, 1932–1937." *positions* 12, no. 2 (2004): 457–78.
Hanan, Patrick. *The Chinese Short Story: Studies in Dating, Authorship, and Composition*. Cambridge, Mass.: Harvard University Press, 1973.
——. *The Chinese Vernacular Story*. Cambridge, Mass.: Harvard University Press, 1981.
——. "The Early Chinese Short Story: A Critical Theory in Outline." *Harvard Journal of Asiatic Studies* 27 (1967): 168–207.
——. "The *Yün-men chuan*: From *Chantefable* to Short Story." *Bulletin of the School of Oriental and African Studies* 36, no. 2 (1973): 299–308.
Hanscomb, Christopher P., and Dennis Washburn, eds. *The Affect of Difference: Representations of Race in East Asian Empire*. Honolulu: University of Hawai`i Press, 2016.
Hanshu. Academia Sinica Scripta Sinica (Hanji quanwen ziliaoku). http://hanchi.ihp.sinica.edu.tw/ihp/hanji.htm.
Hara Nensai. *Sentetsu sōdan*. In *Nihon tetsugaku shisō zensho*, ed. Saigusa Hiroto et al., vol. 20. Tokyo: Heibonsha, 1956.
Harootunian, H. D. *Overcome by Modernity: History, Culture, and Community in Interwar Japan*. Princeton, N.J.: Princeton University Press, 2000.
——. *Things Seen and Unseen: Discourse and Ideology in Tokugawa Nativism*. Chicago: University of Chicago Press, 1988.
Harrell, Paula. *Sowing the Seeds of Change: Chinese Students, Japanese Teachers, 1895–1905*. Stanford, Calif.: Stanford University Press, 1992.

Hartley, L. P. *The Go-Between*. New York: New York Review of Books, 2002.

Hashimoto, Satoru. "Afterlives of the Culture: Engaging with the Trans–East Asian Cultural Tradition in Modern Chinese, Japanese, Korean, and Taiwanese Literatures, 1880s–1940s." Ph.D. diss., Harvard University, 2014.

Hedberg, William C. "Akutagawa Ryūnosuke's Uncanny Travels in Republican-Era China." *Japan Forum* 29, no. 2 (2017): 236–56.

——. "Reclaiming the Margins: Seita Tansō's *Suikoden hihyōkai* and the Poetics of Cross-Cultural Influence." *International Journal of Asian Studies* 12, no. 2 (2015): 193–215.

——. "Separating the Word and the Way: Suyama Nantō's *Chūgi Suikodenkai* and Edo-Period Vernacular Philology." *Journal of Japanese Studies* 41, no. 2 (2015): 343–67.

Hegel, Robert E. *Reading Illustrated Fiction in Late Imperial China*. Stanford, Calif.: Stanford University Press, 1998.

Higashi Kan'ichi. *Nihon risshihen*. Osaka: Yoshioka Heisuke, 1882.

Hiraga Gennai. *Fūryū Shidōkenden*. Ed. Nakamura Yukihiko. In *Nihon koten bungaku taikei*, 55: 153–224. Tokyo: Iwanami shoten, 1961.

Hisamatsu Sen'ichi, ed. *Ochiai Naobumi, Ueda Kazutoshi, Haga Yaichi, Fujioka Sakutarō shū*. In *Meiji bungaku zenshū*, vol. 44. Tokyo: Chikuma shobō, 1984.

——, ed. *Shioi Ukō, Takeshima Hagoromo, Ōmachi Keigetsu, Kubo Tenzui, Sasagawa Rinpū, Higuchi Ryūkō shū*. In *Meiji bungaku zenshū*, vol. 41. Tokyo: Chikuma shobō, 1971.

Hobsbawm, Eric. *Bandits*. London: Abacus, 2010.

Howland, Douglas. *Borders of Chinese Civilization: Geography and History at Empire's End*. Durham, N.C.: Duke University Press, 1996.

——. *Translating the West: Language and Political Reason in Nineteenth-Century Japan*. Honolulu: University of Hawai'i Press, 2002.

Hsia, C. T. *The Classic Chinese Novel: A Critical Introduction*. New York: Columbia University Press, 1968.

——. "Yen Fu and Liang Ch'i-ch'ao as Advocates of New Fiction." In *C. T. Hsia on Chinese Literature*, 223–46. New York: Columbia University Press, 2004.

Huang, Martin W. *Negotiating Masculinities in Late Imperial China*. Honolulu: University of Hawai'i Press, 2006.

Huang Lin and Han Tongwen. *Zhongguo lidai xiaoshuo lunzhu xuan*. 3 vols. Nanchang: Jiangxi renmin chubanshe, 2000.

Huffman, James L. *Creating a Public: People and Press in Meiji Japan*. Honolulu: University of Hawai'i Press, 1997.

Hutcheon, Linda. *A Theory of Adaptation*. 2nd ed. London: Routledge, 2013.

Huters, Theodore. *Bringing the World Home: Appropriating the West in Late Qing and Early Republican China*. Honolulu: University of Hawai'i Press, 2005.

Hu Yinglin. *Shaoshi shanfang bicong*. Shanghai: Shanghai guji chubanshe, 2009.

Idema, W. L. *Chinese Vernacular Fiction: The Formative Period*. Leiden: Brill, 1974.

——. *The Dramatic Oeuvre of Chu Yu-Tun (1379–1439)*. Leiden: Brill, 1985.

Idema, W. L., and Lloyd Haft. *A Guide to Chinese Literature*. Ann Arbor, Mich.: Center for Chinese Studies, 1997.

Inada Atsunobu. "*Suikoden* no shōgeki." In *Ajia yūgaku*, no. 131, ed. Inada Atsunobu. Tokyo: Bensei shuppan, 2010.

Inoue Keiji. "Kyōden *Chūshin Suikoden* to *Suikoden* sanshu." In Suikoden *no shōgeki,* ed. Inada Atsunobu, 150–59. Tokyo: Bensei shuppan, 2010.

Inoguchi Atsushi. *Nihon kanbungakushi.* Tokyo: Kadokawa shoten, 1984.

Irwin, Richard Gregg. *The Evolution of a Chinese Novel: Shui-hu-chuan.* Cambridge, Mass.: Harvard University Press, 1953.

Ishizaki Matazō. *Kinsei Nihon ni okeru Shina zokugo bungakushi.* Tokyo: Kōbundō shobō, 1940.

Itō Jinsai. *Yōjikaku.* Woodblock edition with 1703 preface in Special Collections, Waseda University Library, Waseda University, Tokyo.

Jansen, Marius B. *China in the Tokugawa World.* Cambridge, Mass.: Harvard University Press, 1992.

Jin Makabe. *Tokugawa kōki no gakumon to seiji: Shōheizaka gakumonjo jusha to bakumatsu gaikō hen'yō.* Nagoya: Nagoya daigaku shuppankai, 2007.

Jones, Stanleigh Hopkins, Jr. "Scholar, Scientist, Popular Author Hiraga Gennai, 1728–1780." Ph.D. diss., Columbia University, 1968.

Kamei Hideo. "*Shōsetsu*" ron: *Shōsetsu shinzui to kindai.* Tokyo: Iwanami shoten, 2001.

Kanda Masayuki. "*Suikoden* no shohon to Bakin." In *Fukkō suru Hakkenden,* ed. Suwa Haruo and Takada Mamoru, 249–86. Tokyo: Bensei shuppan, 2008.

Kano Naoki. *Shinagaku bunsō.* Tokyo: Misuzu shobō, 1973.

——. *Shina shōsetsu gikyoku shi.* Tokyo: Misuzu shobō, 1992.

Karatani Kōjin. *Origins of Modern Japanese Literature.* Trans. Brett de Bary. Durham, N.C.: Duke University Press, 1992.

Katanuma Seiji. "Okajima Kanzan no kenkyū." *Kokugo kokubungaku kenkyū* 45 (1970): 73–82.

——. "Okajima Kanzan no kenkyū (3): *Taiheiki engi no isō.*" *Kokugo kokubungaku kenkyū* 49 (1972): 42–54.

Katō Masanobu, ed. *Nihongo no rekishi chiri kōzō.* Tokyo: Meiji shoin, 1997.

Kawai Kōzō, ed. *Chūgoku no bungaku shikan.* Tokyo: Sōbunsha, 2002.

Kazantzakis, Nikos. *The Odyssey: A Modern Sequel.* Trans. Kimon Friar. New York: Simon and Schuster, 1958.

Keene, Donald, trans. *Chūshingura: The Treasury of Loyal Retainers.* New York: Columbia University Press, 1971.

——. *Dawn to the West: Japanese Literature of the Modern Era.* New York: Holt, Rinehart, and Winston, 1984.

——, trans. *Four Major Plays of Chikamatsu.* New York: Columbia University Press, 1966.

——. *World Within Walls: Japanese Literature of the Premodern Era, 1600–1867.* New York: Columbia University Press, 1999.

Kitamura Saburō. *Sekai hyakketsuden.* Tokyo: Hakubunkan, 1890.

Klompmakers, Inge. *Of Brigands and Bravery: Kuniyoshi's Heroes of the* Suikoden. Leiden: Hotei, 1998.

Knechtges, David R. *Wen xuan, or Selections of Refined Literature, Volume 1: Rhapsodies on Metropolises and Capitals.* Princeton, N.J.: Princeton University Press, 1982.

Kockum, Keiko. "Liang Qichao: The Japanese Years." *Cina* 21 (1988): 195–203.

Kōda Rohan. "Kin Seitan." *Bungei shunjū* 5, no. 6 (1923): 2–5.

——. *Rohan zenshū.* 42 vols. Tokyo: Iwanami shoten, 1978–1980.

Kojima Kenkichirō. *Shina bungaku shikō.* Tokyo: Fuzanbō, 1912.

Kojō Teikichi. *Shina bungakushi*. Tokyo: Keizai zasshisha, 1897.

———. "Yoron." In *Shina bungakushi*, 576–85. Tokyo: Fuzanbō, 1902.

Komatsu Ken. *Chūgoku rekishi shōsetsu kenkyū*. Tokyo: Kyūko shoin, 2001.

Kōno Kimiko, Wiebke Denecke, and Jinnō Hidenori, eds. *Nihon "bun"gakushi*. 2 vols. Tokyo: Bensei shuppan, 2015.

Kornicki, Peter. *The Book in Japan: A Cultural History from the Beginnings to the Nineteenth Century*. Leiden: Brill, 1988.

———. "The Enmeiin Affair of 1803: The Spread of Information in the Tokugawa Period." *Harvard Journal of Asiatic Studies* 42 (1982): 503–33.

———. *The Reform of Fiction in Meiji Japan*. London: Ithaca Press, 1982.

———. "The Survival of Tokugawa Fiction in the Meiji Period." *Harvard Journal of Asiatic Studies* 41, no. 2 (1981): 461–82.

———. "Unsuitable Books for Women? *Genji monogatari* and *Ise monogatari* in Late Seventeenth-Century Japan." *Monumenta Nipponica* 60, no. 2 (2005): 147–93.

Kōtoku Shūsui. "*Sen-Shin bungaku to Shina bungakushi*." *Tōyō tetsugaku* 4, no. 6 (1897): 313–14.

Koyamoto Rumiko. "*Tōwa jisho Chūgi Suikodenkai* ni tsuite." *Kōchidai kokubun* 31 (2000): 21–37.

Kubo Tenzui. *Shina bungakushi*. Tokyo: Jinbunsha, 1903.

Kyokutei Bakin. *Bakin shokan shūsei*. Ed. Shibata Mitsuhiko and Kanda Masayuki. 7 vols. Tokyo: Yagi shoten, 2002–2004.

———. *Chinsetsu yumiharizuki*. Ed. Gotō Tanji. In *Nihon koten bungaku taikei*, vols. 60–61. Tokyo: Iwanami shoten, 1958–1962.

———. *Gendō hōgen*. Tokyo: Yoshikawa kōbunkan, 1993.

———. *Keisei Suikoden*. Special Collections, Waseda University Library, Waseda University, Tokyo.

———. *Kinsei mononohon Edo sakusha burui*. Tokyo: Yagi shoten, 1988.

———. *Nansō Satomi hakkenden*. Ed. Hamada Keisuke. 12 vols. Tokyo: Shinchōsha, 2004.

Lamarre, Thomas. *Uncovering Heian Japan: An Archaeology of Sensation and Inscription*. Durham, N.C.: Duke University Press, 2000.

Lee Yeounsuk. *The Ideology of Kokugo: Nationalizing Language in Modern Japan*. Trans. Maki Hirano Hubbard. Honolulu: University of Hawai`i Press, 1996.

Lefevere, André. *Translation, Rewriting, and the Manipulation of Literary Fame*. London: Routledge, 1992.

Legge, James. *The Chinese Classics: With a Translation, Critical and Exegetical Notes, Prolegomena, and Copious Indexes*. Taipei: Southern Materials Center, 1985.

Levy, Indra. *Sirens of the Western Shore: The Westernesque Femme Fatale, Translation, and Vernacular Style in Modern Japanese Literature*. New York: Columbia University Press, 2006.

Lippit, Seiji. *Topographies of Japanese Modernism*. New York: Columbia University Press, 2005.

Li Shuguo. *Riben duben xiaoshuo yu Ming Qing xiaoshuo*. Tianjin: Tianjin renmin chubanshe, 1998.

Liu, Lydia H, ed. *Tokens of Exchange: The Problem of Translation in Global Circulations*. Durham, N.C.: Duke University Press, 1999.

———. *Translingual Practice: Literature, National Culture, and Translated Modernity—China, 1900–1937*. Stanford, Calif.: Stanford University Press, 1995.

Liu Hsieh [Xie]. *The Literary Mind and the Carving of Dragons*. Trans. Vincent Yu-chung Shih. New York: Columbia University Press, 1959.

——. *Zengding Wenxin diaolong*. Ed. Huang Shulin, Li Xiang, and Yang Mingzhao. Beijing: Zhonghua shuju, 2012.

Li Zhi. *A Book to Burn and a Book to Keep (Hidden): Selected Writings*. Ed. and trans. Rivi Handler-Spitz, Pauline C. Lee, and Haun Saussy. New York: Columbia University Press, 2016.

Li Zhi [Zhuowu]. *Fenshu*. Beijing: Zhonghua shuju, 1974.

Lu, Sheldon Hsiao-peng. *From Historicity to Fictionality: The Chinese Poetics of Narrative*. Stanford, Calif.: Stanford University Press, 1994.

Lu Hsun. *A Brief History of Chinese Fiction*. Trans. Yang Hsien-yi and Gladys Yang. Peking: Foreign Languages Press, 1959.

Lu Lin, ed. *Jin Shengtan quanji*. Nanjing: Fenghuang chubanshe, 2008.

Lurie, David. *Realms of Literacy: Early Japan and the History of Writing*. Cambridge, Mass.: Harvard University Asia Center, 2011.

Machida Saburō. *Meiji no kangakusha-tachi*. Tokyo: Kenbun shuppan, 1998.

Maeda Ai. *Kindai dokusha no seiritsu*. Tokyo: Iwanami shoten, 2001.

——. *Kindai Nihon no bungaku kūkan: Rekishi, kotoba, jōkyō*. Tokyo: Heibonsha, 2004.

Mair, Victor. "Buddhism and the Rise of the Written Vernacular in East Asia: The Making of National Languages." *Journal of Asian Studies* 53, no. 3 (1994): 707–51.

——, ed. *The Columbia History of Chinese Literature*. New York: Columbia University Press, 2001.

Marceau, Lawrence E. "Ninjō and the Affective Value of Literature at the Kogidō Academy." *Sino-Japanese Studies* 9, no. 1 (October 1996): 47–56.

Maruyama Masao. *Studies in the Intellectual History of Tokugawa Japan*. Trans. Mikiso Hane. Princeton, N.J.: Princeton University Press, 1974.

Maruyama Masao and Katō Shūichi. *Hon'yaku to Nihon no kindai*. Tokyo: Iwanami shoten, 2001.

Masaoka Shiki. "*Suikoden* to *Hakkenden*." In *Shiki zenshū*, 14: 253–92. Tokyo: Kōdansha, 1976.

McCullough, Helen, trans. *The Taiheiki: A Chronicle of Medieval Japan*. Westport, Conn.: Greenwood Press, 1976.

——, trans. *The Tale of the Heike*. Stanford, Calif.: Stanford University Press, 1988.

——, trans. *Tales of Ise: Lyrical Episodes from Tenth-Century Japan*. Stanford, Calif.: Stanford University Press, 1968.

McMahon, Keith. *Causality and Containment in Seventeenth-Century Chinese Fiction*. Leiden: Brill, 1988.

Mehl, Margaret. *History and the State in Nineteenth-Century Japan*. New York: St. Martin's Press, 1998.

——. *Private Academies of Chinese Learning in Meiji Japan: The Decline and Transformation of the* Kangaku Juku. Copenhagen: NIAS, 2005.

Mikami Sanji and Takatsu Kuwasaburō. *Nihon bungakushi*. Meiji Taishō bungakushi shūsei, nos. 1–2. Tokyo: Nihon tosho sentā, 1982.

Miner, Richard H., ed. and trans. "Ogyū Sorai's *Instructions for Students*: A Translation and Commentary." *Harvard Journal of Asiatic Studies* 36 (1976): 5–81.

Minford, John, and Joseph S. M. Lau, eds. *Classical Chinese Literature: An Anthology of Translations*. New York: Columbia University Press, 2000.

Ming Qing shanben xiaoshuo congkan. Taipei: Tianyi chubanshe, 1985.

Miura Kanō. *Meiji no kangaku.* Tokyo: Kyūko shoin, 1998.

Miyata Yasushi, ed. *Tō tsūji kakei ronkō.* Nagasaki: Nagasaki bunkensha, 1979.

Miyazaki Shigekichi, *Shina kinsei bungakushi.* Tokyo: Waseda shuppanbu, 1905.

Mori Kainan. *Sakushihō.* Tokyo: Bunkaidō, 1911.

——. "Shina shōsetsu no hanashi." *Waseda bungaku* (1891–1892).

Mori Ōgai, ed. *Mezamashigusa* 20 (May 1897).

Morishima Chūryō. *Zokugokai.* In Nagasawa, *Tōwa jisho ruishū,* vol. 11.

Mote, F. W. *Imperial China: 900–1800.* Cambridge, Mass.: Harvard University Press, 1999.

Nagasawa Kikuya, ed. *Nikkōsan Tenkaizō shuyō kosho kaidai.* Nikkō: Nikkōsan Rinnōji, 1966.

——. ed. *Tōwa jisho ruishū.* 21 vols. Tokyo: Kyūko shoin, 1969–1977.

Najita, Tetsuo, ed. and trans. *Tokugawa Political Writings.* Cambridge: Cambridge University Press, 1998.

Nakai, Kate Wildman. "The Naturalization of Confucianism in Tokugawa Japan: The Problem of Sinocentrism." *Harvard Journal of Asiatic Studies* 40, no. 1 (1980): 157–99.

——. "Tokugawa Confucian Historiography: The Hayashi, Early Mito School, and Arai Hakuseki." In *Confucianism and Tokugawa Culture,* ed. Peter Nosco, 62–92. Honolulu: University of Hawai`i Press, 1997.

Nakamura Aya. "*Suikoden* wakokubon to tsūzokubon—*Chūgi Suikodenkai* hanrei to Kin Seitan hon o megutte." In Suikoden *no shōgeki,* in *Ajia yūgaku,* no. 131, ed. Inada Atsunobu, 113–24. Tokyo: Bensei shuppan, 2010.

——. "*Taiheiki engi* ni okeru Kanzan no yakkai taido o megutte." *Edo bungaku* 38 (2008): 70–89.

Nakamura Yukihiko. *Kinsei bungei shichōkō.* Tokyo: Iwanami shoten, 1975.

——, ed. *Kinsei hakuwa shōsetsu shū.* 13 vols. Tokyo: Kyūko shoin, 1984–1988.

——. *Nakamura Yukihiko chojutsushū.* 15 vols. Tokyo: Chūō kōronsha, 1984.

Nakane Kiyoshi. *Shina bungaku shiyō.* Tokyo: Kinkadō, 1900.

Nakano Mitsutoshi. *Edo bunka hyōbanki: Gazoku yūwa no sekai.* Tokyo: Chūō kōronsha, 1992.

——. *Jūhasseiki no Edo bungei: Ga to zoku no seijuku.* Tokyo: Iwanami shoten, 1999.

——. "The Role of Traditional Aesthetics." In *18th Century Japan: Culture and Society,* ed. C. Andrew Gerstle, 124–32. Sydney: Allen and Unwin, 1989.

Nishihara Daisuke. "Edo jidai no Chūgoku kenkyū: Okajima Kanzan to Ogyū Sorai." *Hikaku bungaku / Bunka ronshū* 9 (1992): 13–20.

Nosco, Peter. "Man'yōshū Studies in Tokugawa Japan." *Transactions of the Asiatic Society of Japan* 4, no. 1 (1986): 109–46.

——. *Remembering Paradise: Nativism and Nostalgia in Eighteenth-Century Japan.* Cambridge, Mass.: Harvard University Press, 1998.

Ōba Osamu. *Edo jidai ni okeru Chūgoku juyō no kenkyū.* Kyoto: Dōhōsha, 1984.

——, ed. *Hakusai shomoku.* 2 vols. Fukita: Kansai daigaku tōzai gakujutsu kenkyūjo, 1972.

——. "Sino-Japanese Relations in the Edo Period." Trans. Joshua A. Fogel. Eleven-part series, *Sino-Japanese Studies* 8, no. 1–13, no. 1 (October 1995–October 2000).

Ogyū Sorai. *Bunkai*. In *Ogyū Sorai zenshū*, ed. Yoshikawa Kōjirō and Maruyama Masao, vol. 17. Tokyo: Misuzu shobō, 1976.

——. *Ken'en zatsuwa*. In *Zoku Nihon zuihitsu taisei*, ed. Mori Senzō and Kitagawa Hirokuni, vol. 4. Tokyo: Yoshikawa Kōbunkan, 1979.

——. *Ogyū Sorai*. In *Nihon shisō taikei*, vol. 36, ed. Yoshikawa Kōjirō. Tokyo: Iwanami shoten, 1973.

——. *Ogyū Sorai zenshū*. Ed. Yoshikawa Kōjirō and Maruyama Masao. 18 vols. Tokyo: Misuzu shobō, 1976.

——. *Yakubun sentei*. 1711 edition. Special Collections, Waseda University Library, Waseda University, Tokyo.

——. *Yakusha yaku*. In *Kinsei juka bunshū shūsei*, ed. Hiraishi Naoaki, 186–87. Tokyo: Perikansha, 1985.

Okada Kesao. *Edo igengo sesshoku: Rango, Tōwa to kindai Nihongo*. Tokyo: Kasama shoin, 2006.

Oka Hakku. *Joji yakutsū*. 1762 edition. In National Diet Library, Tokyo.

——. *Shōsetsu seigen* and *Shōsetsu kigen*. Photoreproduced in *Shōsetsu sangen*, ed. Ogata Tsutomu. Tokyo: Yumani shobō, 1976.

——. *Suikoden yakkai*. In Nagasawa, *Tōwa jisho ruishū*, vol. 13.

Okajima Kanzan. *Jikai benran*. In Nagasawa, *Tōwa jisho ruishū*, vol. 14.

——. *Taiheiki engi*. 1719 edition. National Archives of Japan, Tokyo.

——. *Tō'on gazoku gorui*. In Nagasawa, *Tōwa jisho ruishū*, vol. 6.

——. *Tōwa ben'yō*. In Nagasawa, *Tōwa jisho ruishū*, vol. 7.

——. *Tōwa san'yō*. In Nagasawa, *Tōwa jisho ruishū*, vol. 6.

——. *Tōyaku benran*. In Nagasawa, *Tōwa jisho ruishū*, vol. 7.

——. trans. *Tsūzoku Gen Min gundan*. Microfilm of 1705 edition. National Institute of Japanese Literature, Tokyo.

Okumura Kayoko. "*Chūshingura engi* to *Kaigai kidan*." *Chūgokugo kenkyū* 44 (2002): 64–80.

——. *Edo jidai no Tōwa ni kansuru kiso kenkyū*. Suita-shi: Kansai daigaku shuppankai, 2007.

——. "Ken'en ni okeru Chūgokugo juyō to zokugokan: *Tōwa gazoku gorui* no gago to zokugo ni tsuite." *Kansai daigaku Chūgoku bungakkai kiyō* 23 (2002): 1–24.

——. "Okajima Kanzan *Tōwa san'yō* kō." *Kansai daigaku Chūgoku bungakkai kiyō* 99 (1996): 99–113.

——. "*Taiheiki engi* no kotoba: *Taiheiki* hon'yaku ni arawareta hakuwakan." *Kansai daigaku Chūgoku bungakkai kiyō* 24 (2003): 113–31.

——. "*Yakka hitsubi*, *Chūshingura engi* to *Kaigai kidan*." *Kansai daigaku Chūgoku bungakkai kiyō* 26 (2005): 55–73.

Ōmachi Keigetsu et al., eds. *Shina bungaku taikō*. Tokyo: Dai Nihon tosho kabushiki gaisha, 1897–1904.

Ooms, Herman. *Tokugawa Ideology: Early Constructs, 1570–1680*. Princeton, N.J.: Princeton University Press, 1989.

Owen, Stephen. *Readings in Chinese Literary Thought*. Cambridge, Mass.: Harvard University Press, 1992.

——. *Remembrances: The Experience of the Past in Classical Chinese Literature*. Cambridge, Mass.: Harvard University Press, 1986.

Paramore, Kiri. *Japanese Confucianism: A Cultural History*. Cambridge: Cambridge University Press, 2016.

Pastreich, Emanuel. "An Alien Vernacular: Okajima Kanzan's Popularization of the Chinese Vernacular Novel in Eighteenth-Century Japan." *Sino-Japanese Studies* 11, no. 2 (1999): 39–50.

——. "Grappling with Chinese Writing as a Material Language: Ogyū Sorai's *Yakubunsentei*." *Harvard Journal of Asiatic Studies* 61, no. 1 (2001): 119–70.

——. *The Observable Mundane: Vernacular Chinese and the Emergence of a Literary Discourse on Popular Narrative in Edo Japan*. Seoul: Seoul National University Press, 2011.

——. "The Pleasure Quarters of Edo and Nanjing as Metaphor: The Records of Yu Huai and Narushima Ryūhoku." *Monumenta Nipponica* 55, no. 2 (2000): 199–224.

——. "The Projection of Quotidian Japan on the Chinese Vernacular: The Case of Sawada Issai's 'Vernacular Tale of the Chivalrous Courtesan.'" Occasional Paper presented at Harvard University Japan Forum, February 15, 2002.

Perkins, David. *Is Literary History Possible?* Baltimore: Johns Hopkins University Press, 1992.

Perry, Elizabeth J. *Rebels and Revolutionaries in North China, 1845–1945*. Stanford, Calif.: Stanford University Press, 1980.

Plaks, Andrew. *The Four Masterworks of the Ming Novel*. Princeton, N.J.: Princeton University Press, 1987.

Pollack, David. *The Fracture of Meaning: Japan's Synthesis of China from the Eighth to the Eighteenth Centuries*. Princeton, N.J.: Princeton University Press, 1988.

Pollock, Sheldon. *The Language of the Gods in the World of Men: Sanskrit, Culture, and Power in Premodern India*. Berkeley: University of California Press, 2006.

Posnett, Hutcheson Macaulay. *Comparative Literature*. New York: Appleton, 1886.

Pyle, Kenneth B. *The New Generation in Meiji Japan*. Stanford, Calif.: Stanford University Press, 1969.

Reitan, Richard M. *Making a Moral Society: Ethics and the State in Meiji Japan*. Honolulu: University of Hawai'i Press, 2010.

Robertson, Jennifer, ed. *A Companion to the Anthropology of Japan*. Malden, Mass.: Blackwell Publishing, 2005.

Rodd, Laurel Rasplica, trans., with Mary Catherine Henkenius. *Kokinshū: A Collection of Poems Ancient and Modern*. Princeton, N.J.: Princeton University Press, 1984.

Rolston, David, ed. *How to Read the Chinese Novel*. Princeton, N.J.: Princeton University Press, 1990.

——. "'Point of View' in the Writings of Traditional Chinese Fiction Critics." *CLEAR* 15 (1993): 113–42.

——. *Traditional Chinese Fiction and Fiction Commentary: Reading and Writing Between the Lines*. Stanford, Calif.: Stanford University Press, 1997.

Saitō Mareshi. "Gen to bun no aida." *Bungaku* 6, no. 8 (2007): 91–98.

——. *Kanbunmyaku no kindai: Shin-matsu = Meiji no bungakuken*. Nagoya: Nagoya daigaku shuppankai, 2005.

Sakai, Naoki. *Voices of the Past: The Status of Language in Eighteenth-Century Japanese Discourse*. Ithaca, N.Y.: Cornell University Press, 1991.

Sakaki, Atsuko. *Obsessions with the Sino-Japanese Polarity in Japanese Literature*. Honolulu: University of Hawai'i Press, 2006.

Sakakura Atsuyoshi et al., eds. *Taketori monogatari, Ise monogatari, Yamato monogatari*. In *Nihon koten bungaku taikei*, vol. 9. Tokyo: Iwanami shoten, 1957.

Sakano Tōru. *Teikoku Nihon to jinruigakusha 1884–1952 nen*. Tokyo: Keisō shobō, 2008.

Salmon, Claudine, ed. *Literary Migrations: Traditional Chinese Fiction in Asia (17–20th Centuries)*. Beijing: International Culture Publishing, 1987.

Sanguo yanyi xiaozhu. Taipei: Liren shuju, 1994.

Santō Kyōden. *Santō Kyōden zenshū*. Ed. Mizuno Minoru et al. Tokyo: Perikansha, 1992.

Sasagawa Taneo [Rinpū]. *Shina bungakushi*. Tokyo: Hakubunkan, 1898.

——. *Shina shōsetsu gikyoku shōshi*. Tokyo: Tōkadō, 1897.

Sato, Kazuki. "'Same Language, Same Race': The Dilemma of *Kanbun* in Modern Japan." In *The Construction of Racial Identities in China and Japan*, ed. Frank Dikötter, 118–35. Honolulu: University of Hawai'i Press, 1997.

Seely, Christopher. *A History of Writing in Japan*. Leiden: Brill, 1991.

Seidensticker, Edward G., trans. *The Tale of Genji*. London: Penguin Books, 1981.

Seita Tansō. *Kujakurō hikki*. Ed. Nakamura Yukihiko et al. In *Nihon koten bungaku taikei*, vol. 96. Tokyo: Iwanami shoten, 1965.

——, trans. *Morokoshi kōteiki*. 1769 edition. Special Collections, Waseda University Library, Waseda University, Tokyo.

——, trans. *Shōseihai*. Photoreproduced in *Shōseihai*, ed. Tokuda Takeshi. Tokyo: Yumani shobō, 1976.

——. *Suikoden hihyōkai*. In Nagasawa, *Tōwa jisho ruishū*, vol. 3.

"*Sen-Shin bungaku to Shina shōsetsu gikyoku shōshi* o hyō-su." *Teikoku bungaku* 3, no. 7 (1897): 89–95.

Shen Defu. *Wanli ye huo bian*. Beijing: Beijing yanshan chubanshe, 1998.

Shigeno Yasutsugu. "Kangaku yoroshiku seisoku ikka o mōke shōnen shūsai o erami Shin-koku ni ryūgaku seshimu-beki ronsetsu." *Tōkyō gakushi kaiin zasshi*, vol. 1 (1879): 76–93.

Shiji. Academia Sinica Scripta Sinica (Hanji quanwen ziliaoku). http://hanchi.ihp.sinica.edu.tw/ihp/hanji.htm.

Shimura Ryōji. "Tōwa to sharebon." In *Edo kōki no hikaku bunka kenkyū*, ed. Minamoto Ryōen, 370–419. Tokyo: Perikansha, 1990.

Shionoya On. *Shina bungaku gairon kōwa*. Tokyo: Dai Nihon yūbenkai, 1919.

Shirane, Haruo, ed. *Early Modern Japanese Literature: An Anthology, 1600–1900*. New York: Columbia University Press, 2002.

——. *Traces of Dreams: Landscape, Cultural Memory, and the Poetry of Bashō*. Stanford, Calif.: Stanford University Press, 1998.

Shirane, Haruo, and Tomi Suzuki, eds. *Inventing the Classics: Modernity, National Identity, and Japanese Literature*. Stanford, Calif.: Stanford University Press, 2000.

Shiroki Naoya. "Wakokubon *Suikoden* no kenkyū." *Hiroshima daigaku bungakubu kiyō* 28 (1968): 277–304.

——. "Wakokubon *Suikoden* no kenkyū: Shōzen." *Hiroshima daigaku bungakubu kiyō* 29 (1970): 120–44.

Sieber, Patricia. *Theaters of Desire: Authors, Readers, and the Reproduction of Early Chinese Song-Drama, 1300–2000*. New York: Palgrave Macmillan, 2003.

Simmons, Richard VanNess. "A Second Look at the *Tōwa Sanyō*: Clues to the Nature of the *Guanhuah* Studied by Japanese in the Early Eighteenth Century." *Journal of the American Oriental Society* 117, no. 3 (1997): 419–26.

Songshi. Academia Sinica Scripta Sinica (Hanji quanwen ziliaoku). http://hanchi.ihp .sinica.edu.tw/ihp/hanji.htm.

Steininger, Brian. *Chinese Literary Forms in Heian Japan.* Cambridge, Mass.: Harvard University Asia Center, 2017.

Suematsu Kenchō. *Shina kobungaku ryakushi.* 2 vols. Tokyo, 1882.

Suyama Nantō. *Chūgi Suikodenkai.* In Nagasawa, *Tōwa jisho ruishū,* vol. 3.

——. *Chūgi Suikoden shōyaku.* In Nagasawa, *Tōwa jisho ruishū,* vol. 3.

Suzuki, Keiko. "The Making of Tōjin Construction of the Other in Early Modern Japan." *Asian Folklore Studies* 66 (2007): 83–105.

Suzuki, Tomi. *Narrating the Self: Fictions of Japanese Modernity.* Stanford, Calif.: Stanford University Press, 1996.

Taguchi Ukichi. *Shina kaika shōshi.* Tokyo: Keizai zasshisha, 1887.

Taine, Hippolyte. *History of English Literature.* Trans. H. Van Laun. New York: Holt, 1883.

Takashima Toshio. *Suikoden to Nihonjin: Edo kara Shōwa made.* Tokyo: Taishūkan shoten, 1991.

Takayama Chogyū. *Chogyū zenshū.* Ed. Saitō Shinsaku and Anezaki Masaharu. Tokyo: Hakubunkan, 1912.

Takebe Ayatari. *Honchō suikoden.* Ed. Takada Mamoru et al. In *Shin Nihon koten bungaku taikei,* vol. 79. Tokyo: Iwanami shoten, 1992.

Tanaka, Stefan. *Japan's Orient: Rendering Pasts into History.* Berkeley: University of California Press, 1993.

Thompson, Hunter S. *Hell's Angels: A Strange and Terrible Saga.* New York: Ballantine Books, 1995.

Thompson, Sarah E. *Tattoos in Japanese Prints.* Boston: MFA Publications, 2017.

Thornber, Karen Laura. *Empire of Texts in Motion: Chinese, Korean, and Taiwanese Transculturations of Japanese Literature.* Cambridge, Mass.: Harvard University Asia Center, 2009.

Tierney, Robert Thomas. *Tropics of Savagery: The Culture of Japanese Empire in Comparative Frame.* Berkeley: University of California Press, 2010.

Tinios, Ellis. "Kuniyoshi and Chinese Subjects: Pushing the Boundaries." *Impressions* 31 (2010): 88–99.

Toby, Ronald. "Carnival of the Aliens: Korean Embassies in Edo-Period Art and Popular Culture." *Monumenta Nipponica* 41, no. 4 (1986): 415–56

——. *State and Diplomacy in Early Modern Japan: Asia in the Development of the Tokugawa Bakufu.* Stanford, Calif.: Stanford University Press, 1991.

Tōjō Kindai. *Sentetsu sōdan kōhen.* In *Dai Nihon bunko: Jukyō hen,* vol. 17, ed. Oyanagi Shigeta. Tokyo: Shun'yōdō shoten, 1936.

Tokuda Takeshi. *Edo Kangaku no sekai.* Tokyo: Perikansha, 1990.

——. *Nihon kinsei shōsetsu to Chūgoku shōsetsu.* Musashimurayama-shi: Seishōdō, 1987.

Tokutomi Sohō. *Shina man'yūki.* Tokyo: Min'yūsha, 1918.

Toury, Gideon. *Descriptive Translation Studies and Beyond.* Amsterdam: John Benjamins, 2012.

Treat, John Whittier. *The Rise and Fall of Modern Japanese Literature.* Chicago: University of Chicago Press, 2018.

Tsūzoku rekkokushi jūni chō gundan. Microfilm of 1712 edition. National Institute of Japanese Literature, Tokyo.

Tsūzoku Sōshi gundan. Microfilm of 1719 edition. National Institute of Japanese Literature, Tokyo.

Tsūzoku Tō Taisō gunkan. Microfilm of 1696 edition. National Institute of Japanese Literature, Tokyo.

Ueda Akinari. *Ueda Akinari shū.* Ed. Nakamura Yukihiko. In *Nihon koten bungaku taikei,* vol. 56. Tokyo: Iwanami shoten, 1959.

Ueda Atsuko. *Concealment of Politics, Politics of Concealment: The Production of "Literature" in Meiji Japan.* Stanford, Calif.: Stanford University Press, 2007.

——. "Sound, Script, and Styles: *Kanbun kundokutai* and the National Language Reforms of 1880s Japan." *Review of Japanese Culture and Society* 20 (December 2008): 133–54.

Ueda Atsuo. "Okajima Kanzan hen'yaku *Tsūzoku Chūgi Suikoden* kō." *Journal of Chinese Literature* 19 (1994): 119–31.

van Bremen, Jan, and Akitoshi Shimizu. *Anthropology and Colonialism in Asia and Oceania.* Richmond, Surrey, UK: Routledge Curzon, 1999.

Venuti, Lawrence, ed. *The Translation Studies Reader.* New York: Routledge, 2004.

——. *The Translator's Invisibility: A History of Translation.* New York: Routledge, 2008.

Wakabayashi, Judy. "The Reconceptualization of Translation from Chinese in 18th-Century Japan." In *Translation and Cultural Change,* ed. Eva Hung, 119–45. Amsterdam: John Benjamins, 2005.

Waley, Arthur, trans. *The Book of Songs.* New York: Grove Press, 1960.

Walley, Glynne. *Good Dogs: Edification, Entertainment, and Kyokutei Bakin's Nansō Satomi hakkenden.* Ithaca, N.Y.: Cornell University East Asia Program, 2017.

Wang, David Der-wei. *Fin-de-Siècle Splendor: Repressed Modernities of Late Qing Fiction, 1849–1911.* Stanford, Calif.: Stanford University Press, 1997.

——. ed. *A New Literary History of Modern China.* Cambridge, Mass.: Belknap Press, 2017.

Wang, John C. Y. *Chin Sheng-t'an.* New York: Twayne, 1972.

Washburn, Dennis. *Translating Mount Fuji: Modern Japanese Fiction and the Ethics of Identity.* New York: Columbia University Press, 2007.

Watanabe Kazuyasu. *Meiji shisōshi: Jukyōteki dentō to kindai ninshikiron.* Tokyo: Perikansha, 1985.

Watson, Burton, trans. *The Complete Works of Chuang Tzu.* New York: Columbia University Press, 1968.

Weiner, Michael. "The Invention of Identity: Race and Nation in Pre-War Japan." In *The Construction of Racial Identities in China and Japan,* ed. Frank Dikötter, 96–117. Honolulu: University of Hawai'i Press, 1997.

Wellek, René. *Discriminations: Further Concepts of Criticism.* New Haven, Conn.: Yale University Press, 1970.

——. *A History of Modern Criticism.* 8 vols. New Haven, Conn.: Yale University Press, 1955–1992.

Widmer, Ellen. "Island Paradises: Travel and Utopia in Three East Asian Offshoots of *Shuihu zhuan.*" *Sino-Japanese Studies* 13, no. 1 (2000): 20–33.

——. *The Margins of Utopia: Shui-hu hou-chuan and the Literature of Ming Loyalism.* Cambridge, Mass.: Council on East Asian Studies, Harvard University, 1987.

Wigen, Kären. "Mapping Early Modernity: Geographical Meditations on a Comparative Concept." *Early Modern Japan* 5 (1995): 1–13.

Xie Zhaozhe. *Wu za zu*. Beijing: Zhonghua shuju, 1959.

Xiong Damu. *Da Song zhongxing tongsu yanyi*. In *Ming Qing shanben xiaoshuo congkan*. Taipei: Tianyi chubanshe, 1985.

Yamaji Aizan. *Dokuritsu hyōron*. Tokyo: Misuzu shobō, 1988.

Yanada Zeigan. *Zeigan shū*. Ed. Tokuda Takeshi. Tokyo: Perikansha, 1985.

Yanagisawa Kien. *Hitorine*. In *Nihon koten bungaku taikei*, vol. 96. Tokyo: Iwanami shoten, 1965.

Yeh, Catherine Vance. *The Chinese Political Novel: Migration of a World Genre*. Cambridge, Mass.: Harvard University Press, 2015.

Yoda, Tomiko. *Gender and National Literature: Heian Texts in the Constructions of Japanese Modernity*. Durham, N.C.: Duke University Press, 2004.

Yonemoto, Marcia. *Mapping Early Modern Japan: Space, Place, and Culture in the Tokugawa Period, 1603–1868*. Berkeley: University of California Press, 2003.

Yoshida Seiichi et al., eds. *Kindai bungaku hyōron taikei*. 10 vols. Tokyo: Kadokawa shoten, 1971–1975.

Yoshikawa Kōjirō. *Jinsai, Sorai, Norinaga*. Tokyo: Iwanami shoten, 1975.

——. *Jinsai, Sorai, Norinaga: Three Classical Philosophers of Mid-Tokugawa Japan*. Trans. Yūji Kikuchi. Tokyo: Tōhō gakkai, 1983.

Zachmann, Urs Matthias. "Blowing Up a Double Portrait in Black and White: The Concept of Asia in the Writings of Fukuzawa Yukichi and Okakura Tenshin." *positions* 15, no. 2 (2007): 345–68.

——. *China and Japan in the Late Meiji Period: China Policy and the Japanese Discourse on National Identity, 1895–1904*. London: Routledge, 2011.

Zang Maoxun, ed. *Yuan qu xuan*. 4 vols. Beijing: Zhonghua shuju, 1989.

Zhang Xiaogang. "Kin Seitan to Seita Tansō no shōsetsu ron ni tsuite no hikaku kenkyū: Shōsetsu to shisho no shiten kara." In *Aiura Takashi sensei tsuitō Chūgoku bungaku ronshū*. Tokyo: Hakubaijo tōhō shoten, 1992.

Zhu Xi. *Shiji zhuan*. Ed. Wang Huabao. Nanjing: Fenghuang chubanshe, 2007.

——, comp. *Sishu zhangju jizhu*. Beijing: Zhonghua shuju, 1982.

Zhu Yixuan, ed. *Ming Qing xiaoshuo ziliao xuanbian*. 2 vols. Jinan: Ji Lu shushe, 1989.

Zhu Yixuan and Liu Yuchen, eds. *Shuihu zhuan ziliao huibian*. Tianjin: Nankai daxue chubanshe, 2002.

Zhu Yixuan, Ning Jiayu, and Chen Guisheng, eds. *Zhongguo gudai xiaoshuo zongmu tiyao*. Beijing: Renmin wenxue chubanshe, 2005.

Zwicker, Jonathan E. *Practices of the Sentimental Imagination: Melodrama, the Novel, and the Social Imaginary in Nineteenth-Century Japan*. Cambridge, Mass.: Harvard East Asia Center, 2006.

INDEX

245

INDEX

Sakaki, Atsuko, 7, 8

Santō Kyōden, 21, 85–90, 91, 180, 201n3; commentarial tradition and, 23; as mentor to Kyokutei Bakin, 85. See also *Chūshin Suikoden*

Sasagawa Rinpū, 100, 103, 121, 123, 147, 210n88, 211n103; on Chinese fiction and drama, 134; on disruption of Confucian hegemony in China, 137; influence of Taine on, 138; "inner China" and, 143; on institutional shake-up and authentic Chinese voice, 142; interest in Yuan period, 139. See also *Shina shōsetsu gikyoku shōshi*

scholar-and-beauty (*caizi jiaren*) romances, 156

seiji shōsetsu, 100

Seita Tansō, 13, 53, 80, 91, 178, 195n28, 196n38; commentarial tradition and, 23; historiography as interest of, 71, 74; on Jin Shengtan, 71–79, 81, 180–81; Kujaku Dōjin (The Peacock Adept) nom de plume, 71; *Suikoden hihyōkai* [Explication of *The Water Margin*], 72–79, 178; on "universal" Confucian norms, 148; Yanada Zeigan as mentor to, 66

Sekai hyakketsuden [One hundred biographies of world heroes] (Kitamura Saburō), 98, 101, 206n9

Self Help (Smiles), 52

senryū, 55

Sen-Shin bungaku [Pre-Qin literature] (Fujita, 1897), 103, 150, 152

Sentetsu sōdan kōhen [Collected tales of former worthies, part 2] (Tōjō Kindai), 51

sentiment (*ninjō*), 52

sewamono, 153

Shakespeare, William, 98, 111, 148

Shang dynasty, 102, 135

Shanghai Classic Works Publishing House (Shanghai guji chubanshe), 62

Shaoshi shanfang bicong [Collected jotting from the Shaoshi Retreat] (Hu Yinglin), 76

Shen Deqian, 129

shi (events related in the text), 69

Shigeno Yasutsugu, 50–51, 64

Shina (Japanese name for China), 14, 104–5, 140

Shina bungaku (Chinese literature), 7, 9, 100

Shina bungaku gairon kōwa [Lectures on the outlines of Chinese literature] (Shionoya, 1919), 125–26

Shina bungakushi (Chinese-literature historiography), 100, 101–2, 120, 147, 205–6n8, 206n13, 207n38; China as literature itself, 173; climate and race as factors in development of, 135–36; equated with Western genre of "literary history," 101; first wave of, 120–21; hidden and authentic self revealed in, 143; Japanese adaptations of Chinese novels, 153; key figures in, 121; northern and southern literary traditions, 134–35, 136, 137–39; Western standards of culture and, 177

Shina bungakushi (Fujita), 124

Shina bungakushi [A history of Chinese literature] (Kojō, 1897), 100, 102, 121, 122–23, 134–37, 150, 209n80; on antiquity of Chinese civilization, 126; reprint (1920) of, 151

Shina bungaku shikan (Kawai Kōzō), 214n58

Shina bungaku shikō [An outline of Chinese literature] (Kojima), 124

Shina bungaku taikō (journal), 167

Shi Nai'an, 18, 20, 67, 73, 144, 196n38; attention to characterization, 151, 153–54; authorial intention of, 81; Jin Shengtan's praise and critique of, 69, 151; placed among Western literary and political figures, 96–97, 101; view of rebel leaders, 70

Shina kinsei gikyoku shi [History of Chinese Drama of the Early Modern Period] (Aoki, 1930), 142

Shina kobungaku ryakushi [A short history of classical Chinese culture] (Suematsu, 1882), 121–22